Globalization and Religion

About the Editors

Scaria Pannackal is the Director of The Institute of Indian Culture a Research Centre for the study of Culture, Religion and Society. He has his Doctorate in Social Philosophy from the University of Pune. He has Published Articles on various aspects of Culture and Religion. Presently, he also teaches at St. Xavier's College, Mumbai.

V. Mohan retired as an Associate Professor from The University of Mumbai (From the Dept. of Eurasian Studies). She has her Doctorate (in Political Science) from The University of Rajasthan, Jaipur. She has travelled extensively in USA, Europe and Russia in connection with her Research work. She has published a numbers of Research Articles both in Foreign and Indian Journals. She has Eight books to her Credit. Presently, she is working as the Programme Director at IIC.

Globalization and Religion

Interactions and Divergences

Edited by

Scaria Pannackal SVD
Vasundhara Mohan

Published for

INSTITUTE OF INDIAN CULTURE
MUMBAI–400093

by

CONCEPT PUBLISHING COMPANY PVT. LTD.
NEW DELHI–110059

ISBN-13: 978-93-5125-282-5

First Published 2017

Published and Printed by

Concept Since 1974

Concept Publishing Company Pvt. Ltd.
Regd. Office:
A/15-16, Commercial Block, Mohan Garden,
New Delhi-110059 (INDIA)
Phones : 25351460, 25351794, *Fax* : 091-11-25357109
E-mail : publishing@conceptpub.com
Website: www.conceptpub.com

Editorial Office: H-13, Bali Nagar, New Delhi-110 015, India.

Cataloging in Publication Data—DK Courtesy: D.K. Agencies (P) Ltd. <docinfo@dkagencies.com>

National Seminar on Globalization and Religion: Interactions and Divergences (2016: Mumbai, India)

Globalization and religion : interactions and divergences / edited by Scaria Pannackal SVD, Vasundhara Mohan.
pages cm
Papers presented at a National Seminar on Globalization and Religion: Interactions and Divergences, organized by and held at the Institute of Indian Culture, Mumbai, India, during 27th-28th January, 2016.
Includes bibliographical references and index.
ISBN 9789351252825

1. Globalization—Religious aspects—Congresses. 2. Culture and globalization—India—Congresses. 3. Globalization—Social aspects—India—Congresses. I. Pannackal, Scaria, editor. II. Mohan, Vasundhara, 1947- editor. III. Institute of Indian Culture (Mumbai, India), organizer. IV. Title.

HN683.5.N38 2016 DDC 303.48254 23

Foreword

Globalization has created great discontinuities. Its inner logic of hankering after profit is making people more acquisitive in terms of status, power and the yearning for consumer goods. There is a sense of disorientation and helplessness that is reflected in the increasing religiosity among people.

The National Seminar on *Globalization and Religion: Interactions and Divergences* at the Institute of Indian Culture, Mumbai brought together minds and ideas that triggered a fresh look at the phenomenon of globalization which invariably has accompanied the processes of Privatization and Liberalization.

The major insight of the seminar, clearly presented in the various chapters included in the book, is the overwhelming influence of globalization forces on the cultural dimension of life, especially on Religion, Identities, Environment, Education, Dalits and Women. The various papers bring together this overpowering influence of a globalized world.

The unique contribution of this book is the focus on the cultural impact of globalization. While the economic and political impact of globalization has been studied substantially and written about, awareness on the cultural significance has been few, particularly in the Indian context. Take for instance the increasing religiosity in the urban centres of India. In the context of an aggressive economic policies and growth strategies, more and more people are marginalised and many more feel insecure. As a consequence, there is a great resurgence in religion which makes people turn to and depend on gods and rituals. Whether such religiosity has resulted in lesser corruption, more ethical way of living and deeper humanization processes is a moot question. What is confusing is the increasing religiosity and corresponding levels of de-humanization. Extreme forms of violence towards humans, animals and nature are in principle irreconcilable with religion. But everyday reality is replete with reports of growing violence in the world. Thus, religiosity *vs.* spirituality becomes a major concern for discussion.

Take another example, education, especially in India. There has been a total neglect of state supported, secular and liberal education. In its place, privatized and self-financing education focussing more on technical skills which prepare workers for a globalized economy, supported by a neo-liberal economy and the increasing number of middle class in India, is growing at break-neck speed. The exclusion of vast number of the most marginalized from the processes of education and consequent economic and social growth is clearly an impact of globalization. Critical reflections in the Seminar are reflected in the chapters of the book which will help the reader to respond proactively to the situation.

Similar presentations on other areas like environment, identities etc. make this book a welcome addition to the vast literature on the impact of Globalization. The core argument in the book is to humanize the process of globalization, so that, the marginalization of substantial sections of people is avoided and nature is protected to provide for the future generations.

The seminar and the book owe their gratitude to ICSSR and the Institute of Indian Culture, Mumbai particularly its Director, Dr. Scaria Pannackal and its Programme Director, Dr. (Mrs.) Vasundhara Mohan and their team.

4th July, 2016
Christ Hall
Kozhikode

Dr. M. K. George Mutholil SJ
Provincial, Kerala Province

Preface

When globalization was recommended as a strategy to overcome the economic problems of Latin America in early 1990s, it was believed by the proponents that it would help the poor and rich countries alike. If the U.S. and European consumers would have their pick of inexpensive items made by people whose pay was much lower than theirs, the abolition of trade barriers would help expansion of multinationals and the developing countries would benefit through increased employment opportunities. Geo-political cooperation was expected to flourish. It is true that globalization has enabled many developing countries with access to markets, and employment opportunities have increased. But, Globalization is a complicated issue and is not as simple a phenomenon as it may appear to be.

Supporters of globalization argue that it has the potential to make the world a better place to live and solve some of the deep-seated problems like poverty and unemployment. They foresaw globalization ushering in free trade and promoting global economic growth, creating jobs, making companies more competitive to the benefit of consumers. However, free trade is not entirely free as some of the developed countries have added more restrictive export and import measures to safeguard their own interests.

Globalization has facilitated influx of information between countries which do not have anything in common and there is cultural intermingling and each country is learning more about other cultures. Socially, people have become more open and in most cases, tolerant towards each other. For many, the speedy travel, mass communications and quick dissemination of information through the Internet are the true benefits of globalization. Globalization has also enabled labour to move from country to country to market their skills, although such migration of labour hired at lower wages often leads to problems with the local labour. At the same time, transnational companies investing in other countries provide employment for the people in those countries often getting them out of poverty.

In spite of the above benefits, the real goal that poor countries would flourish on account of infusions of foreign capital and technology and will have a chance to develop economically and by spreading prosperity, has not been achieved by many countries. Experience has shown that globalization has made the rich richer while making the poor poorer. The biggest grouse of the developed countries is that jobs are lost and transferred to lower cost countries. Large multinational corporations are accused of social injustice, unfair working conditions as well as lack of concern for environment, mismanagement of natural resources, and ecological damage. Multinational corporations are increasingly influencing political decisions in the countries in which they operate.

The anti-globalists also claim that globalization is not working for the majority of the world and that inequality is becoming worse both internationally and within countries. Experts think that globalization is also leading to human trafficking and incursion of communicable diseases. Globalization has led to exploitation of labour, with some developing countries making workers (especially women and children) work in inhuman conditions ignoring safety standards, with the sole intention of producing cheap goods. Social welfare schemes or "safety nets" are under great pressure in developing countries because of cutting down government spending.

But, Globalization is an economic tsunami that is sweeping the planet. We cannot stop it but there are many things we can do to slow it down and make it more equitable.

It is in the above background that the Institute of Indian Culture organized a 2-day seminar on 27th-28th January, 2016, to deliberate on various issues concerned with globalization from an Indian perspective. Unlike other countries, India is beset with problems arising out of the existence of Scheduled Castes and Scheduled Tribes population, religious differences, the caste system and still not-so-empowered women who are fighting for parity in different fields. The Seminar was supported by the Indian Council of Social Science Research, New Delhi.

Reputed academicians presented papers on a variety of issues emerging from globalization in the Indian context. *Professor Muzaffar Assadi* of the Mysore University dealt with the theoretical aspects of

Globalization. Holding that there are ambiguities with regard to the very term Globalization, he has dealt with the different schools of thought about globalization, right from Karl Marx.

Dr. Scaria Pannackal, Dr. (Ms.) Leela D'Souza (both of the Institute of Indian Culture) and *Dr. G. Ramachandram* (retired Principal and an authority on Jawaharlal Nehru, besides being a prolific writer on contemporary issues) expressed their views on the impact of globalization on religion and religious identity. Dr. Leela D'Souza pointed out that both individuals and collectivities, marginalized by the globalization processes; struggle to establish coherent identities, as the earlier ones are being threatened by contradictory social imperatives. She stressed that religion today is not being abolished, but is taking on a new character; religious revival at the individual leveland religious activism at the collective level. There is a search for a new consciousness; a new identity, in response to the new demands of a globaiizing world. Cultural survival in the face of globalization is one of the causes of religious revivalism and religious activism. And religious revival, in the face of globalization, is using the technology offered by globalization very effectively, to communicate instantly and globally; both directly to individual persons and to establish collectivities across the globe.

In his presentation, *Dr. M.K. George SJ* has made a clear distinction between religiosity and spirituality, stating that in the globalised world, while religiosity divides, spirituality unites.

Dr. Mangesh Kulkarni (Pune University) presented an interesting chapter on the Masculinities in the Matrix of Globalization. It is under the influence of globalization that "a new species, metro-sexual, has entered the zoo of Indian masculinity." Unlike in the past, a man's favourite haunts now include the fashion industry and the audio-visual media. Unlike their conventional counterparts, men have been taking keen interest in personal grooming, developed an open attitude to sexuality, and in touch with the 'feminine' side. Kulkarni cites the example of the Hindi film star Shahrukh Khan, who has featured in a gender-bender soap advertisement, and who is often cited as a metro-sexual icon.

Professor Nalini Kant Jha (Pondicherry University) has discussed at length the effect of globalization on the culture and society in India. In spite of the advantages, globalization has its adverse effects on Indian culture and society. As it cannot be wished away and one cannot turn back the wheels of history, Prof. Jha opines that instead of searching for an alternative to Globalization and IT revolution, one has to think of ways and means of minimizing the negative implications and take maximum advantage of globalization.

Dr. S.M. Michael (IIC, Mumbai) points out that today's world is characterized by contradicting forces of post-modernism and multiculturalism on the one hand, and Globalization, Nationalism and Fundamentalism on the other. He points out that Globalization, which supports a secular and liberal culture also, creates a troubled relationship between the local and the international. The sense of fear that the emergence and spread of global culture was destroying the local values and posing a threat to national identities was responsible for the birth of fundamentalism.

Economic aspects being the crux of globalization, chapters were presented by *Dr. P. Nataraja Murthy* (Inflationary Trends after Globalization and its Impact on Indian Economy) and *Dr. N. Prasanna* (Analysis of the Relationship between Economic Growth and FDI Inflows in India) both of Bharatidasan University, Tiruchirapalli. A chapter on the effects of Globalization on Ecology (Towards a Spiritual Ecology of Global Modernity: A Rudimentary Outline of Globalization on the Ecology) was presented by *Dr. Aseem Srivatsava*, an Environmentalist and writer from Gurgaon.

The effects of globalization on women formed the subject of the chapters presented by *Dr. Vasundhara Mohan* (Institute of Indian Culture), *Dr. Archana Sinha* (Institute of Social Studies, New Delhi) and *Dr. Moly Kuruvilla* (Calicut University), which extensively discussed the benefits and problems that Indian women were facing due to globalization. As Globalization has encouraged private sector to enter the field of education, *Dr. Manisha Madhava* (SNDT University, Mumbai) discusses whether the private sector education is better than that in the public sector.

As stated above, while globalization has benefitted the rich (both individuals and multinational corporations), it has devastating effects on the poor. This aspect was ably discussed in the chapter presented by *Dr. G. Palanithurai* (Gandhigram Rural University, Tamilnadu). Palanithurai blames the political parties and intellectual classes for not adopting strategic approaches to enable the poor to take advantage of democracy and decentralization on account of which the poor have not been able to claim any benefits out of globalization. As an extrapolation of this subject, *Dr. Tej Pratap Singh* (Banaras Hindu University, Varanasi) presented a chapter on Globalization, Inequality and Violence in India. Tej Pratap Singh argues that there is a direct correlation between the adoption of neo-liberal policies by India in the wake of globalization, liberalization and privatisation and the rise of Maoist insurgency in India. The exclusion of the vast number of people from growth process created lot of resentment and discontent amongst the masses swelling the ranks of Maoists.

Professor Chandrakant Puri of the Rajiv Gandhi Institute of Contemporary Studies, Mumbai University presented his findings on the effects of Globalization on the Nomadic community of Maharashtra.

Effect of globalization on Human Rights formed the subject of the chapters presented by *Dr. Homi Dhalla* (Violations of Human Rights in a Globalized World) and *Dr. Allwyn D'Silva* (Globalization and Human Rights). Homi Dhalla cites a statement issued by Human Rights Watch which said that many governments view Human Rights as a "luxury" that they cannot afford. According to Homi Dhalla and Allwyn D'Silva, the emphasis on economic development and international competitiveness has resulted in new onslaughts on the rights of indigenous people. As natural resources are found through out the world on indigenous lands and prospectors and entrepreneurs are permitted to encroach on them in the name of economic development, the rights of indigenous rights all over the world are under threat.

The seminar witnessed an enthusiastic participation by the faculty, students and research scholars from Mumbai University and other colleges in Mumbai, who raised very pertinent questions.

The unanimous view at the conclusion of the seminar was that we need a political leadership that keeps the interests of the vulnerable sections of the population when globalization is inevitable and is here to stay. While there could be many ways in which government could reduce its expenditure, it should not be at the cost of denying the social safety measures to the poor. Similarly, the rolling out of red carpet to multinational corporations need not be at the expense of the green belt and the dislocation of the lives of the indigenous populations.

The speakers did not oppose globalization which is good for the country as it brings in new technologies and opens up employment opportunities. But it should be ensured that the multinationals do not exploit the environment and human labour. Special attention also needs to be paid to issues related to Religion as well as Women in the matter of employment and wage parity. Globalization is like being overwhelmed by a snow avalanche or a tsunami. One cannot stop it; but one can only swim in the snow and hope to stay on top. We cannot stop globalization but there are many policies and strategies we can use to make it more equitable.

Scaria Pannackal SVD
Director

(Mrs.) Vasundhara Mohan
Programme Director

Inaugural Address

REV. FR. PAUL VATTATHARA SVD
Provincial Superior, India, Mumbai Province

I have great pleasure in welcoming all the participants of this 2-day National Seminar on "Globalization and Religion: Interactions and Divergences" organized by the Institute of Indian Culture, with support from the Indian Council of Social Science Research, Government of India, New Delhi. What gives me immense pleasure is the enthusiastic participation of acclaimed academicians from different parts of the country, to share their views on the subject.

The objective of the Seminar, as I understand, is to analyse the relationship between globalization and religion through a dispassionate and thorough discussion of the positive and negative interactions and repercussions upon each other. It is also aimed at examining the relationship between religion and globalization from the perspective of religion and proposing recommendations that are crucial for bringing about equality within the process of globalization.

Globalization is a process where political, economic, social and cultural relationships are not restricted to territorial boundaries. It alters the cultural make up of the globe and makes the world a smaller place in which political, social and economic events elsewhere affect individuals anywhere. Globalization has, in fact, removed the cultural differences, and eroded local customs and beliefs and spread a secular way of life which is often at odds with religions. Nationalism comes into play when certain aspects of westernization are seen as challenges to nation's ethos. Individuals feel insecure when the life once they led becomes contested and changed due to globalization.

At the same time, religion and globalization can be seen as partners in historical change, for religions have become a carrier of globalising tendencies in the world. Globalization offers immense possibilities not only for promoting religion but also in posing challenges. It not only engenders greater religious tolerance, but also disrupts traditional communities; brings religion to a circle of conflicts that reinforces their specific identities. Globalization has also brought about a culture of pluralism, which is central to religious teachings. With most of the world and its diverse religions, cultures, languages having become an integral part of globalization, it is crucial that we look upon something that is more definite to unify us in a positive direction. By using the free flow of communication available through advanced technology, religions could focus more on the humanitarian and pluralistic aspects of their teachings as a means to lessen the divide. Religious understanding can be one of the most essential means by which foundations of peace and harmony can be achieved.

I sincerely hope that this seminar will thoroughly discuss the pros and cons of globalization and offer valuable suggestions. I wish the participants a pleasant stay in Mumbai and the seminar a great success.

Acknowledgements

The two-day National Seminar on "*Globalization and Religion: Interactions and Divergences*" was organised with financial support from the Indian Council of Social Science Research, Government of India, New Delhi. Without ICSSR's support it would not have been possible to invite reputed scholars from far and wide. We therefore gratefully acknowledge the support extended by the ICSSR.

We would also like to thank the various scholars who made it convenient to participate in the Seminar and present papers on various facets of Globalization. We found that some of them cancelled their earlier commitments to participate in this Seminar. We are thankful to them. Their contribution to the success of the seminar was evident from the interest that was generated among the students and research scholars who attended the Seminar and raised several relevant questions.

Our thanks are also due to Rev. Fr. Paul Vattathara SVD, Provincial Superior, India, Mumbai Province of the SVD Congregation for gracing the occasion and delivering the Inaugural Address. We are also grateful to Dr. M.K. George SJ for writing the Foreword as well as delivering the Valedictory Address.

We acknowledge with thanks the support that we received from Mr. Anwar Hussain, Research Scholar, Mr. Kishor and others who lent a big helping hand with paper work and outdoor jobs. Our greatest support in bringing out the seminar presentations in a book form has been from Mr. R. Mohan and Mr. P.K. Nair, who did meticulous editing of the papers.

Scaria Pannackal SVD
Director

(Mrs.) Vasundhara Mohan
Programme Director

Contents

List of Contributors

Allwyn D'Souza, Human Rights Activist, Mumbai.
E-mail: blaseallwyn97@rediffmail.com

Archana Sinha (Mrs.), Senior Fellow & Head, Rural and Urban Development Department, Indian Social Institute, New Delhi.
E-mail: sinha3may@gmail.com

Aseem Srivatsava, Environmental Economist, Formerly visiting Professor, Nordic College, Norway and freelance writer.
E-mail: maybeaseem@gmail.com

Chandrakant Puri, Professor, Chair Professor, Rajiv Gandhi Centre for Contemporary Studies, Mumbai University, Mumbai.
E-mail: chandrakant.puri@gmail.com

G. Palanithurai, Professor, Rajiv Gandhi Chair Professor for Panchayat Studies, Gandhigram Rural Institute, Deemed University, Gandhigram, Tamilnadu.
E-mail: gpalanithurai@gmail.com

G. Ramachandram, Professor, Formerly Professor, Political Science and retired Principal.
E-mail: g_ramachandram@yahoo.com

Homi Dhalla, Founder President, Zarathrushta World and Featured Speaker in numerous International Conferences, Mumbai.
E-mail: wzcf@bom8.vsnl.net.in

Leela D'Souza (Ms.), Faculty, Institute of Indian Culture, Mumbai.
E-mail: leelads2005@yahoo.co.in

M.K. George SJ, Formerly Director, Indian Social Institute, Bangalore.
E-mail: gmutholil@gmail.com

Mangesh Kulkarni, Professor, Department of Political Science, Savitribai Phule Pune University, Pune.
E-mail: mangshra@yahoo.co.in

Manisha Madhava (Mrs.), Associate Professor, Department of Political Science, SNDT Women's University, Mumbai.
E-mail: m.manisha@gmail.com

Moly Kuruvilla (Mrs.), Associate Professor, Director, Women's Studies Centre, Calicut, Kerala.
E-mail: molykuruvilla@gmail.com

Muzaffar Assadi, Professor and Head, Department of Political Science, University of Mysore, Manasa Gangotri, Mysore.
E-mail: muzaffar.assadi@gmail.com

N. Prasanna, Associate Professor, Department of Economics, Bharatidasan University, Tiruchirapalli, Tamilnadu.
E-mail: npeco@bdu.ac.in

Nalini Kant Jha, Professor, Director, South Asia Studies School of Social Sciences and International Studies, Pondicherry University, Puducherry.
E-mail: jhank59@gmail.com

P. Nataraja Murthy, Assistant Professor, Department of Economics, Bharatidasan University, Tiruchirapalli, Tamilnadu.
E-mail: nataraja_23@yahoo.co.in

S.M. Michael, Formerly Professor, Department of Sociology, Mumbai University, Mumbai.
E-mail: smmichael2000@hotmail.com

Scaria Pannackal, Director, Institute of Indian Culture, Mumbai.
E-mail: spannackal@rediffmail.com

Tej Pratap Singh, Professor, Department of Political Science, Banaras Hindu University, Varanasi.
E-mail: tejpratapbhu@gmail.com

Vasundhara Mohan (Mrs.), Programme Director, Formerly Associate Professor, Centre for Central Eurasian Studies, University of Mumbai.
E-mail: mohan_rallapalli@hotmail.com

1

Theorising Globalization

MUZAFFAR ASSADI

Decade of 1990s saw a large number of debates in the domain of public policy, scholarship and academia, with each contending, contradicting and critiquing the term globalization. The difference is apparent in the way globalization is perceived, analysed, encountered and debated There is a possibility that the word would become a cliché in the years to come. This is mainly because of curiosity and the anxiety that the word had created.

One of the reasons why globalization is much debated is the fact that there are ambiguities with regard to the very term itself. A Question quite often raised is as to whether globalization is a "phenomenon", a "process", a "phase", a "stage of development", a "programme" or an "agenda", "end of an ideology" or a "buzz word" of the "decade. Finally, one can ask the following question: How far globalization has become an intellectual and cultural current? Has it become what is called "major concern" in academics and public policy?

David Renton, a Marxist, for example, would view globalization in terms of "long process" and has "long history."[1] On the contrary, for Chamsy el-Ojeili and Patrick Hayden, globalization is a "major concern of contemporary world."[2] Nonetheless, war historians such as Martin Walker predict the emergence of new stage in human history.[3] There are others who would argue that globalization has become a completed event, so as to argue for "post-globalization" phase and others who view the arrival of "second globalization."[4] or "second wave of globalization" reversing the earlier process from developed countries to developing countries (India and China).

It is true that there are others who tried to look at globalization as a phenomenon of the contemporary period, beginning from 1990s. That's why 1990s is called "decade of globalization." But for others including World Bank, it all started "immediately after world war Second, but accelerated considerably after 1980s."[5] It viewed globalization as "the growing interdependence of countries resulting from the increasing integration of trade, finance, people, and ideas in one global market place. International trade and cross-border investment flows are the main elements of this integration."

Baldwin and Martin hold that globalization is not a new phenomenon; rather it dates back to the nineteenth century. They believed that there were two trends of globalization in history; one trend, beginning with the middle of nineteenth century till the beginning of world war I and the second beginning after First World War and continuing even today.[6]

David Held, on the other hand, has tried to locate the historicity of globalization in the imagined past and in a phased manner. He divides history into different phases beginning with pre-modern globalization. The first phase is stretched from the Neolithic Revolution to 1500 AD; the second phase, the modern globalization, stretching from 1500 and 1850 AD and the third phase stretching from 1850 AD and 1945. The last phase is the contemporary phase of globalization, starting from the Second World War until today.[7] In his argument, Held dismisses the arguments of the globalists. On the contrary he supports the thesis of traditionalists who believe in historicizing the process of globalization. Interestingly, his argument also dismisses the myth that globalization was started by the European conquerors.

Adding to the above arguments, another scholar, Tehranian, holds "Globalization is a process that has been going on for the past 5000 years, but it has significantly accelerated since the demise of the Soviet Union in 1991."[8] Similar arguments have been advanced by others to show that the globalization has a very long history; even beyond colonial past.

But there are many who look at the phenomenon in the colonial past, suggesting that globalization needs to be looked at from the beginning of colonialism. They hold that the shrinkage of world began with the beginning of colonialism, despite the fact that the British, Spanish, Portuguese and French colonialism were no different in their basic structures. They all carried the task of interlinking colonized south with colonial west or north, since colonialism carried along with it the seeds of capitalism in the form of trans-border trade, mass migration of citizens, wars of different scale etc. It is obvious that colonialism changed the land scape of global history. Its legacy is still continued in different forms. In the contemporary period, market has taken over the colonial legacy, and global capital has replaced the colonial state.

But, one can not negate the contribution of World system theorists towards understanding globalization. They represent dependency theorists too and are known as neo-Marxists. A.G. Frank, Wallenstein, Arrighi and others have been arguing that the world system has grown out of capitalism. It all began after the sixteenth century when accumulation at global scale required constant innovation in technology, constant colonization of regions through plunder or market. All these have allowed the growth of hegemonic power at the global level, by a few countries over rest of the world. Initially, it all began with Spaniards and Portuguese then moved on to France and Britain and finally settling with the US; the latter is now, what Negeri, one of the well known scholars of the contemporary politics, calls, the "Empire."

Many of them would look at Globalization in the "Washington Consensus." There are a couple of them who would try to look at the phenomenon of globalization in the Structural Adjustment Programmes of the State. But, what is commonly agreed is that globalization is thrust upon third world or the developing countries from the above, particularly the International Multilateral agencies and the western world to change the paradigm of development. This is because most of the third world countries were reeling under poverty, backwardness, and uneven development. To overcome such economic ills, globalization was offered as a "prescription." This is the reason why multilateral institutions look at globalization as a phenomenon working on the basis of three issues. IMF for example argued that globalization has four important aspects: trade and transactions, movement, migration of people, and finally the dissemination of knowledge.[9]

Nonetheless there are other ways of viewing globalization. Anthony Giddens, one of the well-known globalists, looks at globalization as "intensification of worldwide social relations which link distant localities in such a way that local happenings are shaped by events occurring many miles away and *vice versa*."[10]

Chamsy el-Ojeili and Patrick Hayden look at globalization in terms of four conceptual categories: one, stretched social relations (events and processes happening in one corner of the world will have its ramification elsewhere at the global level); two, intensification of flows, due to social, cultural and economic changes and subsequent increase in the flow of interaction; third, increasing interpenetration (making cultures of distant places to come to face to face with each other) and finally, global infrastructures working as globalized networks.[11]

Globalization as New Idea and Ideology

How far Globalization is a New Idea and Ideology? For a large number of Western scholars it is an "idea"; a "big idea of twentieth century." This is because it is based on the new idea of inter-connectedness in all spheres of life; from culture to criminality to terrorism. In other words, the world is inter-connected; any event happening in one part of the world has its impact on other parts of the world. Tribal struggle for example in the remote parts of Chile would have its impact on the tribal struggle in Australia. In this interconnectedness, it is not necessary that each be known to other by face, rather it connects the world without "faces." A man playing poker in India might be playing poker with a person from Papua New Guinea or from a remote corner of Argentina. In other words, the idea of globalization creates interconnectedness without dislocation.

Secondly globalization is also seen as an idea or ideology to conceal the reality of human life. For scholars such as Barrett, it is used as a legitimating cover for ideology; "a set of ideas that distorts reality so as to serve particular interests."[12]

As an extension of the previous argument, there are Sociologists who look at globalization as a "key idea", which helps us to understand the transition to the third millennium. At the same time this new idea has created conditions for collapse of nation-states or erasing the boundaries of nation states. In fact this idea is not a new one. Way back in 1844-46, Marx viewed the traits of globalization, although he never used the term "globalization" as such. Rather, he viewed the tendencies towards globalization in many of his works such as the Communist Manifesto, Das Kapital, Bourgeois and Proletarians (with Engels), Theses on Feuerbach, First War of India's Independence etc. He saw the tendencies of globalization in such issues as enveloping of the world by capitalism, growth of monopoly capitalism, domination of world by capital, flexibility of labour, trans-border exchange of finance etc. Incidentally the World Development Report of 1996 refers to a passage from the Communist Manifesto while advocating market reforms in different countries. This text along with other texts such as from Das Kapital has reference to the way capitalism would become unifying, universalizing and dominating power in the years to come. In the Communist Manifesto following passage is important: "The need of a constantly expanding market for its products chases the bourgeoisie over the whole surface of the globe. It must nestle everywhere, settle everywhere, and establish connections everywhere."[13]

Nonetheless, one cannot help but state that globalization represents a larger ideology as well. The argument that "ideology has come to an end in the context of globalization is largely a myth. One cannot but negate the fact that globalization inherently carried the ideology of domination, the ideology of hegemony and the ideology of universalism. In fact, capitalism mediating through globalization has all these traits; it tries to dominate each and every social category through market and culture, it tries hegemony in each and every aspect including politics and economies and finally it tries to univerzalise the ideology saying that there is no escape from it nor alternative. It reminds one of the word TINA coined by Margaret Thatcher; *There Is No Alternative*. Hence, globalization is an ideology of capitalism engulfing each and every social aspect including politics and economy."

Globalization as different "Projects"

In fact, globalization is seen as a larger project imposed by the western world including the global capital, on the developing or underdeveloped world more from the above than from below. These impositions came at a time when Soviet Union was collapsing as a Super power. This phase is often celebrated and conceptualized as "triumph of capitalism." Nonetheless, there are scholars who argue that globalization carried "multiple projects" which cannot be simply understood in terms of the goodies it offers to the third world.

(a) As a Liberal Project

Globalization is viewed as a "liberal project" of the decade and claimed that this is the reflection of "triumph of capitalism" over

Marxism. It emerged at a time when Marxism was receding as a political project across the world, particularly after the collapse of the Soviet Union and the subsequent disintegration of Soviet bloc. Globalization came handy to spread the western values of democracy, freedom, and liberty. It was argued that globalization has the task of "converging democracy with capitalism." This is the reason why convergence theory has been advocated. On one hand it was argued that globalization would help in democratization of countries on a large scale, while at the same time help in developing capitalism as "universal and dominant mode of development" and that it would help in Marketization of economy rather than strengthening democracy. This is the reason why Samir Amir, a well known dependency theorist dismisses this "convergence theory" advocated to justify the need for universalizing globalization argument.

It is true that liberal project identifies globalization with the beginning of liberalization and privatization. Globalization was viewed not only in terms of increasing interconnectedness of social relations between communities, but also integration of the market. For them anything happening in one part of the world will have its implications on another part of the world. Farmers' suicide in India, they would believe, will have its larger implications on the larger agrarian economy of the world. An attack on Kentucky Fried Chicken would also have its implications in other parts of the world. Such interconnectedness has not only shrunk the gap between time and space, but also geography. Liberal project believed that the nation-state was a conceptual category, which would collapse with the collapse of "boundaries and with the end of geography." States will also lose their importance as the nature of state would undergo transformation.

(b) As "Western Project"

Secondly, Globalization is seen as a "western project"; a project of the US and its allies to univerzalise the values of freedom, market and capitalism. This reflects what Fukuyama argued "end of history" wherein liberal democracy alone would triumph and would become universal ideology. This is because liberal democracy is "free from internal contradictions." This is the extension of Kantian philosophy of universalism of liberal ideology. However, what lies in this "western project" is establishing western domination over the south through the means of universal values as well as technology. Western project is hegemonic too; it establishes hegemony through cultural industries, symbols, military power and capital. Shani, incidentally, believed that this liberal project is a failed concept as it has flaws right from the beginning and secondly this failure lies in the very dynamics of modernity.

(c) Modernity Project

In one of his articles on globalization, Zuhair Djibaja has argued that "Globalization received its sustenance from the failure of modernity", which obviously means that globalization tried to be a modernity project of, once again, the same western world including the multinational companies and multilateral institutions. This modernity has created homogeneity of cultural tastes and practices, which, Featherstone calls as "Americanization." This is also called "McDonaldization" of the world culture. The latter is available in the same size, same taste, and same structure in Mysore, Karachi, Moscow or Washington DC or even in Cairo. It has created uniformity in taste and cultural practices. This modernity was incidentally pushed through by Multinationals whose power of the capital is much larger than many countries. In fact there are around 33,000 McDonald Restaurants in 118 countries in the world. Subway is another restaurant, which is incidentally larger than McDonald. It has more than 44,000 restaurants in more than 100 countries. Similar is the case of Coca Cola and Pepsi Cola. All these have created modernity of culture and life styles.

Giorgio Shani, Japanese Sociologist, has gone a step further to argue that globalization in the conventional sense is nothing, but "globalization of liberal-capitalist modernity." This liberal modernity project is advocated by the US whose aim is to univerzalise "liberal capitalist modernity." This is manifested through multiple means: political, economic and cultural homogenization on a global scale.

Marx was one of those who saw globalization and modernity as intertwined projects of colonial capitalism. Weber went further with his argument of rationality and capitalism. But both saw modernity as a universal process and carrying universal project. Marx, however, particularized liberal capitalist modernity; Weber on the contrary looked at the cultural roots of liberal capitalist modernity project in protestant ethics. However what problematized the issue was the fact that "modernity had different languages" and different faces.

However, one cannot deny that capitalism has acted both progressively in the case of Colonial County and in a destructive way in the colonized world. At the same time a number of Marxist have argued that the modernity project in the context of colonized world, such as India, has remained half done. In some cases it never reached many social categories, which remained excluded from the project of modernity. Even capitalism did the same thing. In the colonized world capitalism came from the above; it did not allow its natural growth from within. Hence, the argument that capitalism did more harm in the colonized world by compromising with pre-capitalist social relations and co-existed along with it. The consequence was twofold: uneven and lopsided development on the one hand and destruction of native communities on the other. Samir Amir for example calls it as the first stage of capitalism wherein the latter became more destructive. It destroyed the natives of Haiti, destroyed the indigenous industries in India, the natives of America etc.

(d) Laminated Project of Post-Modernity

There are arguments stating that globalization would lead to "post-modernity" trend too. This is because it reduces the importance of class politics, which would be replaced by identity politics. Traditional social movements would be replaced by New Social Movements. On the contrary there are others who viewed globalization as a method or model to understand post-modernism, adopted by the western, particularly American and British scholars. This is apparent in the argument of Omar Lizardo and Michael Strand: "Globalization theory has become the province of British and American theorists because of a contiguity that extends back to a propitious model employed to understand post-modernism."[14]

It is in this context that one can ask: does globalization represent a new form of modernity or post-modernity? Or does it represent a hybrid? If globalization is understood as changing process or phenomenon of capitalism, which is trying to envelop the whole world through different means, including culture and market, then obviously it can be treated as a phenomenon of a new form of modernity. It is trying to complete what the earlier modernity had not done; trying to reach each and every social category and interconnect them with the larger market.

Schools/Perspectives/Thoughts on Globalization

There are three schools of thought that have viewed Globalization differently, although it does not mean that there are no other perspectives available. These three schools are called, Hyper-globalist, Sceptics and Transformationalists.

The first school represented by Ohmae and others looks at globalization as a phenomenon that would bring in profound changes in the contemporary period. To quote, "contemporary globalization defines a new era in which peoples everywhere are increasingly subject to the disciplines of the global marketplace."[15] People are profoundly influenced by the market forces. In this context the traditional nation-states have become unwanted business units. Their places have been taken over by the Market. Ohame's central argument is that the states are increasingly coming under economic and political process and change. In this process of change, market has become the unifying and universal force to link up each and every social category in the larger market. This market is decided by MNC and Transnational global capitalists. All these have created what is called "borderless" global space and also global production at a scale unprecedented in the history of the world. Nation-states are becoming redundant and the role of states is now reduced to "receive decisions" from without and from within. It is in this context that the argument of Soros, a well-known financier, needs to be stressed. In his book on Globalization, he argued that "globalization is most powerful and unstoppable process."[16] His argument reflects the views of the hyper-globalist. Even Soros' argument sometimes reflects those of the sceptics, as he claims that even globalization, particularly transnational financial markets, can also become a destabilizing force. This overlapping is apparent in other schools of thought too.

On the contrary, sceptics such as Thomson and Hirst argue that "globalization is a myth" and that it "conceals the reality of an international economy increasingly segmented into three major regional blocs in which National Governments remain very powerful."[17] They believe that globalization is not a new phenomenon. Hirst and Thomson point out that trade and investment flows were higher between 1890 and 1914 than at present. This is the reason why they are opposed to celebrating globalization as new process of modernity and economic development. Further, they argue that more than globalization, regionalism is growing with such regional blocks as ASEAN, NAFTA, EU etc. They also point out that not all the countries are involved in the regulations of market or finance; rather it is confined to a few countries of the OECD.

Rosanau belongs to the third important school, the Transformationalists. David Held argues that globalization has brought profound changes, but changes are uncertain in nature. To quote them: "States and societies across the globe are experiencing a process of profound change as they try to adapt to a more interconnected but highly uncertain world."[18]

Other than these three schools of thought, there are two more perspectives available: one is globalists, who believe that globalization has arrived as a social process and that there is no escape from it, as it mediated through different forms—from financial form to cultural form. In fact cultural form is so strong that it cannot be brushed aside. In this perceptive one can find two categories emerging: optimist and pessimist. The optimists see in globalization a chance to reclaim democracy, improve standards of life, decrease poverty and achieve over all development. On the contrary, the pessimists hold that more than solving the problems of hunger, under-development, and backwardness, globalization will sharpen the same over time. They also believe that it would aggravate violence, conflict and contradiction across regions and between social categories.

In a second perspective, the traditionalists try to view globalization as an old phenomenon, dating either back to colonial period or to the period of modernity. Marx is one those who viewed the beginning of globalization in transfer of capital and the subsequent conquest of world by the colonial powers in Asia, Africa and North American continent. There are others too who would argue that globalization is a myth on the grounds that nation-states are still the strong reference point in the contemporary politics, and that the culture of a country cannot be destroyed as it has internal mechanisms to protect and defend it.

Globalization has also created two broad schools of thought: one group of scholars looking at the process in an optimistic way. This includes liberal economist such as Bhagawathi and Nigel Harris. If Bhagawathi looks at globalization as "panacea," as a solution to all the problems afflicting population, Harris argues that globalization would bridge the gap between first and third world countries as it allows free flow of capital without any barriers. Secondly, he is optimistic that globalization would allow the emergence of regional economic blocks which would bring in economic equality between the regions.

There are others too who fall under the "optimistic" category. Giorgio Shani argues that even though globalization is liberal capitalist project, it has the larger project of creating "liberal global civil society." This is referred to as "a society where social life (the public sphere) is modelled on exchange and persons meet in order to arbitrate their pre-existing interests which have been self-authored."[19]

On the contrary, the pessimists look at globalization as a process of disempowerment, displacement, and dispossession. One important pessimist is Zygmunt Bauman feels that "globalization is the cause of our unhappiness" although he also argues that "Globalization" is on everybody's lips; a fad word fast turning into a shibboleth, a magic incantation, a pass-key meant to unlock the gates to all present and future mysteries."[20]

Pessimists also argue in terms of binary opposition of "Old Leviathan" and "New Leviathan." In the case of "Old Leviathan" the state is powerful, would control the economy, market and would provide social safety networks. It would withstand the power of the "capital." On the contrary, the "New Leviathan" justifies the entry of global capital, retrenchment of work force, reduction of wages of the workers, and the withdrawal of the state from the realm of social welfare and large scale privatization and outsourcing of economy. They are better known as critiques of globalization. These critics also accuse that more than creating mass production, globalization has created flexible production.

Apart from the optimists and pessimists, we have Critical Globalists. Ideologically, they criticise globalization and do not look at globalization as a "panacea" like the liberal globalists do. That does not mean that every globalist would argue in similar fashion. The best example of a critical globalist is Stiglitz. Initially, he believed that globalization would be an answer for the problem afflicting the global poverty, backwardness and underdevelopment. But later he began to understand the fact that instead of becoming a solution, globalization was becoming a "problem itself". This is because instead of solving a problem "globalization" was intensifying the problem.

Another critical globalist, Prabhat Patnaik, who is also a left economist, sees the process of globalization in "late capitalism." In the late capitalism, which he believed is also phase of finance capital,[21] he sees the features of Imperialism again re-emerging and recapitulating the world economy. He equated globalization with "Imperialism" and believes that there "is a tremendous globalization of capital in the form of finance." Secondly, he also believed that "globalization of capital-in-finance was taking place instead of globalization of capital-in-production." Thirdly, he argues that "tremendous fluidity of finance capital has undermined the ability of nation-states to intervene in the economy to retain the high level of activity."[22]

There are other critical globalists too who look at globalization as a problem. Stiglitz, the former Chief Economist of IMF, in his pioneer book, "Globalization and Its Discontent" made scathing attack on the neo-liberal policies advanced by the World Bank and IMF. He dismissed the "efficient outcomes" argument inherent in neo-liberalism. He wrote: "Behind the free market ideology there is a model, often attributed to Adam Smith, which argues that market forces—the profit motive—drive the economy to efficient outcomes as if by an invisible hand."[23] Interestingly, he was not out rightly opposed to Market; rather he wanted to rework the framework of the market in such a way that it helps the poor or development of a country. This does not mean that these schools and perspectives have not been contested. They have been contested but for lack of empirical substantiation, they are too ambiguous to reflect upon.

Four-scapes and Globalization

One of the questions often asked is whether we can imagine the growth of new scapes that the globalization has created. In his seminal work "Modernity At large: Cultural Dimension of Globalization" (Minnesota, 1996) Arjun Appadurai, a Cultural Anthropologist, argues that globalization has the tendency to create five scapes: these are ethno-, media-, techno-, finance-, and ideo-. They offer radical cultural interpretations to the issues of globalization. Further, these 'scape arguments' are advanced to overcome insufficiency in the centre-periphery debate. Further, it was also meant to demonstrate that globalization is not only rooted in the expansion of global capitalism, but also the fact that the modernity of globalization mediates and circulates through diasporic, imaginary, and geographic means. This creates irregularities in globalization.

First scape is ethno, which is nothing but deterritorialized and re-territorialized scape that the globalization creates. This scape also maps different categories of social agents such as tourists, immigrants, exiles, guest workers who represent disorganized, dispersed capitalism.[24] These categories are in constant struggle to define their identity as well as territory in the "imagined world", as Arjun Appadurai argues.

Second is the establishment of media-scape. Appadurai explores how imaginations of individuals are affected by interconnectedness of migration including mass media. In the latter case he believed that media has the potentiality to create conditions to think about the notions of neighbourhood and nationhood. He further believed that media and migration have de-territorialized people to a large extent and have created long distance nationalism, ethnic violence, and "Diaspora public sphere and also they have created disjuncture between economic, cultural, and political aspects of daily life."[25] In fact his ideas corroborate with the ideas of Anderson in his *Imagined Communities*.

As regards the third scape (the techno-scape), one is reminded of Daniel J. Boorstin who argued that the contemporary age is driven by what is called "Republic of Technology" (Theodore Levitt, "The Globalization of Markets", in the *McKinsey Quarterly*, Available at http://www.lapres.net/levitt.pdf), whose main aim is "convergence" of everything under the rubric of technology. The technology, incidentally, has pushed the market into global commonality; commonality in the adoption of technology, commonality in the usage of technology, and commonality in the reach or inter linkage between the social categories. It also transformed the nature of commodity consumption, commodity distribution and commodity transmission. This is visible in the way internet is universally and uniformly adopted everywhere as a medium of interaction, and as a medium of consumption. In fact, techno-scape has shrunk the gap between Time and space. Time and Space have been conscripted with the technology creating a new scape. This is nothing but creating techno scape; globalization has done it. Many social movements use this scape, despite critiquing globalization, to register their protest against globalization.

Fourth one is Ideo-scapes. This is meant to capture the ideas of the state, state power and also counter-ideologies to modern and dominant political discourse of contemporary period. The last one is finance-scape. The increasing flow of finance across borders and countries has created finance-scape at the global level unprecedented in the history.

Different Types of Globalization: One or Multiple Globalization

Often globalization is seen as homogenous and unilinear and single process without understanding the fact that Globalization is perceived in multiple ways. Cheng, for example (2006), has come out with a series of globalization processes, which he categorized as technological globalization, economic globalization, social globalization, political globalization, cultural globalization and learning globalization.[26] What is missing in this analysis is the presence of other forms of globalization. One such globalization is capitalist globalization.

There are others who have tried to argue that primarily there are three types of globalization: Political, Economic and Cultural. In the first case of political globalization, the argument centred around the importance of International agencies such as the UN. It is also argued that political globalization has made the boundaries of the nation-state redundant, creating conditions for the "collapse of boundaries or geography." It has reduced the importance of nation-state in the overall sphere of international politics. Their arguments represent the voice of Transformationalists' school led by David Held who believed that political globalization has brought in a paradigm shift in the reach of political power, authority and forms of rule. These are brought in by transnational and multilateral agencies. At the same time, Marxist scholar such as Heberamassee see in political globalization a space for "democratic deficit" as the decisions in this contemporary world are taken not within the national boundaries, but outside its realms. He argues that one can no longer count on its own forces to provide its citizens with adequate protection from the external effects of decisions taken by *other* actors, or from the knock-on effects of processes originating beyond its boundaries." The result is the growth or the emergence of multiple social movements, challenging the larger agenda of globalization. In the second case, it is argued that globalization is necessarily an economic process wherein the economic resources are transferred from one country to another without the loss of time and space. National boundaries simply collapse in the context of increasing interlinkage between countries.

Proponents of Cultural globalization look at globalization in terms of growing homogeneity of world in the recent past. In this context, the argument in favour of national culture is given up on the grounds that world today is becoming multi-cultural. Masao Miyoshi, Japanese scholar argues that "national culture is increasingly irrelevant; multi-culturalism holds the day."[27] At the same time it is true that cultures are undergoing tremendous transformation; the linkage on the one hand given rise to a situation of "glocalization" (a product or service tailored to conform to the local laws, customs or consumer preferences), i.e., globalization is negotiating with local culture. On the other hand, a new global culture is allowed to replace the local culture. It is true that in the contemporary context symbols of culture have changed; Coca-Cola is now replacing local drinking habit of developing world. Bisleri Bottles have replaced the habit of drinking water, Maggi noodles have replaced the habit of eating, This is why Anthony Giddens[28] argument that, "local happenings are shaped by events occurring many miles away and *vice versa*" holds good. This is because globalization has created "linked trends"—any happening in parts of the world has its impact on other parts of the world.

Further, it is argued that the everyday cultural practices have been transformed into commodities. Cultural industries such as malls, cinemas, music, movies, TVs, pop shows etc. have pushed the globalization to a marked level. The cultural industries have created a new category of consumers who are linked to global market. Global market, backed by global capitalist or Multinationals, has become the centre of cultural production, creating new culture of lifestyle and uniformity in practices throughout the world. In other words, popular culture has become a part of homogenization process towards integrating world, particularly global market. This has transmitted to the cultural practices at domestic level. On civil society, McLibel, once claimed that, "today children at home decide what to eat, what to bring and what to dispose off." A paradigm shift has taken place in the cultural practices. Cultural symbols like English books have global readers. Harry Potter, for example, now symbolized the new culture of reading, Pepsi-Cola and Coca-Cola have emerged as alternative cultures of drinking. Fast foods have become the symbol of modernity. All these have the potentiality to flatten cultural differences. This is what Thomas Friedman calls the "World is Flat."

There are other ways of dividing globalization. Thomas Friedman, a journalist turned globalist, divided the globalization into three forms:

Globalization (1) wherein the government and the countries are the main protagonists; Globalization; (2) wherein the multinationals plays a dominant role in accentuating globalization, and finally Globalization; (3) wherein personal computers, cables etc. play the dominant role. This is being criticised for its too naive arguments.

Finally, one may ask as to what prompted globalization. The World Bank argues in favour of Globalization with two factors: firstly, technological advancement in recent years, which has resulted in the reduction of the cost of production, and consequently investment. This helped a large number of firms to relocate the production facilities from one country to another. Secondly, the growing liberalization of economy in different countries has helped the integration of local economy with the larger economy or the market. However, the Trinity—World Bank, IMF and WTO, has pushed the process of globalization at different intervals.

There are other factors that have pushed globalization. The collapse of Soviet Union helped the west to celebrate the same as "triumph of capitalism" and reaffirm its domination over global market by means of large scale democratization of either dictatorial countries, or former socialist blocs. It is said that decade of 1990s saw democratization or what is called "third wave" in more than one hundred countries. A survey conducted by Freedom House has revealed that (the 2001-2002 survey) "about 65 per cent of the world's population lives in free or partly free states that afford their citizens some degree of basic rights and civil liberties. The Survey also showed that of the world's 192 countries, 121 (63%) were "electoral democracies."[29] Such political freedoms were used as a pretext and as a barometer to enter into domestic market and integrate the same with the global market in the name of democracy. This market had mediated through multiple means: cultural symbolism, virtual markets, bio-diversity, Intellectual Property Rights, Super Bazaars, miracle seeds including cultural industries. In these countries the market had created "homogenization" of culture, which sometimes, as Featherstone called, created conditions for "Americanization of culture." These markets became the fountain of global capital and also the terrain of individual freedom and new rights on the one hand, and terrain of dislocation, deprivation, dispossession on the other. This is the reason why large number of social movements grew in these countries wherein Market and Global capital became the target of different social categories/social movements in the name of loss of identity, culture, community life including farmers' suicide.

REFERENCES

1. David Renton, (2001), *Marx on Globalization*, (Ed.) London (reprint): Lawrence and Wishart, p. 1.
2. Chamsy el-Ojeili, Chamsy and Patrick Hayden. *Critical Theories of Globalization*: *An Introduction*, Houndmills, Basingstoke, Hampshire, UK (2006) Palgrave MacMillan, p. 1.
3. *Ibid.*
4. OC and C, *Second Globalization,: How is it reshaping the corporate governance* and *CEOs Agenda*, 2012.
5. http://www.worldbank.org/depweb/beyond/beyondco/beg_12.pdf.
6. This is reported in WTOs report on "Globalization and Trade" http://www.wto.org/english/res_e/booksp_e/anrep_e/wtr08-2b_e.pdf.
7. David Held, 1996.
8. http://www2.hawaii.edu/~fredr/glotexts.htm#TEHRANIAN
9. International Monetary Fund (2000). "*Globalization: Threats or Opportunity*." 12th April, 2000: IMF Publications.
10. Giddens, Anthony, (1991), *The Consequences of Modernity,* Cambridge: UK Polity Press.
11. Chamsy el-Ojeili, *op. cit.*, p. 1.
12. Barrett, M. (1991), *The Politics of Truth: From Marx to Foucault,* Cambridge: UK Polity Press.
13. Karl Marx, (1982), *Communist Manifesto*, Moscow: UK Progress Publishers.
14. Omar Lizardo and Michael Strand. Post-modernism and Globalization (Available at http://www3.nd.edu/~olizardo/chapters/ps-pomo-glob.pdf)
15. Held, D., A. McGrew, D. Goldblatt, and J. Perraton. (1999). *Global Transformations: Politics, Economics and Culture*. Stanford CA, Polity and Stanford University Press.
16. Soros, George (2002). *On Globalization*, New York: Public Affairs Publishers.
17. Held, D. and A. McGrew (2001). Globalization, in *Oxford Companion to the Politics of the World* (Ed.) Joel Krieger, Oxford University Press.
18. Quoted in Bryane Michael, Theorising the Politics of Globalization: A Critique of Held *et al.*'s "Transformationalism," in *Journal of Economic and Social Research,* Vol. 4, No. 2, pp. 3-17 (Available at http://jesr.journal.faith.edu.tr/globalization.pdf).

19. Giorgio, Shani. 2003, *The Liberal Project: Globalization, Modernity and Identity*, The International Studies Association of Ritsumeikan University: Ritsumeikan Annual Review of International Studies, Vol. 2, pp. 37-57.
20. Quoted in Chamsy el-Ojeili Patrick Hayden, (2006), *Critical Theories of Globalization: An Introduction*, London: Palgrave MacMillan.
21. Patnaik, Prabhat, *Globalization of Capital and Terms of Trade Movement,* Centre for Economic Studies and Planning, JNU, New Delhi, (chapter presented at the International Conference on *Agrarian Reforms and Rural Development in Less Developed Countries*, January 3-6, 2002, Kolkata. (Available at http://www.networkideas.org/featart/mar2002/globalization_1.pdf).
22. Patnaik, Prabhat, Globalization of Capital and the Theory of Imperialism, in *Social Scientist*, Vol. 24, Nos. 11-12, November-December 20, 1996.
23. Stiglitz, Joseph, (2002), *Globalization and its Discontents*, London : Penguin Books.
24. Kostas Maronitis, *Threat and Defence: Diaspora and the Creation of Ethnoscapes*, Chapter from the Conference "INTER: A European Cultural Studies Conference in Sweden", organised by the Advanced Cultural Studies Institute of Sweden (ACSIS) in Norrköping 11-13 June, 2007. Conference Proceedings published by Linköping University at www.ep.liu.se/ecp/025/.
25. Oonk, Gijsbert, Modernity at Large: Cultural Dimensions of Globalization (review) in *Journal of World History*, Volume 11, Number 1, Spring 2000, pp. 157-159.
26. Cheng, Yin Cheong, *Fostering Local Knowledge and Wisdom in Globalized Education: Multiple Theories,* Centre for Research and International Collaboration, Keynote Speech Presented at The 8th International Conference on *"Globalization and Localization Enmeshed: Searching for a Balance in Education"*, Organized by Faculty of Education of Chulalongkorn University Hong Kong Institute of Education, November 18-21, 2002.
27. Miyoshi, M. "Sites of Resistance in the Global Economy", in *Cultural Readings of Imperialism: Edward Said and the Gravity of History*, K. Ansell-Pearson, M. Parry and J. Squires (Eds.), London (1997), Lawrence and Wishart, pp. 49-66.
28. Giddens, Anthony (1991), *The Consequences of Modernity*, Redwood City CA Stanford University Press, p. 64.
29. Freedom House, 2001, *Freedom in the World 2001-2002*, New York, December 18, Press Release.

2

The Changing Face of Religion in a Globalizing World

SCARIA PANNACKAL SVD

Globalization is a metaphor for a world that is seen as increasingly interconnected, where borders and boundaries are becoming porous, where a great deal of interaction and exchange between people of different nationalities, cultures and religions is taking place. Globalization is characterized by an exclusive, unprecedented movement of capital, goods, technology, people, cultural patterns, ideas and images. A great deal of hope and euphoria surrounds the process of globalization. The protagonists of globalization speak of a borderless world, de-territorisation and the end of geography, and the global village. In reality, globalization is a paradoxical phenomenon. It represents a mixed bag of positive and beneficial as well as negative and socially disruptive elements and features. Thus, on the one hand, it has brought about a great deal of uniformity and homogenization in respect of economic and technological processes, political structures and institutions, lifestyles and entertainment; on the other hand, it has led to a strengthening and revival of ethnic and religious consciousness and identities in large parts of the world.

There has been a good deal of discussion and debate, especially in Western Sociology about the process of secularization. The Enlightenment project repudiated the world view of medieval Christianity and sought to replace it with secular nationalism. From the middle of the nineteenth century, religion began to experience a steady decline in power, prestige and popularity in large parts of the Western world. For example, between 1965 and 1999, the percentage of church-goers in West Germany dropped from 75 per cent to less than 30 per cent. In 1851, about 60 per cent of the population of England and Wales attended church. By the end of the twentieth century this figure dropped to 10 per cent. The steady decline of religion in Europe is also reflected in the shortage of priests. Thus, though the population of England grew by 35 per cent between 1900 and 1984, the number of Christian Clergy halved from 20,000 to 10,000. The available survey data indicate that in most European countries as well as in the United States and Canada, there has been a general erosion of religious beliefs and a steady decline in church membership and attendance.

Sociologists have a tendency which is far from healthy to jump to generalizations on the basis of limited data. This has particularly been the case with the Sociology of Religion, especially with what has come to be known as the secularization thesis. More than a quarter century ago, a well-known American sociologist, Peter Berger, asserted that modernization would inevitably lead to a decline of religion in the public and private spheres. This, however, did not happen. In fact, in the last couple of decades, there has come about an evident resurgence of ethnic and religious consciousness in large parts of the world. This development has taken sociologists like Berger by surprise. Peter Berger has recently confessed that the secularization thesis has been falsified by the revival of ethnic and religious consciousness in many countries, including the United States. He points out that the project of secularization has been successful only in one small corner of the world, namely, Western Europe. The rest of the world, he says, continues to be as fervently religious as before. The point is that secularization is neither universal nor inevitable. In fact, one of the most modernized nations in the world, the United States, has witnessed a remarkable resurgence of evangelism in recent years, which has also played an important role in domestic politics as well as foreign policy. The debate about creationism or intelligence design *vs.* evolutionism has resurfaced and is currently the subject of a heated controversy in the country. A recent incident reflects the strengthening of religious consciousness in the United States. Shortly after he took office as Chief Justice of Alabama Supreme Court in 2001, Roy Moore caused a national furore when he commissioned and installed a granite monument of the Ten Commandments in the State Supreme Court building and refused to remove it. When Moore defied a Federal Court order to remove the monument, thousands of his supporters from across the country descended in the city of

Montgomery offering him moral and social support. They squatted on the steps of the Supreme Court building, praying, singing and blowing ram's horns.

Modern information and communication technologies are the lifeline of globalization. It is interesting to note that modern information and communication technology has played and continues to play a highly significant role in the global dissemination of religious ideas and beliefs and in the revival of religious consciousness. Many of America's biggest publishing and media corporations are pushing into the religious market for the simple reason that the religious market in the country is experiencing a huge, unprecedented boom. It is estimated that in 2003, the market for religious products in the US alone was worth 8.6 billion dollars. The market for religious books, mainly evangelical literature, grew by 37 per cent in 2003. The *Purpose-driven Life,* by Rick Warren, an evangelical preacher in the US is the best-selling hard-cover book in American history, with more than 25 million copies sold. The growing popularity of religious literature is also reflected in the consumer market. Thus, Wal-Mart, America's largest chain of supermarkets, now sells Christian diet books and Christian detective stories.

Zygmunt Bauman, an eminent contemporary Sociologist, has coined the word globalization to highlight the fact that globalization seems to reinforce not only global and transnational, but also local ethnic identities. Thus, in Thailand, Buddhist monks are making increasing use of the internet for disseminating their traditions through 200 websites. In the US, the television shows of the evangelist Billy Graham enjoy enormous popularity across the country. This phenomenon is not confined to the developed world; there are several television channels in India which are devoted to religious discourses, *yoga*, and meditation. One of them, the Astha TV, set-up in 2000, is beamed to 160 countries. Swami Ramdev, who regularly appears on Astha TV, has become a cult figure with hundreds of thousands of followers not only in India, but also in countries which have large number of NRIs. There are more than 17,000 web pages on Google on Swami Ramdev. Books, cassettes and VCDs containing his discourses are widely circulated in India and abroad.

One of the highly significant features of globalization is the existence of transnational communities or Diaspora which maintain a vast network of communication and culture with their homelands. Modern information and communication technology, especially telephone, satellite television and the Internet, plays a highly important role in connecting these diasporic communities to their cultural roots and their homelands. Hundreds of local news chapters and magazines in scores of languages are available online, which allow the overseas immigrants to keep in touch with their religious and cultural traditions as well as developments in their native countries. With the creation of the state of Israel in 1948, more than 50 per cent of the local Palestinian population was driven out of their homeland. More than four million of the refugees took shelter in Europe and North America. A whole generation was born and brought up in foreign lands, cut off from their roots. The members of this generation are now rediscovering, thanks to home pages on the Internet, their religious and cultural traditions as well as the villages from which their parents migrated. The Internet is thus serving as a source of virtual rootedness. It is also becoming an instrument for transnational political mobilization, as in the case of Kurdish and Palestinian refugees in Europe.

The process of globalization has greatly contributed to the growing popularity of Eastern cults in the Western world. The International Society for Krishna Consciousness (ISKCON) now has a million followers worldwide, including such notables as a scion of the Ford family and Beatle George Harrison. The global popularity of *yoga*, the discourses of Hindu spiritual leaders and the quasi-spiritual works of Deepak Chopra owe a great deal to modern information and communication technologies.

The fascination with Eastern philosophies and cults in Europe and North America needs to be viewed in the social and cultural context of contemporary Western societies. Several Western social scientists, writers and commentators have pointed out that, by and large, Western societies are faced with fracture, fragmentation and atomization and that this fragmentation is evidenced in the lies of individuals as well as in the institutional structure and cultural patterns. It is manifested in the falling apart and decomposing of human relationships, in the growing feelings of insecurity, vulnerability and uncertainty, living alone as well as people who experience feelings of loneliness. In Western societies, social institutions—family, neighbourhood, church, community—that once provided common bonds and sense of belonging and served as a bulwark in the face of life's inevitable uncertainties and crises, have nearly disappeared and have not been replaced by any viable alternatives. Living in the abstract and disquieting spaces of late modernity and globalization—characterized by gigantic, impersonal structures, fragmented social fabric, atomized relationships, stressful lifestyles—the individual inevitably feels diminished, alienated, depersonalized. It is hardly surprising that many people in Western countries are turning to Eastern philosophies in search of spiritual solace and fulfilment.

I mentioned earlier that globalization has paradoxical features and consequences. Thus, on the one hand, one notices a good deal of exposure to ethnic, cultural and religious diversity and consequently a substantial measure of inter-cultural and inter-religious sensitivity and tolerance. This is an important dimension of contemporary multiculturalism. Candy producers in Europe, like Haribo and Van Melle, are now substituting their meat-produced gelatine with alternative substances, so that they will be acceptable to Jewish and Muslim consumers who prefer kosher and halal meat products. The global fast-food chain McDonald's displays appreciable cultural sensitivity in not serving beef burgers in India or hamburgers in Islamic countries.

On the other hand, one finds that the cultural atmosphere in many Western countries is suffused with Xenophobia, exclusion and discrimination against ethnic and religious minorities. The 2004 annual report of the European Monitoring Centre on Racism and Xenophobia points out that the record of EU Governments in combating Racism and Xenophobia is at best mixed and at worst deplorable. The report says that some EU countries are either too slow to enact anti-racism laws or pass measures that actually restrict the rights of immigrants. The report reveals that the British police received nearly 53,000 complaints of racist incidents in 2004, followed by Germany which received 6,474 complaints. According to the report, religious and ethnic minorities, particularly the Gypsies and Muslims, face discrimination and exclusion in many different forms, from education and poor housing to ghettoization to restricted employment opportunities.

In many purportedly multicultural societies of Europe, there is an evident chasm between legal norms (such as equality, citizenship) and the social reality of exclusion and discrimination. France, for example, swears by the ideals of liberty, equality and fraternity. In reality, widespread discrimination and exclusion, especially in the case of immigrants from North Africa, expose the hypocrisy of the French system. In Britain, racial discrimination, in overt or covert form, is still widely prevalent. The non-white elite schools in the UK require a record of regular church attendance on the part of parents, which automatically excludes people from other religious backgrounds. According to British law, blasphemy against Christianity is a punishable offence. This provision, however, is not applicable to Islam or other religions. Thousands of Anglican, Catholic and Jewish religious schools are funded by the state in Britain. Until recently, such funding was not available to Muslim schools. In the US, despite the existence of legal mechanisms such as the Equal Opportunity Agency, discrimination against the African-Americans, Hispanics and other minority groups continues unabated.

In most Western countries, immigration, cultural diversity and the integration of immigrants into mainstream society have become sites of intense contestation. By and large, the immigrants face discrimination, lack of legal security, unclear citizenship status and institutionalized racism. During the past couple of decades, racist sentiments and violence against foreigners and immigrants have been on the rise in many Western countries. Ethnic and religious minorities often bear the brunt of attacks by neo-Nazi groups and other racist outfits. The growing popularity of racist, ultra right-wing political parties such as the British National Party and *Front Nationale* in France indicate that racist sentiments are getting strengthened.

Racist sentiments are so deeply embedded in the consciousness of people in many Western societies that even the mainstream churches do not seem to be immune to its insidious influence. This is borne out by the experience of immigrants from the Caribbean islands who began migrating to Britain from the 1950s onwards. They saw Britain as the mother country where they would find honour and economic well-being. Their hopes were dashed when they began to experience discrimination and vilification by the established churches. Some of them were so disillusioned that they eventually turned to Pentecostalism which promises salvation in the next life.

There has been a good deal of debate in the US about racial profiling in the aftermath of 9/11. Certain sections of the population, notably ethnic and religious minorities from West Asia and the Middle East, have been subjected to a process whereby information about their beliefs, background and activities is secretly collected by the FBI. Nearly 32 million people in the US, mostly Muslims, have reported that they have been racially profiled. A recent report by the Amnesty International points out that nearly 87 million people in the

US are at high risk of being victimized because they belong to ethnic or religious minorities.

A dark side of globalization is the global campaign of hatred against ethnic and religious minorities and its clandestine funding by sections of diasporic communities. For example, an affluent section of the Indian Diaspora in the US has been an important source of funding as well as political and moral support for quasi-political organizations such as the Rashtriya Swayam Sevak Sangh (RSS). It was recently revealed that for the past 13 years, the India Development and Relief Fund (IDRF) has been misusing funds donated by the corporate sector in the US to support RSS and affiliated organizations in India. The IDRF receives every year hundreds of thousands of dollars from corporate houses and business establishments in the US. In 2000, for example, it collected 1.7 million dollars. Most of the four million dollars collected by the IDRF between 1994 and 2000 was used against Christians and Muslims in India. These startling revelations were brought out by the Campaign to Stop Funding Hate, a coalition of Indian professionals, students, artists and intellectuals in the US.

Modern information and communication technologies are being increasingly used for global dissemination and export of extremist political and religious ideologies and the cult of violence and terrorism associated with them. The globalization of reckless terrorism, in the guise of religion, poses an ominous threat to world peace.

A relatively recent phenomenon which has attracted worldwide attention, especially in the aftermath of 9/11, is what has come to be known as *Islamophobia*: fear of and hatred towards Islam and Muslims. A set of factors, including the role of the global media, the writings and utterances of some influential writers and intellectuals and the growing global network of terrorism, has contributed to the negative perception about Muslims. The currently prevailing perception about Islam in the Western World is that it is devoid of progressive values, that it incites violent passions in its followers, and that it poses a serious threat to world peace. Shortly after 9/11, Nobel Laureate V.S. Naipaul asserted that Islam enslaved and attempted to wipe out other cultures and that it had a calamitous effect on converted people. Samuel Huntington described the contemporary period as the "age of Muslim wars" in which Muslims are fighting each other and non-Muslims alike. He asserts that these wars have replaced the Cold War as the principal form of international conflict, and that there is a danger that the current situation could produce a clash of civilizations between the Islamic world and the West. Francis Fukuyama argued that the September 11 attack on the US represents a "desperate backlash against the modern world by those who either do not understand modernity or do not want to understand it." He characterizes the challenge faced by the West as a struggle between Western liberal democracy and what he calls Islamo-fascism. A British historian Niall Ferguson has recently said that even if the Muslims in Europe are the citizens of the countries where they live, they cannot be true citizens.

The global media has played a significant role in popularizing and strengthening stereotypes about Muslims. Disney's 1993 animated film *Aladdin* referred to Arabs as "barbaric." The Hollywood film *True Lies* stereotypes Arabs as violent anti-American fanatics who launch terrorist attacks for no apparent reason. This kind of stereotyping and labelling not only distorts and misrepresents reality, but also fails to take cognizance of the fact that there are more than 15 million Arab Christians in the Middle East.

In many Western countries, Muslim immigrants regularly experience discrimination and exclusion in respect of housing, education and employment. According to the French policy of colour-blind cultural assimilation, the immigrants are required to eschew their cultural, religious and political distinctiveness and allegiances and assimilate into the French system. Notwithstanding the lofty ideals of liberty, equality and fraternity, a mixture of class, religion and race differentiates the French population. The suburbs, where the majority of Muslim immigrants from North Africa and their second and third generation descendants live, are characterized by poverty, high unemployment rate and crime. The unemployment rate among the North African immigrants is 30 per cent to 40 per cent as compared to the national average of 10 per cent. Mainstream jobs and positions remain largely with a white, upper class, Christian majority. Faced with this depressing situation, many Muslim youth born and brought up in France are forced to change their names from Fatima and Muhammad to Sandrine and Laurent to conceal their religious identity. Many of them hide their local addresses for fear that this might jeopardize their chances of getting a job. In November 2005 there was large-scale rioting and vandalism on the streets of Paris carried out by North African youth, triggered by the accidental death by electrocution of two of their colleagues who were being chased by the police. The riots exposed the fragility and failure of the French system and the marginalization and vulnerability of the immigrants.

The discrimination and exclusion experienced by Muslims living in Western countries is reflected in the denial of their cultural and religious rights. A couple of years ago, the French President Jacques Chirac commissioned the Bernard Stasi report, which recommended a ban on school children wearing religious symbols, including the Jewish *yarmulke,* the Christian cross, the Islamic headdress and the Sikh turban. The Netherlands is currently considering a ban on the Islamic headdress. The southern state of Baden-Wurttemberg in Germany has created its own searching examination exclusively for Muslim applicants seeking German citizenship. Questions in the examination include the following: If your son told you he was homosexual and wanted to live with another man, how would you react?

The disquieting climate of our time has produced some prophets of doom such as Samuel Huntington. He argues that future international conflicts will no longer be based on the clash of political ideologies or economic interests but on civilizations or cultural-religious communities. He believes that the renewed aggression and hostility in many Islamic countries directed against the West is the root cause of many present-day problems. He sees Western Christianity and Islam as potentially pitted against each other as the defining feature of the unfolding global scenario.

Huntington's argument is true neither from the historical point of view nor in the context of present times. The assumptions on which he bases his conclusions are fallacious, naïve and contestable. He takes an essentialized, fossilized view of cultures and civilizations. His view is not only myopic, but also fraught with dangerous implications and insinuations. Thankfully, the hollowness this argument has been exposed by some of the world's leading thinkers and intellectuals. Edward Said, for example, decries the clash of civilization thesis as a deplorable attempt to revive the good *vs.* evil dichotomy prevalent during the cold War era. Huntington's views have been publicly denounced by heads of states, statesmen and politicians in many Western countries. Thus, in a speech to the Jordanian Parliament in 1994, President Bill Clinton strongly repudiated the clash of civilizations thesis, noting that "there are those who insist that there are impassable religious and other obstacles to harmony that our beliefs and our cultures must somehow inevitably clash. America refuses to accept that our civilizations must collide." The massive anti-war protests and demonstrations across Europe, North America and the rest of the world before the American-led invasion of Iraq and the sharp differences between the European Union and the United States and its allies before and after the invasion exposed the absurdity of the clash of civilizations thesis.

A notable development in recent years, which has been facilitated by the process of globalization, is inter-religious or inter-faith dialogues. Inter-faith activities in the West have been initiated by Christian and Jewish groups. The World Council of Churches in Geneva opened an office that deals with inter-faith issues. In Sweden, inter-faith programmes are supported by the state. A small group comprising of a Christian Priest, a Jewish Rabbi and a Muslim Imam held public dialogue session in which churches, universities and the media were also involved. This was followed by the establishment in 1996 of the Nordic Centre for Inter-religious Dialogue. Many people who are active in inter-religious dialogue emphasize that religion needs to be reinterpreted and reinvented in the context of present times and in the service of good will, tolerance and harmonious coexistence between followers of different religious traditions. They also emphasize that world religions need to regulate the narrow sectarian and polemical issues to the background and concentrate on harnessing their creative potentialities in the service of human welfare and world peace. Today we need to distinguish between religiosity and spirituality because religiosity is dividing the globe at a disastrously fast pace. We definitely need to focus on spirituality that unites.

Religiosity stems from the word religion, which denotes basically three things: creed, cult and code. If a person abides faithfully to these three aspects of a particular religion, he or she should be considered a pious or religious person. It refers to the numerous aspects of religious activities, pious practices, devotional undertakings, ritual observances and following up of a particular set of moral code. All of these are observable, measurable and can remain in the realm of externality. What matters in religiosity is what you do and how well you perform. They differ from one religion to another, since the belief systems, worship formulae and the accepted religious codes are diverse.

Spirituality on the other hand, focuses on who you are and what you are becoming as a person because of what you do, including religious performances and pious activities. It is something that deals with one's quality of being, living and relating. It is intrinsic to and focuses upon the process of becoming more and more attuned to one's own true inner self, spiritual self or soul. And so, it is possible to be filled with religiosity without being religiously inclined. Each one is one's own spirituality. In that perspective, I see Jesus, Buddha and Gandhi truly spiritual at the very core, exceptional in the lives they lived and yet religiously belonging to the back benches.

REFERENCES

Albrow, Martin, 1997, *The Global Age*, Cambridge: Stanford University Press.

Bardhan, P. 2001, Social Justice in the Global Economy in *Economic and Political Weekly*, 36, February, pp. 3-10, 467-480.

Corea, Gamani (1999), *The Challenge of Globalization: Main Issues Around Colonialism and Globalization*, New Delhi: Indian Social Institute, pp. 14-21.

Dhanagare, D.N. 2003, Globalization: Towards an Alternative View in *Sociological Bulletin*, Vol. 52, No. 1, March, pp. 4-31.

Farquhar, J.N. 1998, *Modern Religious Movements in India*, Delhi: Munshiram Manoharlal Publishers Private Ltd. [originally published New York (1915), MacMillan & Company].

Giddens, Anthony, 2001, Dimensions of Globalization in Steven Siedman, and Alexander, Jeffry, C., (Eds.) *The New Social Theory Reader*, London and New York: Routledge.

Held, David, 1999, *et al.*, *Global Transformations: Politics, Economics and Culture*, Cambridge: Cambridge University Press.

Manorama Year Book 1997, Kottayam (1997), Malayala Manorama.

Rao, V.M. 2000, Mapping the Periphery: The Poor Communities in the Southern States in the *Journal of the Indian School of Political Economy*, Vol. 12, No. 2, April-June, pp. 235-264.

Robertson, Roland. (1991), The Globalization Paradigm: Thinking Globally in *Religion and Social Order*, Greenwich JAI Press, pp. 207-224.

Sen, Chandra. Conceptualizing Globalization Issues and Implications in *Seminar*, Vol. 34, August, 2001.

Sharma, S.L. (2003) Globalization and its Socio-cultural Discontents in Judge, P.S. (Ed.) *Development: Gender and Diaspora*, New Delhi: Rawat.

Tomlinson, J. (1999), *Globalization and Culture*, Cambridge: UK Polity Press.

Wiseman, John (1997), (Ed.) *Alternatives to Globalization: An Asia-Pacific Perspective,* Melbourne: Community Aid Abroad.

3

Religion and Identity in the Context of Globalization

LEELA D'SOUZA

Introduction

Globalization today is no longer just a concept, but has become a social reality. The discourse on globalization in recent times is taking three major directions: (i) World Polity theory, (ii) World system theory and a globalizing economy, and (iii) World Culture theory. We are concerned in this chapter with the third dimension. In the west, tradition is seen as opposed to modernizing processes; two different points in time. In India and in many of the developing nations, we see the co-existence of tradition and modernizing processes.

At the cultural level, we are observing globalizing trends in the areas of education, mass media, consumerism and lifestyles; the last especially of the middle and upper classes. The social structure is also changing, where human rights are becoming a dominant force, propelled by the active participation of the civil society—areas of women's rights, dalit rights, and gay movement etc. Religious revival and religious activism that is being observed today, is also closely linked to globalization.

Globalization

Globalization resulted with the invention, during the 1970s, of the electronic chip, which led to a new technology, very different from the earlier invention of electricity, which ushered in the industrial period of the modern era; a progress over horse power of the medieval period. By the late 1980s/early 1990s, a new age was dawning in human history—the electronic period.

The use of the term 'Globalization' in the contemporary period, as a specifically sociological concept, owes greatest debt to R. Robertson (Waters, 1995:38), which he used in preference to the then existing terms like 'internationalization' and 'trans-nationalization', as a more suitable concept for describing the ever-intensifying networks of cross-border human interaction (Hoogvelt, 1997:114). Robertson's chief rival for the mantle of parent of the concept was A. Giddens (Waters, 1995:17).

The term 'Globalization', which referred to an empirical condition of complex connectivity, i.e., the rapidly developing inter-connectedness and interdependencies that characterized the modernization period, is now taking on a qualitative change in the electronic era, resulting in the compression of the world. It both increasingly imposes constraints, but also differentially empowers (Robertson, 1998:8). As Giddens explained, the intensification of world-wide social relations links different localities in such a way that local happenings are shaped by events occurring many miles away and *vice versa* (Giddens, 1990:64). Another aspect of globalization is the intensification of global consciousness, which implies that individual phenomenology is addressed to the entire world, rather than to just local or national sectors (Waters, 1995:42).

The effects of globalization can be seen in areas of economic impact/development, military and political issues, mass media, consumer preferences, religious issues, and issues like citizenship, environment and global warming, status of women and so on. No longer are these issues viewed only from a local perspective, but are seen from both global interaction and simultaneity of frames of reference. The global impact can also be seen in greater unification and systematization of various services like banking and political governance, and in symbolizations of national expressions like the national flag, national anthem etc.

Several scholars like Held, are of the view that Globalization is neither a wholly novel, nor primarily a modern social phenomenon; only its form has changed over time and across key domains of human interaction. But although important continuities with previous phases of Globalization exist, the contemporary patterns of Globalization constitute a distinctive historical form; the electronic age (Held,

1999:414). In Sociological theory, one of the debates of Globalization is over when it began. Sociologists largely see globalization through the mediating category of Modernization. Two broad patterns are suggested:

(1) **The Emergence of a New Age:** Martin Albrow (1997:6) speaks of a 'Global Age' that replaces the 'Modern Age'. The shift lies in the axial principles that put communication, mobility and connectivity at the centre of human lives (see Tomlinson, 1999:38-48).

(2) Through the powerful mediating category of modernity, (Waters, 1995:4) three possibilities are suggested:

(a) *Globalization seen in the historical context of modernity*: Robertson is of the view that the nexus of institutions of modernity is necessary for the rise of Globalization. Modernity tended to accelerate the Globalization process. Robertson maintains that globalization of the contemporary type was set in motion long before modernity; in the economic sphere it predated even the rise of capitalism. But he does not deny that modernization did accelerate the process of globalization (Robertson, 1998:170; Hoogvelt, 1997:116).

(b) *Globalization as a consequence of modernity*: A. Giddens is of the view that globalization is a consequence of the inherently expansive characteristics of modernity. Like Robertson, he sees the ascendancy of the nation-state, which has become a universal political unit, is simultaneous with the development of Globalization. The world is seen as a network of national societies in a global system of international relationships. In 'Consequence of Modernity' (1990), he offers one of the most sophisticated analysis of modernity and its inherently globalizing properties. Using concepts of time-space distanciation, disembedding and reflexivity, he explains how complex relationships develop between local activities and across distances. While Giddens' approach to Globalization is historically discontinuous, Robertson's approach is historically continuous. According to Giddens, modernity implies universalizing tendencies, which make possible global networks of relationships and more basically extend temporal-spatial distance of social relationships (Waters, 1995:48-50). Rather than focusing on society, which implies a bounded system, Giddens suggests that starting points should be how social life is ordered across time and space (Giddens, 1990:64).

(c) *Globalization is the result of the hegemony of modernity*: I. Wallerstein is of the view that Globalization is the result of western cultural dominance and its universalizing and hegemonic tendencies; an ideological, economic, political and cultural dominance (See Hoogvelt, 1997:65-67; Waters, 1995:23-26).

Globalization and Identity

Globalization does not imply a simplistic uniformity like a world culture, which all people of the world supposedly share. Rather, it is more about how people increasingly form local cultures and identities, in terms of general global models (Beyer, 1998:305). These global models are being framed increasingly by the dominant western nations. It is a complex social and phenomenological condition, in which different aspects of human life are brought into articulation with one another. In its current manifestation, globalization involves the relativization of individual and national reference points, to general and supra-national ones (Waters, 1995:42).

One of the sub-concerns of Globalization is the need to create viable identities. As Giddens explains, modernization, with its basic tendency to differentiation and increased possibilities of choice, has, created problems of identity at both the individual and the collective levels. Both individuals and collectivities, marginalized by the globalization processes, struggle to establish coherent identities, where the earlier ones are being threatened by contradictory social imperatives (see, Bendle, 2002:3). But it also allows for new identities to be created across national boundaries.

Other scholars, exploring the crisis of identity in the context of high modernity or globalization, argue that the fragmented nature of identities in the face of differentiation, has led marginalized groups to participate in social movements, in search of new identities. In other words, one of the responses to globalization is the participation in projects to change the system. For example, while on one hand, the local community identity is being threatened, at the broader level, new identities are being formed-based on consumer fora, lifestyle groups, Area Level Management (ALMs) and so on. At the global level, transnational identities are being forged—identity of women, transgender groups, etc.,—which globally address how these issues can be addressed/resolved.

Identities in pre-modern societies are seen as synonymous with the 'core' or centre of existence. Post-modernity or globalization views reject the notion of 'core', and consider identity to be something more superficial, transient, multiple and constructed in the course of discourse. Giddens regards the transformation in self-identity, as one of the requirements in the dialectic of local-global conditions. Bendle observed, that the greater the de-traditionalization of a society, the more the need to negotiate lifestyle choices from the diversity of options (see Bendle, 2002:7).

Thus, the formation of identity becomes a key component in the social dynamics of Globalization. As Heelas explained, in traditional societies, identity is largely ascriptive and based on an authoritative taken-for-grantedness, whereas in a de-traditionalized society, identity is more achieved or constructed. Identity is no longer seen as involving the self's non-reflective, unquestioning 'ascription' within a tradition; rather it emerges in a discourse. In a globalized society, it is seen as a shift from a passive level of acceptance, to an active level of reflexivity and critique (See Bendle, 2002:7).

Identity is an intrinsic human need to establish, "Who am I?" which takes place at the individual, community and national levels. Identity is the basis of self-existence, a sense of belongingness within a community and a nation. It is established by stating difference from 'other', and is constructed on the basis of collective experiences of a group/society, which are then internalized by its members. Collective identity reflects the sameness of identity, that a people with a shared history and ancestry hold in common; a sense of religious and cultural belongingness. Today, the norm that seems to be emerging is that a minority group (economic, political, or cultural), that has less bargaining power across the table, can express its demands and identity more forcefully through collective action (D'Souza, 2002: 414-427; 2010:14-26).

Today, religion is emerging as an important criterion of global identity. It is providing a rallying ground for cultures, unable to compete with global powers; a response to rejection of global economic/political domination.

Globalization and Religion

Robertson is of the view that the world religions of Islam and

Christianity, have played an important role in the process of globalization; the former (Islam) in its military expansions during the twelfth to fifteenth centuries, during the Arab and Ottoman empires. By the eighteenth century it had achieved a considerable presence in diverse regions; the latter (Christianity) in its military expansions and subsequent colonization in the sixteenth and seventeenth centuries across the globe. These two universalizing religions became the most effective globalizers. Their beliefs spread across ethnicities, nations and classes. These religions became the single, moral ethic for diverse cultures—a common value reference for diverse peoples (Waters, 1995:127-28).

In the modern period, society has undergone a process of secularization, i.e. the influence of religion being replaced by a rationalist and scientific temper. Sociologists put forward the idea that religion in the contemporary western world has become increasingly privatized. Scholars like T. Parsons (1966:134), P.L. Berger (1973:133), T. Luckmann (1967:103) and R. Bellah (1970:43) have interpreted secularization in the modern world to mean that traditional religion is now primarily the concern of the individual and has therefore lost its 'public' relevance (Berger, 1973:137). Institutional differentiation, (which Luckmann called functionally differentiated societal sub-systems), and pluralistic, individual identities, are the basic features of modern societies. Secularization is the consequence of the relative independence of these initial sub-systems of society, from religious norms, values and justifications, i.e. religion now has a limited legitimating role, in a highly differentiated society (Beyer, 1999:373-74).

The Niklas Luhmann's thesis maintains that globalization of society, while structurally favouring privatization of religion, also provides fertile ground for renewed public influence of religion, i.e. religion not only retreats from important aspects of social life, but also develops an institutionally specialized sub-system of its own. By public influence, he meant that one or more religions could become the source of collective commitment; collective action in the name of specific religious norms now becomes legitimate (Beyer, 1999:373). Religion thus becomes a source of collective commitment. Professionals now become prime, public representatives of societal sub-systems, in a modernizing society. Thus, the public importance of a system rises and falls, with the public influence of its professionals.

In brief, a global focus on religion has emerged because of a cluster of issues:

(i) the debate about whether societies are becoming more or less secularized;
(ii) the resurgence of religion; and
(iii) the emergence in the 1970s and 1980s of Church-state and religion-politics tensions and conflations, across much of the globe (Robertson, 1998:2).

However, religion today is not being abolished, as it was earlier believed; it is only taking on a new character in terms of movements of both religious revival at the individual levels (what are being called 'new religious movements' or NRMs, which are apolitical and seeking for a new spiritual dimension); and religious activism at the collective level (what are being called Religious National Movements or RNMs, which are a political expression of religion, seeking world-wide identities for political gain) (D'Souza, 2005:340-341). These movements are being regarded as a search for a new consciousness; a search for a new identity, in response to the new demands of a globalizing world. Cultural survival in the face of globalization is one of the causes of religious revivalism and religious activism. But it is not simply a revival of traditional religion, rather religion is taking on a new character, where it is using the new electronic technology of the age of globalization very effectively, to communicate instantly and globally; both directly to individual persons and to establish collectivities across the globe.

This retreat from secularization and the revival of religion at the individual level, is taking place because science, technology and rationality have failed to provide meaning and purpose in life. They have failed to provide a guide to the human search for ultimate concern, accepting that by anthropological nature, humans are religious. In other words, the disillusionment with religion is taking place, not because persons have stopped searching for transcendental answers, but because this search has now intensified beyond the limits of an institutional religion (Giri, 1998:41; and D'Souza, 2005:290).

As Weber explained, as long as questions of causes/control of death, disease, sickness and accidents remain unanswered, questions of religion will emerge. Religion is seen as a belief in spiritual beings and humans providing explanations to situations beyond their control, to explain unknown elements, in order to soothe pain and take away their fear of lack of control. At the individual level, religion also provides a stable point of existence in an ever-changing world; a point of security, in a world that has not yet been deciphered or explained by science. In a fluctuating world, where knowledge today may be refuted tomorrow and nothing remains an undisputed fact; nothing remains constant. Religion has become necessary to explain the reality of "Who am I?", "What is my future?".

At the collective level, religion is seen as one of the most fundamental basis of identity in a globalizing, insecure and constantly changing world. Religion has moved into the public domain, largely because of the loss of confusion in identity, as a result of the processes of globalization. The right to an independent identity of a collectivity and struggle for its recognition is justified. Religious activism is an attempt to express the identity of a community/nation, in the context of globalization. As Robertson explained, it is the assertion of a deep particularity, in the context of globalism. It is a quest for community and the assertion of power (Robertson, 1998:175-78).

The role of the West in domination at both the economic and political domains globally, leading to a loss of identity by the smaller nations and a feeling of their being subsumed by a dominant group (especially the G-8 nations), leads these smaller cultures to seek to reassert their identity. This re-assertion of identity, since it cannot take place/compete at the economic/political levels, is increasingly taking place at the religious level. Religion remains one area where regional/local identities can be asserted, to establish a distinct identity from the dominant west. Further, religious identity cuts across nationalities and ethnicities, class and occupational differences, and establishes a new basis of a global identity.

In the twentieth century we see the emergence of these politically motivated, Religious Nationalist Movements at collective levels, seeking a political ideology based on religion, to become the underlying basis of a nation-state,—in India and in Pakistan we see this religious activism in the struggle against colonialism. We see the struggle for identity at the religious level again in national identities in Yugoslavia (Bosnia, Serbia, etc.) and later Indonesia—between Christian and Islamic communities. Today, in the twenty-first century we see this religious struggle for identity taking the face of terrorism, beginning 11 September—a fight by a minority group/country, against the political and economic attempt to domination by the global powers;

an attempt by the dominant West, to change the basic structure of a nation-state, from a religious/secular autocracy to a democracy. We know the control of oil reserves in the past, was an economic motive. Today, it could also include political control, through demand for democratic structures.

Conclusion

Religion is a basic component of human beings and one of the most basic and fundamental basis of identity. There is no collectivity in the world that does not have a religion (no matter how defined), to cement a society. In the early modern or Renaissance period, there was an attempt to replace religion with a legalistic and Constitutional system, as the legitimating power in a secular and democratic society. But these legalistic, normative structures, did not command the same levels of conformity from members of a society, as did religion in the past. Legalistic/Constitutional systems are external to individuals and are imposed from without; religion is internal to individuals and directs conformity from within. Further, a legal system is secondary to/reflects the status of a society. It does not initiate change, but reflects change. In his study of the Protestant Ethic, Weber has shown how religion has the capacity to initiate moral and economic change.

We need to observe the experiment with a Constitutional democracy that we see today in the USA, setting aside the biblical norms that the country was initially founded on and seeking to replace it, with demands of different groups of a civic society, in its commitment to democratic values. How effectively is the USA handling emerging issues like gay rights, gun culture, and breakdown of family as early as 17-18 years of age—a strong individualistic culture, over a group/familial one.

In the language of a more traditional sociology, there is no system of general values, integrating either individuals or classes into the dominant culture. Secular society does not possess any general system of values, to give absolute legitimacy to social, economic and political functions. The coherence of contemporary societies depends increasingly on a variety of regulative practices, economic restraints and ultimately force. The central paradox of secular society for sociology of religion is to reconcile the facts of secularization with the centrality of religion, especially on a global scale (Turner, 1991:201).

In multi-cultural or pluralistic societies, the nation-state is required to allow individual religions the right to exist/express themselves. Minority religions cannot be subsumed under a single religious umbrella; be it the USA, India, or elsewhere in the world. Today we are witnessing a struggle by religious leaders to establish their political authority in society (Islamic States, Hindu State in India; Religious Fundamentalists in USA), often on one hand, regressing to traditional demands of allegiance and on the other, seeking to maintain growth of the nation-state on political/economic global standards/ demands. Religion is thus emerging, in a global context, as the basis of re-establishing a new identity at the collective level. Religion is once again emerging as a dominant constituent of life and a strong basis of individual and collective identity. In a globalizing society, the interweaving of the religious and the secular is observed, not a false divide between them. Religion is attempting to emerge on the one hand, (at the collective level), as the foundation of national and cultural differences and on the other, (at the individual level), as the basis of full humanity. Religion is thus both furthering and resisting globalization. In fact, it is globalization that has revitalized religion.

Note

Globalization, or a concept very much like it, had appeared early in the development of the social sciences. S. Simon noticed that industrialization was inducing commonalities of practice, across the disparate cultures of Europe. E. Durkheim's legacy to globalization was his theories of differentiation; M. Weber identified rationalization as a globalizing solvent. Even in the ancient and medieval periods, globalization at a lower scale was taking place, through trade and markets, between East and West and through wars and extensions of empires.

REFERENCES

Bendle, M.G. 2002, "The crisis of 'identity' in high modernity" in *British Journal of Sociology*, Vol. 53, No. 1, March 2002, pp. 1-18.

Berger, P.L., and T. Luckmann (1967), *The Social Construction of Reality,* London: Penguin Press.

Beyer, P. 'Globalization' in R. Wuthnow (Ed.) (1998), *Encyclopaedia of Politics and Religion,* vol. I, pp. 305-307, London: Routledge.

Beyer, P.F. "Privatization and the Public Influence of Religion in Global Society" in M. Featherstone (Ed.) (1999), *Global Culture: Nationalism, Globalization and Modernity*, pp. 373-395. New Delhi: Sage Publications.

Clarke, P.B. "New Religious Movements: An Introduction" in S. Sutherland *et al.* (Eds.). (1988), *The World's Religions*, pp. 907-911. London: Routledge.

D'Souza, Leela, 2003, "Identity Formation and Pluralism: The Need to Reconstruct Identities" in *Social Action*. Vol. 53, No. 4, Oct-Dec., pp. 413-427.

D'Souza, Leela (2005), *The Sociology of Religion: A Historical Review,* Jaipur/New Delhi: Rawat Publications.

D'Souza, Leela, 2010, Communal Violence and Assertion of Identity, in *Social Action*, Vol. 60, No. 1, January-March, pp. 14-26.

Giddens, A. (1990), *The Consequences of Modernity,* Stanford Stanford: University Press.

Giri, A.K. (1998), *Global Transformations: Post-Modernity and Beyond,* New Delhi: Rawat Publications.

Heelas, (1999), P. *Religion, Modernity and Post-modernity*, Oxford: Blackwell Publishers Ltd.

Held. D. (1999), *et al. Global Transformations: Politics, Economics and Culture,* Cambridge: UK Polity Press.

Hoogvelt, A. (1997), *Globalization and the Post-Colonial World,* London: MacMillan Press Ltd.

Mendieta, E. (2001), "Society's Religion: The Rise of Social Theory, Globalization and the Invention of Religion" in D.N. Hopkins, *et al.* (Eds.), *Religions/Globalizations: Theories and Cases,* London: Duke University Press.

Robertson, R. (1998), *Globalization: Social Theory and Global Culture,* London: Sage Publications.

Tomlinson, J. (1999), *Globalization and Culture,* Cambridge: UK Polity Press.

Turner, B.S. 1991 (1983), *Religion and Social Theory*, London and New Delhi: Sage Publications Ltd.

Waters, M. (1995), *Globalization,* London: Routledge.

Wilson, B. (1966), *Religion in a Secular Society.* England: Penguin Books.

Wilson, B. "Secularization: Religion in the Modern World" in S. Sutherland *et al.* (Eds.), (1988), *The World's Religions*, pp. 953-56. London: Routledge.

4

Effect of Globalization on Religion and Culture in India

G. RAMACHANDRAM

Introduction

Globalization is a process of integration of countries through greater foreign trade and foreign investment. The developed countries have been trying to pursue developing countries to liberalize their economy and trade and allow more flexibility in business policies to provide opportunities to multinational companies in their domestic market. The Indian Government had liberalized the economy in 1991 under pressure from the WTO and the IMF. Globalization has brought to India new technologies, new products and new economic opportunities. The MNCs are looking at India in a big way. India has taken a lead over other growing economies in Information Technology (IT), business processing and investments.

Globalization is synonymous with Westernization and modernization. Globalization is not a new phenomenon as people kept searching new places and avenues to increase their business activities as evident by explorations of Vasco da Gama, Columbus and the East India Company. The bitter experiences of economic exploitation by the East India Company and the British had made India a little bit cautious for adventures of globalization. India had largely and intentionally isolated itself from the world markets, to protect its fledgling economy and to achieve self-reliance.

The concept of globalization is hardly new to India. It had the distinction of being the world's largest economy in the beginning of the Christian era, as it accounted for about 33 per cent share of world GDP. The goods produced in India had long been exported to far off destinations across the world. As Jawaharlal Nehru says in *"The Discovery of India"* it is the British rule that reduced India, for the first time in its history, to a political and economic appendage of a foreign imperial power. Since liberalization, the value of India's international trade has become more broad-based and has risen to Rs. 12.5 billion in 2003-04 from Rs. 1 billion in 1950-51. Still India accounts for only 2.7 per cent of World Trade.

The economies of countries similar to India are blooming as the world is flattening and shrinking due to globalization. Fifty years ago, countries such as India did not have a say in the global market and trade. America and other European powers, once top players in the international market, are now facing competition from countries like India, which is experiencing fastest economic growth. Technology has played a major role in the advancement of globalization in India, enabling it to compete against the first-world countries for jobs.

There is no denying the fact that globalization has brought cheers to people's lives by opening new vistas of employment. There is increasing interaction between people of different countries. Consequently, the food habits, the dress habits and the lifestyles of indigenous people are being westernized.

Globalization has raised the standard of living of the people at large. It has changed the work culture due to computerization and e-governance. The IT revolution has brought a sea change in the communication technology. Today more than 900 million people in India have access to mobile phones; the largest network after China. IT is being used by the governments to improve the efficiency in providing various services to the people, particularly the poor and marginalized. The internet and social media have come to defy the traditional modes of communication. They have become harbingers of change.

However, critics of globalization argue that, even if increased trade promotes material prosperity, it comes with a high spiritual and cultural cost, running roughshod over the world's distinctive cultures, threatening to turn the globe into one big "tawdry strip mall."[1] Globalization has made people more acquisitive, greedy and corrupt. It is a materialistic view of life *vis-à-vis* aesthetic valued based life style.

Globalization has many negative effects. Although India has immense economic growth and is emerging as a major economic power, not all the sectors of the country have benefited. The benefits of development have not reached the poor and the needy. The funds that should have been directed to the agriculture sector are being diverted to private sector enterprises. For instance, growth in the agricultural sector dropped from 3.8 in 2007 to 2.6 in 2008. And since then it is continuously dropping. This decline in growth has greatly affected farmers with production costs being very high, while the market remunerative price for commodities not matching with that, resulting in over 1,50,000 peasant suicides since 1997. Similarly, the funds meant for social sector like education and public health are drastically curtailed. Jobs in the technology and business sectors have many benefits. However, only the people in those sectors are benefiting. The overall employment rate for the country has decreased, while the number of job seekers is increasing at an annual rate of 2.5. Further, the growth is limited to a few sates like Gujarat, Maharashtra, Karnataka, Andhra Pradesh and Tamil Nadu. Other states like Bihar, Uttar Pradesh, Madhya Pradesh, Odisha, Assam and West Bengal etc. remain poverty-stricken. While the globalization has not impacted the rural life much as standards of living are suboptimal, the people from rural areas are migrating to urban areas in search of employment, creating new problems of slums, health and sanitation, crime and violence in cities.

Effect on Religion

India gave birth to four religions—Hinduism, Jainism, Buddhism and Sikhism. It is predominately a religious country. Religion plays a central and definitive role in the lives of most of its people. The *Dharma*—religions, also known as Indian religions, are a major form of world religions next to the Abrahamic ones. India is one of the most religiously diverse nations in the world, with some of the most deeply religious societies and cultures. The relationship between religion and globalization is antagonistic; one of struggle and conflict. The history of Christianity could be understood in part as an early effort to create a global network of believers. Its extraordinary growth and influence as a world religion was the result of its global ambitions. It succeeded as a globalizing force due to proselytization. Along with the Christian religion came the rest of British and Western culture, thought and customs and the gradual end of traditional ways of life. India's traditional religions and cultures were gradually subverted. Globalization spreads secular and capitalist way of life which is at odds with Indian religions and culture. It is resisted by the traditionalists and religious communities as they fear loss of their religious and cultural identities.

The followers of Islam feel threatened by the process of Westernization and modernization. The invasion of Afghanistan and Iraq by the US in order to destroy the unfriendly regimes had devastating effect on the followers of Islam. The emergence of the Islamic State in Iraq and Syria (ISIS) is a reaction to the US policies in the Middle East. The ghastly 13/11 Paris terror strikes have posed a serious challenge before the world community—how to tackle the presence of the IS on social media. The IS uses the social media platforms to radicalize the Muslim youth with a deadly effect to grow into a Frankenstein. According to a study done by Brookings Project in 2014, some 46,000 Twitter accounts were used by the ISIS supporters for recruits to keep the cinders of terrorism burning. The Indian Muslim youth are being radicalized due to the influence of the IS. Afshan Jabeen and four Indian Muslims youths have been arrested recently for having links with the IS. Afshan Jabeen was influenced by the ISIS propaganda on YouTube. She has identified six administrators of her Face Book group "Islam *Vs.* Christianity." And her arrest led intelligence agencies to the IS sympathizers in Delhi, Mumbai, Hyderabad, Bangalore and Kashmir who were active members on her Face Book group.

Linking of some Muslim youth in India with the IS has sent shock waves among modern Muslims. As a New Year resolution, a group of city Muslims in Mumbai launched a campaign "Muslims Against ISIS", denouncing the Jihadist terror organization's brutalities and chalking out a programme to stop Muslim youths from getting recruited by the IS. They are educating the youth that the IS has nothing to do with Islam and its tenets. Some Muslim organizations are working to "ensure the educated young people, who were attracted to the ISIS, are de-radicalised and brought back into the mainstream."[2] According to Justice Srikrishna, the claim of "religious superiority" by religious groups is the cause of all trouble in the world.

Effect on Culture

India, a cradle of ancient civilization, is cracking up. The traditional Indian culture is defined by a relatively strict social hierarchy. India for ages has had a prevailing tradition of the jointly family system. Today, the family as an institution is under threat. Arranged marriages have been the tradition in the Indian society for centuries. Most of the Indians have their marriages planned by their parents and elders. While the traditional values are declining, American festivals like Valentine Day, Friendship Day have become popular among the youth. The cultural vigilantism by the Hindu extreme groups like Vishwa Hindu Parishad, Bajrang Dal, Sri Ram Sena, is a reaction to westernization.

The overwhelming impact of globalization could be observed on the Indian culture. Most of the educated Indians, particularly the youth, seem to believe that nothing in India, past or present, is worth patronizing. There is an all-pervading presence of a positive, if not worshipful, attitude towards everything in Western society and culture; past as well as present, in the name of modernization. The youth are blindly aping the West. They are alienated from their traditional Indian roots. They are floating in the air without a base. Modernization, as reflected by the forces of globalization and westernization, is resented because it encroaches upon the core values of Indian society, its languages, its traditions and social practices and life styles.

The Hindu right wing extremists' campaign of *'Love Jihad'* and *'Ghar Wapsi'* are a reaction to westernization. The Indian deep-rooted traditions and customs have loosened up their hold with the emergence of globalization. The Indian culture, rich in religions, literature, art, communities and multiple ways of living have been overshadowed by the ruthless forces of globalization. This is due to expansion of the Western culture which is a major cause for the decline of the Indian culture, civilization, religion, art, literature and customs. There is no doubt that globalization increases a country's material prosperity, but it is also true that it comes with a high cultural cost. Every person wants to be swayed in the Western light. We are exploiting the term globalization in the name of progress, reason and science, forgetting that ultimately it is our culture that differentiates us from any other country.

The divorce rate among the young couple is rising. China's eye-popping economic growth has caught the world's attention, but it seems to have let the family values behind as over 10,000 couples are splitting daily due to strained marriages. The institution of family has received a serious drubbing in China. The Chinese transformation to a market economy and modernization is beginning to have negative effect on society. It is forced to abandon its one-child policy because of decline in labour force and increase in old age pensioners. According to the Chinese government's official statement, its "one-child" policy has prevented an estimated 400 million births since its inception in 1980." It is "the population control policy, along with economic reforms, that has helped China to become the world's second largest economy." And many experts blame "China's skewed sex-ratio on enforcement of the policy."[3] China is now giving incentives to some 150 million women, who are in reproductive age group, to go for more children. But "For women economic independence has meant power, to be continually more independent making them brave enough to walk out of an unsatisfactory union. There is a new *mantra*....I do not need someone to take care of me... I want love."[4]

The IT city of Bangalore is emerging as a divorce capital of India. The conflicting value system is damaging the lives of the young couples. The tradition *vs.* modernity is taking its toll. The people are modern only because they dress modern and receive education in a modern foreign language, English. But their mind-sets are conservative and backward looking. They are not modern in thought and action. A survey recently conducted has shocking revelations that, in this age of globalization, "57 per cent of teen age boys and 53 per cent teen age girls think that a husband is justified in beating his wife."[5] The girls aged between 15 and 19 years old share the same views as women in the 45-50 age group.

Liberalization has made the young people tech-savvy, but they are not able to rise to the expectation of modern life. A male techie goes over the edge, revealing the stress of trying to achieve the Indian dream without taking his wife along. Men work in companies that techies aspire to like IBM, Infosys, Accenture and Siemens etc. But "almost everywhere the basic issue is the inability to let the wife realize her potential...Men tend to brook or be disturbed if wives earn more than them...happy to have the extra money but secure in the knowledge that she will stay at home when a child is born...circumscribed by old gender roles..."[6]

In 2013, one Madhusudan-working in a IT sector Bangalore—in a murderous rage grabbed a kitchen knife and stabbed his wife Roopa 49 times in their three bed-room flat and jumped to his death from balcony as he wanted her to resign from the job because he could not digest the fact that she was well placed and earning more than him. Of the more than 5,000 divorce cases filed in Bangalore in 2013, some 3,000 are related to the couples employed in the IT sector. The grounds for divorce vary from illicit messages or calls or chats or *WhatsApp* messages or Face book posts on smart phones getting tracked by either of the spouses. Legal experts in Bangalore say that the divorce cases involving social networking sites and smart phones are on the rise. And the e-mails and SMSs are being used to file for divorce. It is anybody's guess where our family system is heading. A survey conducted a few years ago has revealed that in the modern age "aloneness has increasingly become a cause of depression among people…the number of people who say they have no one to discuss important matters has more than doubled. You might have all materialistic comforts …but suddenly feel wrong within… this is the 'aloneness' within. We feel we are loved less and that growing sense of inner emptiness creeps in."[7]

Effect on Children

Globalization is also seriously affecting the value system of our children and how they are brought up. The 'helicopter parenting' is doing irreparable damage to children. The parents, in order to ensure that their children excel in everything, put tremendous pressure, involving them in various activities, leaving no time to rest and relax. The lack of warmth and affection at home is resulting in loss of self-worth and increasing risk behaviour among children. A report about the internet usage among children, released on October 27, 2014, has come out with very disturbing revelations. Almost every child between eight and sixteen years of age is active on social media. In Mumbai, 90 per cent children are addicted to social media.[8] This is leading to high occurrence of cyber bullying-using technology to harass, embarrass or target a person. Venkat Krishnapur, Head of Operations for Intel Security Group's India Development Centre observes: "an unprecedented level of personal data is now available online, expanding the risk-canvas exponentially."

The children as young as three and four are queuing outside the spine and physiotherapy clinics to deal with aches and pains triggered by obsessive use of gadgets—recurrent use of tablets, handheld games and mobile phones for tweeting, browsing or playing—is causing musculo-skeletal discomfort, including neck, back and shoulder pain, affecting posture. The children are predisposed to get spondylitis early in life.[9] And the overuse of gadgets is slowing down the child's cognitive development and causing attrition—deficit disorders—blurry or double vision, redness, hasten near-sightedness and even dry eyes syndrome. It is hampering physical development and impairing social skills. Online gaming is consuming a lot of physical activity, resulting in a sedentary lifestyle leading to diseases like diabetes and hypertension. The children are robbed of their innocence. They are becoming adults in their teens.

The internet—an integral part of globalization—is having yet another negative effect on us. The mobile phone addiction and 24X7 access to the internet seriously compromise our ability to remember the simplest facts leading to memory loss. What we are seeing is "suffering from digital amnesia-using the phones and the internet and the social media as an extension of memory."[10] As we become increasingly dependent on mobile phones and digital media, we tend to rely less on our own cognitive processes.

These are some of the side effects of globalization and modernization in India.

REFERENCES

1. *DNA* (Mumbai) 18 November, 2015.
2. *The Times of India* (Mumbai), 2 January, 2016.
3. *The Times of India* (Mumbai) 4 January, 2016.
4. *The Free Press Journal*, (Mumbai) 14 November, 2011.
5. *The Times of India* (Mumbai) 25 April, 2012.
6. *Hindustan Times* (Mumbai) 26 September, 2013.
7. *Bombay Times*, 14 November, 2009.
8. *Hindustan Times*, (Mumbai) October 28, 2015.
9. *Bombay Times*, 5 August, 2015.
10. *The Times of India* (Mumbai) 18 December, 2015.

5

From a Religiosity that Divides to a Spirituality that Unites

Challenges from a Globalised World

M.K. GEORGE S.J.

The chapter will look at the broad context of social living in the globalized world, characterized by violence and lack of peace, look at it analytically with specific reference to Religion and Spirituality and propose a line of response.

Globalization

We have already heard many elaborate definitions of globalizations. Hence, a summary reference might suffice here. We might look at it "as referring to our shrinking world, where physical distances are made shorter (thanks to automobiles and air travel) and mental and affective spaces are easily filled (with television, telephony and the internet). This has come about largely because of digital technology: computers, telephones, satellites, which have changed the way in which we teach and learn, and have had enormous impact on traditional patterns of education..." (Pereira, Myron, 2015). Globalization has various dimensions: globalization of finance and the movement of capital, of labour, of culture, especially through tourism and entertainment creating a world of leisure industries and even of persecution as in terrorism (Pereira).

Globalization and its Effects

While Globalization (along with its complex paradigm of LPG) has produced some huge benefits in terms of economic growth, better health facilities, democracy and greater social justice to the world, it has created a platform for mutual cultural educational, intellectual, scientific, technological and skills exchange. It has created solidarities which are incomparable in times of calamities and so on.

On the other hand globalization has given rise to huge disparities and discontents (Stiglitz, Samir Dasgupta and others have written widely on this). Just to quote one, "in terms disparity, we remain parts rather than wholes. In terms of a single humanity, we are divided. In terms of possessions, we are either rich or we are destitute...But in the inner space of the earth, we see the tragic division of humanity into hostile groups. Terrorism, sectarianism, bigotry, fundamentalism and its horrible descendants, fanaticism have possessed this beautiful planet" (Samir Dasgupta, 2004). Stiglitz, one of the strident critiques of the current economic globalization argues, "Globalization often seems to replace the old dictatorships of national elites with new dictatorships of international finance. Behind the architecture of a new world order, malignant globalization creates a three-tier structure across the national boundaries. The globalists represent the core of circle. In the second circle are the people who "labour in insecure forms of employment and are thrown into a cut-throat competition in the global market. The outer ring represents the excluded ones" (*Ibid.*).

The recent unprecedented spurt in migrants and refugees and terrorism are manifestations of this discontent. The United Nations forecasts that 3,000 migrants a day—many fleeing wars in Afghanistan, Iraq and Syria—will pour into the Balkans, trying to reach Western Europe in the next few months. So far, the burden to absorb them has been unevenly distributed (Updated, September 3, 2015). Attacks against Migrants have been on the rise. In Germany, for instance, fire-fighters tried on August 24 to extinguish flames in a house that was to be converted into a shelter for asylum seekers in the southern German city of Weissach. Last month, an attack, thought to be arson, destroyed a sports hall in Nauen, Germany, that was going to be used to house migrants. It was the latest of more than 200 attacks directed against migrants in the country this year.

The Age of Discontinuity

We call our times as an "age of discontinuity". Globalization can be seen as one of the most characteristic discontinuities. There seem to be more uncertainties now than of all the previous centuries of human history. Any discontinuity, as most people testify, brings out reactions and humans have to summon resources either to react against the change, (reactionary/conservative) or to invent a new way of coping with it (innovative) (Myron Pereira, Neville, 2010).

One of the characteristic responses of the present age has been a revival of religiosity, which provides people with an identity, which is often denied by a globalized world. While we do call everyone a globalized citizen, for vast majority of the dispossessed, it is a loss of identity and they in turn seem to resort to religion as a way of smoothening their life.

Perhaps the best and succinct way to introduce the context of the globalized world is to quote Pope Francis' words in Rome in late November, 2015. He said, "We should ask for the grace to weep for this world, which does not recognize the path to peace." We are losing the path to peace over the increasing gap between the rich and the poor, over the frightening spread of terrorism, over the ever rising violence against children, women, the tribal, Dalit, the migrants, the refugees. We are losing peace over the increasing personal disintegration—of suicides, addictions, reverting to fascism and fundamentalism. Most importantly, we are losing peace over a nature that is revengeful for the violence we humans inflicted on her.

Analyses tend to look at the crisis in the global reality from two major points-of-view: the developmental model that guides a "peaceless world" and its consequent crises and the ideological and religious framework. These objective and subjective dimensions are really not separate. The development agenda is indeed founded on specific ideological and religious subsystems. In an interesting reference to the Paris terror attack, Vidya Venkat remarked, "climate change and terror are connected by a common source: the greed for fossil fuels without fostering liberal democracy;" an analysis indicative of the dynamic relations of the social, economic, political and cultural, particularly the religious domain.

Understanding Fundamentalism

The discontinuity created by globalization and the consequent uncertainty makes people to turn to fundamentalism, understood as a negative phenomenon. "Fundamentalism is commonly a quest for certainty and security in an uncertain and insecure world. This is precisely why it is a defensive reaction, which cannot but prove to be an inadequate and illusory response, promised more on subjective need than objective reality. For, fundamentalism, in the final analysis, does not make the external world any more certain or secure, nor can the world be exorcised or exiled from the lives of people living in ever grater interdependence on each other and their environment, both natural and social" (Rudolf C. Heredia, 2012).

Globalization of Indifference

What we notice about the globalized world is a widespread indifference to God, to our neighbours and to nature. At times, we are struck by the absolute lack of concern of people for what is happening around them. There is a total indifference to the marginalized. The indifference to the natural environment, by continued abuse of nature like deforestation, pollution and the resultant natural calamities uproot entire communities from their eco-system and create profound insecurity. As a result, there are new forms of poverty and new situations of injustice, often with dire consequences for security and peace. The result of this indifference is the loss of peace. Many religious leaders, noticeably Pope Francis, are calling for a conversion from indifference to mercy; a conversion of hearts. Repeatedly, these leaders tell us that we are called to make compassion, love and mercy and solidarity a true way of life; a rule of conduct in our relationships with one another. In other words, the challenge is to build a culture of solidarity and mercy to overcome indifference.

Religion and Globalization

What is religion? Very broadly, "*Religion is any specific system of belief about deity, often involving rituals, a code of ethics, and a philosophy of life.*" Thus, we include here all of the great monotheistic religions, Eastern religions, Neo-pagan religions, a wide range of other faith groups, spiritual paths, and ethical systems, and beliefs about the existence of God(s) and Goddess/es.

Thus in India we will say, our people are divided into Hindus: 80 per cent; Muslim: 14 per cent, Christian: 2.4 per cent; Sikh: 2 per cent; Buddhists: 0.7 per cent, Jains: 0.5 per cent, Others: 0.4 per cent, Religion not stated: 0.07 per cent. From a global perspective of the 6 billion plus people on this earth, 4.8 billion profess one form or other of religion. Most people define "*religion*" in a much more exclusive manner in India.

The five core dimensions of religion are:

1. The Belief consequence.
2. "The practice consequence"—Ritualized worship.
3. "The Knowledge dimension"—Information and Knowledge about the beliefs.
4. " The Consequence dimension"—Affecting behaviour.
5. "The expectation experience"—Expectations regarding and experience or through prayer (Glock and Stark).

"The contribution the religions can make to an emerging culture (of peace and harmony) is to seek out what is common or universal in all the religions. However, discovering a universal ground upon which the various religions could relate is problematic when it is attempted at the level of belief or ideology or in the doctrinal sphere" (Teasdale, Wayne).

Globalization and Religion

Purely from a practical side, aspects of globalization have been very well used by Religion. In fact when we look at history, colonization and early forms of globalization were introduced by or through religions, especially Christianity and Islam. In that sense, religion and globalization can also be seen as partners in historical change. In times past, religion, in its various manifestations, has been a carrier of globalizing tendencies in the world. The history of Christianity, for instance, can be understood in part as an early effort to create a global network of believers. Its extraordinary growth and influence as a world religion was a result of a link between its own global ambitions and the expansion of various political and economic regimes. It succeeded as a globalising force long before there was a phenomenon called 'globalization'. Interestingly, elements of this historical pattern can be found in Buddhism, Islam and other faiths as well. The terrorist attacks of September 11, 2011 called everyone's attention to another set of problems and the larger puzzle posed by the relationship between religion and globalization.

At the same time, contemporary technological growth is very well used by religions, either for propagation of faith or its sustenance. Look for example at the channels, media programmes and so on. Similarly, in the resurgence of religion too, globalization has played a major role. "Globalization transforms the generic religion into a world-system of competing and conflicting religions. The process of institutional specialization has transformed local, diverse and fragmented cultural practices into recognizable systems of religion. Globalization has therefore had the paradoxical effect of making religions (*via* their religious leaders and elites) more self-conscious of themselves as being world religions" (Bryan S. Turner, 2007).

Thinking about religion and globalization, "first, there is the way in which globalization flattens out cultural differences, erodes local customs and beliefs, and spreads a secular, capitalist way of life that is at odds with religions of all sorts. At the same time, there is another way in which religion serves as the source of globalization's greatest resistance and as a haven for those standing in opposition to its ubiquitous yet often subtle power. In both of these views, the relationship between religion and globalization is antagonistic—one of struggle and conflict" (THR).

Religiosity

When I talk of religiosity, I would like to make a difference between what is called genuine religion or pure religion and what is lived on this earth. We see religiosity growing at a fast pace, conquering the minds of even the so called educated rational people. How do we recognize religiosity and distinguish it from genuine religion. One way to look at is to look at the culture of fear religion most often produces: fear of tradition, fear of relationships, fear of rituals, fear of God's wrath and anger. Simultaneously, it has also created a culture of craving for pleasure, profit and power (Razu Mohan, 2014).

Debate on Tolerance

None other than the President of India lamented recently "whether tolerance and acceptance of dissent are on the wane in the country". He reminded the nation: "Indian civilization has survived for 5,000 years because of its tolerance. It has always accepted dissent and differences. A large number of languages, 1600 dialects and seven religions coexist in India. We have a Constitution that accommodates all these differences. Humanism and pluralism should not be abandoned under any circumstance. Assimilation through receiving is a characteristic of Indian Society. Our collective strength must be harnessed to resist evil powers in society" (*Press Trust of India*, October 19, 2014).

There has been a raging controversy over whether there is tolerance or intolerance in India. The ruling government took almost invariably the position that there has not been any increase in intolerance. The victims claimed that it is not so. They cited cases of intolerance ranging from extreme cases to hidden. The debate still continues. There have been instrumentalist arguments as well as philosophical reflections. For instance, quoting Scanlon, Kranti Saran argued that "tolerance is valuable for its own sake because of the attitude it allows us to bear towards other citizens, an attitude of fraternity and solidarity that is deeper than the intractable disagreements that divide us. Tolerance makes it possible to view all our fellow citizens as equally entitled to participate in defining and determining the shape of society" (Kranti Saran, 2015).

Spirituality

Research by Martsolf and Mickley (1998) has highlighted the following areas as constitutive of Spirituality:

1. *Meaning*—significance of life, making sense of situations, deriving purpose.
2. *Values*—beliefs, standards and ethics that one cherishes.
3. *Transcendence*—experience, awareness, and appreciation of a "transcendent dimension" to life beyond self.
4. *Connecting*—increased awareness of a connection with self, others, God/Spirit/Divine, and nature/Nature.
5. *Becoming*—an unfolding of life that demands reflection and experience; including a sense of who one is and how one knows.

Spirituality is primary, primordial, numinous or religious experience, and the emphasis is decidedly on experience, not on doctrine or belief. As long as the human condition is experienced as separate from Ultimate reality, it is subject to ignorance and illusion, weakness and suffering. Disciplined practice is essential to the spiritual life; yet spiritual attainment is not the result of one's own efforts, but the result of the experience of oneness with Ultimate reality.

Common Practices in all Spiritualities

1. Practice of compassion
2. Service of others
3. Practicing moral precepts and virtues
4. Training in meditation technique and regularity of practice
5. Attention to diet and exercise
6. Fasting and abstinence
7. Relationship with a qualified teacher
8. Repetition of sacred words, *(Mantra, Japa)*
9. Observing periods of silence and solitude
10. Movement and dance
11. Formative community

Towards a Response

The response has to be multi-dimensional. At the same time, a core response has to be at the level of religiosity because religiosity is dividing the globe at a disastrously fast pace. Some even say that religious wars have killed more people than diseases. One answer, then, definitely is to focus on spirituality that unites. That indeed is the main focus of this chapter.

Facilitate a change from religiosity to spirituality. In doing that we do the following:

(a) Transcend the purely personal and develop communitarian consciousness.
(b) We become aware of the world of nature and our indebtedness to the realm of nature which brought us forth and sustains us.
(c) We are able to function as morally responsible and accountable people even in the absence of any coercion or compulsion.
(d) We resonate with others who entertain values similar to which we hold.

(e) We are infused with a sense of dignity and self-respect (Razu Mohan, 2014).

Moving to a Secular Spirituality

'Secular' has become such a contested word that it is a little risky to talk about secular spirituality. But understood in its right meaning, the usage conveys the answer to the need of the hour. "Reconstructing secular spirituality" is itself a radical imperative because it goes beyond the religious spirituality and other fabricated notions' (Razu, 2014). The new secular spirituality must include "all aspects of people transcending" caste, colour, creed, religion, nationality, gender and so on.

1. Confront both with social science insights.
2. Promote a new culture of spiritual activism. Communal disharmony is man-made. Inter religious dialogue has become essential to achieve a common recognition of the importance of respect and love among humans. Through dialogue and respectful encounter we understand each other better and let our spiritual traditions form us.
3. If so, communal harmony can also be the result of a planned action towards a just and humane society.

The world faces unprecedented challenges for justice and peace. The globalized world has become a powerful ally or foe in building peace. The big question is, can we build a world of peace moving away from a religiosity that divides to a spirituality that unites.

REFERENCES

D'Cunha, Neville, 2010, *Religions in Globalizing India*, in VJTR 74/9 September.

Heredia, Rudolf, 2012, *Faith, Reason and Fundamentalism* in VJTR 76/12 December.

Pereira, Myron (2016) *An age of Discontinuity*. https://groups.google.com/forum/#topic/communicating-church/OJDSlviipXM

Razu, Mohan I. J. (2014), *Secular Spirituality: Contesting the Aberrations of Religiosity*, Bangalore: Candid Publications.

6

Masculinities in the Matrix of Globalization

MANGESH KULKARNI

We begin with a provisional definition of the two keenly contested terms used in the title of this chapter viz., 'globalization' and 'masculinity'. Renowned social theorist Anthony Giddens views globalization as an outcome of instantaneous electronic communication across the globe, which has brought about an unprecedented acceleration of the forces of capitalism and industrialism inherent in modernity.[1] Consequently, the largely predictable process of 'simple modernization' has given way to a volatile sequel that he describes as 'reflexive modernization'. This shift leads societies and individuals to continuously rethink, redefine, and record received ideas as also practices in the face of multiple possibilities that open up as cultures freed from geographical barriers interact on a daily basis.

The term 'masculinity' seems deceptively self-evident. However, it is exceedingly difficult to pin down the moment one questions the essentialist and naturalized understanding of manhood. The Australian Sociologist of gender R.W. Connell has tried to capture the lived complexity of masculinity by defining it as "a place in gender relations, practices through which men and women engage that place, and the effects of those practices in bodily experiences, personality and culture".[2] As Connell rightly argues, while masculinity is associated with privilege due to the 'patriarchal dividend' most men seem to enjoy, this is more true of those who can stake a claim to 'hegemonic masculinity' than of men who occupy a subaltern position due to their class location (e.g., working-class men), racial/ethnic background (e.g., black/lower-caste men) and/or sexual orientation (e.g., gay men).

Hence, the dynamics of masculinity can be tracked only through a plural and political perspective. This is the task which the new discipline of Critical Masculinity Studies (CMS) has set for itself.

Interrogating Indian Masculinities

While CMS originated in the West during the last quarter of the twentieth century, it has slowly, but surely gained a foothold in India during the last two decades. Initially, any mention of it in academic and activist circles was often greeted with bemusement or hostility. Sceptics argued that before the rise of Women's Studies, social research amounted to nothing more than Men's Studies in disguise—an andocentric form of inquiry pursued predominantly by male scholars. It is true that men occupied the foreground and women were relegated to the background in traditional social research. But it must be noted that men's lives were not subjected to a critical scrutiny through the lens of gender. The mere fact that research was a male prerogative does not mean that it was necessarily exercised in a self-reflexive manner. The hostile response to CMS generally came from those feminists who saw it as a sort of 'backlash' or as an attempt to trespass on the terrain of Women's Studies. However, it has come to be accepted that the two interrelated disciplines can and should develop in a dialogical fashion.[3]

Systematic research examining different manifestations of masculinity in India is of recent origin, but it has already enriched our understanding of the country's past and present.[4] Sudhir Kakar and Ashis Nandy are among the pioneering contributors to this field. Through a creative deployment of psycho-analysis, Kakar inquired into the normative matrices, family structures and socialisation processes which shape the psyche of Indian men and generate a close mother-son bond, a relatively weak articulation of Oedipal conflict, and a permeable ego formation.[5] Kakar's findings serve as useful points of departure; but his approach seems somewhat static and ahistorical. In contrast, Nandy (whose work defies disciplinary protocols) provided a historically grounded account focussing on the restructuring of masculinities in colonial India.[6] He argued that pre-modern Indian society sustained fluid gender identities. These were warped by the hyper-masculinist British imperial ideology, resulting in the inflation of the martial or Kshatriya model of masculinity, which had earlier occupied a limited social space. Nandy's influential formulation has been cogently problematized by Rosalind O'Hanlon and Mrinalini Sinha.

The British historian O'Hanlon has convincingly demonstrated the centrality of martial masculinity to society and politics in the late Mughal period.[7] The battlefield, hunting expeditions and sports served as sites for the demonstration of the traits associated with martial valour. On the other hand, the court, the household and the harem were seen as abodes of effeteness and luxury. Contra Nandy, the code of martial masculinity was not exclusively modelled on the Kshatriya ideal, and it entered significantly into a wide variety of practices ranging from military recruitment and diplomacy to fellowship among men from different communities. In her insightful work on colonial masculinity, Sinha, a historian of Indian origin, currently based in the U.S., has pointed out that "British manliness" and "Indian effeminacy" were in fact conjointly constructed.[8] Labelled by the British as "effeminate", the Bengali 'babus' sought to recoup their masculinity by resorting to physical culture and political assertion. The tussle over the Age of Consent Bill (1891) in India intersected with the consent debate of 1885 in Britain where sensationalized cases of child-prostitution had led to the mobilization of women. The efforts to weather the feminist challenge to British masculinity converged with the revivalist-nationalist efforts to reassert Indian masculinity.

For a fine-grained account of postcolonial Indian masculinity, we may turn to the writings of Joseph Alter, a U.S.-based anthropologist of Indian origin. In one of his essays, Alter focuses on late-twentieth century popular literature on *brahmacharya*, comprising Hindi booklets and manuals chiefly intended for young men.[9] His analysis of this literature reveals the extent to which the 'spiritual' male body became a focal site for a discourse of nationalism. The pursuit of celibacy here becomes part of a "somatic nationalism", geared to the resistance of dissolute Western ideologies and to the regeneration of the motherland. The legacy of colonial sexuality is incarnated in the postcolonial 'libertine', whose masculinity is based on pathological individualism, domination and self-gratification, leading to a sheer waste of vital fluids. The *brahmachari* (celibate male), with his commitment to self-control, balance and natural truth, represents a nationalist negation of such libertine masculinity. Central to the pursuit of celibacy is the retention of the semen, which is imbued with not just physiological, but also spiritual/moral potency. An elaborate regimen involving the right kind of diet, exercise and various other norms of conduct, such as the avoidance of pornography, is proffered to this end. Alter finds an exacting embodiment of such a regimen in the wrestlers of North India, with the wrestling *akhara* (gymnasium) serving as a medium through which the aforesaid ideas regarding celibacy are put into practice and propagated.

The Discreet Charm of the Metrosexual

If the English language press is to be believed, a new species entered the zoo of Indian masculinity in the wake of globalization, which it termed 'the metrosexual'.[10] As the name suggests, he is a denizen of the urban world. His favourite haunts include the fashion industry and the audio-visual media. Unlike his conventional counterpart, he takes a keen interest in personal grooming, has an open attitude to sexuality, and is in touch with his 'feminine' side. The Hindi film star Shahrukh Khan, who has featured in a gender-bender soap advertisement, is often cited as a metro-sexual icon.

Is metro-sexuality an Indian reality or a figment of the journalistic imagination with its penchant for the latest Western trends? After all the term was coined in 1994 by the British journalist Mark Simpson to refer to a new breed of young metropolitan males who had a strong aesthetic sense and spent a great deal of time and money on their appearance and lifestyle. Not surprisingly, men's fashion magazines eagerly lapped up and used the expression. With the assimilation of gay men in the mainstream society, 'effeminacy' lost its sting and the metro-sexual subculture became quite prominent in many Western countries. The word itself entered popular parlance after Simpson wrote an essay in 2002 projecting the soccer star David Beckham as a metro-sexual par excellence. He clearly explained the political economy of the phenomenon in this essay which appeared on Salon.com:[11]

> For some time now, old-fashioned (re)productive, repressed, unmoisturized heterosexuality has been given the pink slip by consumer capitalism. The stoic, self-denying, modest straight male did not shop enough (his role was to earn money for his wife to spend), and so he had to be replaced by a new kind of man, one less certain of his identity and much more interested in his image—that's to say, one who was much more interested in being looked at (because that's the only way you can be certain

you actually exist). A man, in other words, who is an advertiser's walking wet dream.

Quite logically, marketing agencies deployed metro sexuality, the word and the mindset, extensively both to tap and create demand for a wide variety of products targeting men.

Contemporary urban India reveals many tell-tale marks signalling the arrival of metro sexuality: billboards sporting male models in various state of undress, beauty parlours catering exclusively to men, and proliferation of gay characters on the celluloid screen. In October 2005, Mumbai witnessed "Met-Fest: Masculinities in the City". Described as "India's first ever festival on men and masculinities", the series of events spread over ten days, sought to explore and celebrate indigenous metro sexuality. It offered a rich fare including talks, films, plays and an art exhibition. Himanshu Verma—the young, Delhi-based organizer of the festival, who was himself an incarnation of the Metrosexual persona, had explained his perspective in a pamphlet which offered a critical account of metro sexuality in the West, even as it tracked various sources like the *Kamasutra* to construct an authentic Indian version of the phenomenon. Does all this mean that the stereotypical Indian man is truly undergoing a transmutation? It is not easy to answer the question. There simply is not enough reliable information on the subject. But even if we discount the media hype, it is hard to deny that the era of globalization has brought about significant changes in the domain of Indian masculinity.

Signs of a 'New Age' masculinity are apparent in the urban, upper class milieu centred on the nuclear family, typically comprising well-educated, employed spouses and their children. In such a setting, men often depart from the rigid patriarchal framework by participating in domestic work and child care, forming closer emotional/sexual bonds with their wives, and involving the latter in financial and other decisions formerly considered as male prerogatives. Boys growing up in such families tend to imbibe the new values and modes of behaviour. They are also likely to develop more wholesome ties with their fathers, quite unlike the distant and even sullen filial relations that commonly prevailed. As the earlier account of metro sexuality has revealed, another characteristic of the New Age man, especially evident among the youth, is a preoccupation with the 'body beautiful', and a less inhibited, unconventional attitude to sexuality.

The transformation of masculinity adumbrated above derives from and feeds into the logic of the globally integrated New Economy centred on the knowledge-driven service sector and geared to non-traditional, varied patterns of consumption. Such an economy requires greater participation of educated male and female workers in the production process, enhanced purchasing power, as also demand for novel products like cosmetics for men. This is not to discount the autonomous role of ideologies and movements that have brought about a genuine alteration both in forms of social existence and consciousness. The role played by feminism and the women's movement is of paramount importance in this context.

Mobilized Masculinities in the Era of Globalization

Though the male response to feminism has often involved indifference or even outright hostility, this is not the whole story. Many men have treated the cause of women's liberation with sympathy and solidarity. An organised and self-reflexive manifestation of this affinity may be found in the pro-feminist men's groups that have emerged during the last decade. The Mumbai-based group Men Against Violence and Abuse (MAVA)—claiming to be the oldest group of its kind in the country—is a prominent representative of the pro-feminist tendency.[12] Formed in 1993 and run as a voluntary agency by a small group of middle-class men, MAVA has conducted several awareness-raising/training/counselling programmes and campaigns geared to gender justice. Along with women's groups and other like-minded organizations, it has particularly sought to target the youth through initiatives like sexuality education workshops.

Especially noteworthy is the annual Marathi publication *Purush Spandana* (Men's Heartbeats) that MAVA publishes. Probably the first publication of its kind in India, the magazine focuses on gender issues from the pro-feminist men's point of view. It carries essays, autobiographical narratives, stories and poems voicing the ideas, views and sentiments of men from diverse walks of life. It has a niche readership and has received prizes from various literary bodies in Maharashtra. Since, the late 2000s, *Purush Uvacha*—a like-minded group in Pune, which initially collaborated with MAVA in bringing out *Purush Spandana*—has been publishing a similar annual number of its own.

New Age masculinity is also reflected in the modicum of visibility and social acceptance gained by gay men in recent years. The publication of *Yaraana* (1999)—an anthology of gay literature in India—by a mainstream publisher like Penguin heralded this changed scenario.[13] But discrimination against homosexuals continues and groups championing the gay cause seek to end it through different forms of intervention. Specifically, they target Section 377 of the Indian Penal Code—a colonial piece of legislation that criminalizes homosexuality by treating it as an "unnatural offence" involving "carnal intercourse against the order of nature". Their efforts to get this Section repealed or amended have run into rough weather and it continues to hang over the gay community like the sword of Damocles.

However, the concerns of the gay rights groups are gaining a wider audience in the aftermath of the HIV/AIDS epidemic. The gay cause has vocal and media-savvy spokesmen like the Mumbai-based activist Ashok Row Kavi. He launched the newsletter *Bombay Dost* in 1991 to provide a forum for the lesbian, gay, bisexual and transgender community. As it could not adequately address the problems of the community, the *Humsafar* Trust was formed in 1994.[14] Over the last decade, the Trust has grown into a recognized organization dealing with issues concerning gay men and men-who-have-sex-with-men (MSM). It seeks to free these men from the bane of invisibility and infamy. It is active in educating them about Sexually Transmitted Diseases. It also provides them support structures and access to health facilities.

All this is not to claim that patriarchal masculinity has ceased to hold sway or that feminist intervention have met with no organized resistance from men. The depressing statistics of violence against women and the declining sex-ratio sufficiently testify to the ravages of patriarchy. And as Anand Patwardhan has vividly demonstrated in his film *Father, Son and Holy War* (1995), the mainstream constructs of aggressive, sexually warped and misogynist masculinity feed sinisterly into the communal politics that has been playing havoc with our society. Moreover, the limited, but very real achievements of the women's movement in the field of legal, institutional and policy reform have provoked palpable anxiety and resentment among certain sections of men, who have sought to defend their supposedly threatened rights.

Thus, an Ahmedabad-based group of men, the *Akhil Bharatiya Patṇi Atyachar Virodhi Sangh* (All India Federation of Opposition to

Crime by Wives), which was launched in the 1990s, sought to safeguard the interests of 'harassed husbands' and their relatives, who were said to be victims of Section 498A of the Indian Penal Code.[15] Similar groups have emerged in many other parts of the country. The said Section was inserted in 1983 to combat the menace of dowry deaths. It makes the harassment of a woman by her husband or his relatives a non-bailable, non-compoundable, cognisable offence. Police complaints filed under the Section may result in the immediate imprisonment of the accused. The men's rights groups allege that it has been widely abused with the connivance of women's organizations. Yet, the fact remains that an unprecedented transformation of Indian masculinity is occurring in the vast grey zone between the media-bolstered façade of metro sexuality and the deep-rooted structures of hetero-patriarchy. This is the space to watch for those seeking to understand and shape the country's gender dynamics in the era of globalization.

NOTES & REFERENCES

1. Giddens, Anthony (2000), "The Social Revolutions of Our Time" in Kate Nash (Ed.) *Readings in Contemporary Political Sociology,* pp. 83-99. Oxford: Blackwell.
2. Connell, R.W. (2005), *Masculinities,* Crow's Nest NSW Allen & Unwin.
3. This spirit of dialogue is evident in writings such as the following: Md. Nazrul Islam and K.E. Kuah-Pearce, 2013, "he Promotion of Masculinity and Femininity through Ayurveda in Modern India", *Indian Journal of Gender Studies*, October, Vol. 20 (3), pp. 415-434.
4. Kulkarni, Mangesh, (2014), "Critical Masculinity Studies in India" in *Masculinity and Its Challenges in India: Essays on Changing Perceptions,* (Eds.) Rohit K. Dasgupta and K. Moti Gokulsing, Jefferson, NC and London: McFarland & Company.
5. Kakar, Sudhir (1978), *The Inner World: A Psychoanalytic Study of Childhood and Society in India*, New Delhi: Oxford University Press.
6. Nandy, Ashis (1983), *The Intimate Enemy: Loss and Recovery of Self under Colonialism*, New Delhi: Oxford University Press.
7. O'Hanlon, Rosalind. "Issues of Masculinity in North Indian History: The Bangash Nawabs of Farrukhabad", in *Indian Journal of Gender Studies*, 4 (1), January-June 1997.
8. Sinha, Mrinalini (1997), *Colonial Masculinity: The 'Manly Englishman' and the 'Effeminate Bengali' in the Late Nineteenth Century*, New Delhi: Kali.

9. Alter, Joseph, 1994, "Celibacy, Sexuality, and Nationalism in North India", *The Journal of Asian Studies*, February.
10. This section draws on Mangesh Kulkarni, "Is There Such A Thing As The Metro-sexual Male?" *Info Change Agenda*, January 2006, pp. 16-17.
11. www.marksimpson.com.
12. MAVA website: www.mavaindia.org
13. Merchant, Hoshan (1999), (Ed.) *Yaraana: Gay Writing from India,* New Delhi: Penguin.
14. Humsafar Trust website: www.humsafar.org
15. Mahurkar, Uday, 1999, "Protesting Partners" in *India Today*, August 30.

7

Impact of Globalization on Culture and Society in India

NALINI KANT JHA

"The era of Globalization" is fast becoming the preferred term in describing the contemporary world. Just as the Depression, the Cold War, the Détente, etc., are used to describe particular periods of history, Globalization describes the political, economic, and cultural environment of today. People around the globe are more connected to each other today than ever before in the history of mankind. Information and money flow more quickly than ever. Goods and services produced in one part of the globe are increasingly available in all parts of the world. International travel is more frequent and international communication has become common.

Globalization should not however be regarded as a unidimensional process symbolizing merely economic integration of the world, as some scholars tend to believe. It is in fact a multi-dimensional process that encompasses economic, cultural, social and political integration of the globe. In other words, globalization is not merely a synonymous for global business. It is much more than that. The same forces that allow businesses to operate, as if national borders do not exist, also allow social activists, labour organizers, journalists, academics, international terrorists and many others to work on a global stage. We indeed live today in an interdependent world in which people in different parts of the globe are compressed together in an instant communication, notwithstanding the immense differences in their socio-cultural and historical experiences.

Needless to add, such a facility of instant communication and increases in the movement of goods, labour, and services have weakened national barriers and restrictions that are imposed by a nation states. Some identify this with the emergence of a new "global village." Amartya Sen, a Nobel Laureate, therefore observes:

> "Global interaction, rather than insulated isolation, has been the basis of economic progress in the world. Trade, along with migration, communication, and dissemination of scientific and technical knowledge, has helped to break the dominance of rampant poverty and the pervasiveness of 'nasty, brutish and short' lives that characterized the world. And yet, despite all the progress, life is still severely nasty, brutish and short for a large part of the world population. The great rewards of globalised trade have come to some, but not to others.[1]

Not surprisingly, Globalization has immensely influenced our life, generating intense debate about its impact on people in the world. Proponents and opponents of Globalization have marshalled facts and figures to substantiate their respective views about the beneficial or adverse implications of Globalization.

In this chapter, however, we propose to confine our discussion to the impact of Globalization on religion and society in India with particular reference to Hindus and Christians. We also suggest how the Hindus and Christians in India can work together to minimize the negative fallouts of Globalization on their religion and society.

** ** **

It is, of course, erroneous to assume that the present conjuncture, when globalization is changing the character of the world in diverse ways, is altogether new and represents a fundamental departure from the past. Globalization is not new. In many ways, the world economy in the late twentieth century resembles the world economy in the late nineteenth century. And there is much that we can learn from history, for there is the past in our present. In the case of India as well, Globalization is hardly a new force affecting this country. To think so is to ignore a diverse and pluralistic long-standing civilization that was shaped by a long list of "invading" (globalizing) cultures that became what we now know as India. The previous globalizers of India include the Greeks, Turks, Afghans, Muslims and most recently, the Europeans, Portuguese, French, Dutch and finally the English.

What is, however, new is that the former globalizers that came with invading armies have replaced now by less violent but equally, if not more, powerful globalizers. The revolution in Information Technology has immensely facilitated the task of globalizers. The instruments of IT such as internet, cable TV and mobile phones etc., have extended the reach of Western culture to bed rooms as well. It is, of course, true that TV channels like Astha, Sanskar and Sadhana, etc., are spreading the great spiritual messages of great Indian saints and philosophers. Several Internet sites too enable us to know about Indian heritage and culture. On balance, however, most of the channels and much larger number of web sites offer commercial entertainment, which most of the people, especially younger generation, prefer to view or visit.

This has facilitated the task of Western civilization to promote monoculture—the same basic values, institutions and points of view for everyone, which it calls Globalization, notwithstanding its claim to support diversity and multi-culturalism. The brutal and stark truth is that Western culture, with its declared pursuit of markets and commodities, eliminates all true cultures, which are based on quality and not quantity. It creates a culture of filthy lucre and lust for money all the way that submerges any true culture of refinement or spirituality; a dismal culture in which everything can be bought and sold, possessed or capitalized on. All our capitalists and businessmen in India today are gloating and bloating about the ever rising tide of consumerism and consumer culture brought about by the ruthless march of Globalization.[2]

Macaulayism of British India, which symbolized colouring of Indian mind with western ideas, has become in letter and spirit the Globalization of today. Pound Sterling has been replaced by the US Dollar. To the people of India in general and educated Indians in particular, Globalization seems to be rather mild and well meaning, more like an imperceptible breeze, which blows in silently, fills up the psychological atmosphere, creates a mental mood, inspires an intellectual attitude and finally settles down as a cultural climate—pervasive, potent and ubiquitous. It is not out to use a specified section of Indian society as a vehicle of its virulence. It is not like Islamism which wants to destroy the body of a culture in one fell sweep. And its target is every section of Indian society.[3]

Since Christians in India too have become a part and parcel of the Indian society, they are not immune from the all pervasive influence of Globalization. Like their Hindu brothers, Indian Christians, who are mostly converts from Hindus and constitute about 2.3 per cent of the country's over one billion people, which makes it a whopping 50 million people, are too affected by Globalization. However, before discussing the impact of Globalization on the Hindu and Christian societies in India, it is worthwhile to mention first the psychological implications of Globalization, as changes in mental outlook leads to changes in the outer behaviour of people.

** ** **

One can identify the psychological transformation brought by Globalization in the manner in which Globalization has altered one's identity; in terms of how people think about themselves in relation to the social environment. According to Jeffrey Arnett, there are four major issues related to identity, which develop due to Globalization.[4]

The first is the development of a bicultural identity or perhaps a hybrid identity, which means that part of one's identity is rooted in the local culture while another part stems from an awareness of one's relation to the global world. The development of global identities is no longer just a part of immigrants and ethnic minorities. People today, especially the young, develop an identity that gives them a sense of belonging to a worldwide culture, which includes an awareness of events, practices, styles and information that are a part of the global culture. Media such as television and especially the Internet, which allows for instant communication with any place in the world, play an important part in developing a global identity. Yet, along with this new global identity people continue to retain and develop their local identity for daily interactions with their family, friends and community. A good example of bicultural identity is among the educated youth in India who despite being integrated into the global fast paced technological world, may continue to have deep rooted traditional Indian values with respect to their personal lives and choices such as preference for an arranged marriage, caring for parents in their old age etc. Although developing a bicultural identity means that a local identity is retained alongside a global identity, there is no doubt that local cultures are being modified by Globalization. This is especially true with immigrants. This author, during his recent visit to Washington DC as a Fulbright Professor at Johns Hopkins University, found that Indian Hindus were arranging special classes on holidays for imparting Hindu values to their children.

The attempt to preserve non-western cultures along with western culture, what they call "global" culture, however generates certain amount of confusion among the youth. While people may adapt to changes and develop bicultural or hybrid, or multicultural identities, some may find it difficult to adapt to even undermining their own cultural values and beliefs. Instead of becoming bicultural, they may feel isolated and excluded from both their local culture and the global culture, thereby belonging to neither. The terms delocalization and displacement have been used to describe these processes. For some young people, however, de-localization may result in an acute sense of alienation and impermanence as they grow up with a lack of cultural certainty, a lack of clear guidelines about how life is to be lived and how to interpret their experience. Identity confusion among young people may be reflected in problems such as depression, suicide, and substance use. This is the second psychological impact of globalization.

While most young people may jump to accept Globalization and its changes, there will always be some, especially with strong traditional cultural background, who will remain out of it by joining a self-selected culture of fellow dissenters. Such groups can have a religious basis, which can result in fundamentalism or espouse clear non-religious anti-western or anti-American views. Accordingly, the third change brought about by Globalization is the growth of the self-selected culture, which means people choose to form groups with like-minded persons who wish to have an identity that is untainted by the "global" culture that it threatens to create one homogeneous worldwide culture in which all children growup wanting to be like the latest pop music star, eat Big Macs, vacation at Disney World, and wear blue jeans, and Nikes. This has encouraged extremism and fundamentalism in some parts of the world and in India.

Finally, Globalization is contributing to emerging adulthood. The timing of transitions to adult roles such as work, marriage and parenthood are occurring at later stages in most parts of the world as the need for preparing for jobs in an economy that is highly technological and information-based is slowly extending from the late teens to the mid-twenties. Additionally, as the traditional hierarchies of authority weaken and break down under the pressure of Globalization, the youth are forced to develop control over their own lives including marriage and parenthood. This spread of emerging adulthood is related to issues of identity. Where a period of emerging adulthood is present, young people have a longer period for identity explorations in love and work before they commit themselves to long-term choices. By experiencing different love relationships, different educational possibilities, and different jobs, they learn more about themselves and their preferences and abilities.

Emerging adulthood is, however, possible only in societies where economic development is high enough that the labour of young people is not urgently needed. They are allowed to spend their late teens and early to mid-twenties exploring possibilities for self development because there is no pressing need for them to contribute to the economic well being of their families.[5] On the other hand, poor young people, especially in rural areas, have no emerging adulthood and may even have no adolescence because they begin adult like work at an early age and begin marriage and parenthood relatively early. In this sense, lives of middle class youth in India, South East Asia, and Europe have more in common with each other than they do with those of poor youth in their own countries.

On the whole, however, globalization appears to be a significant force in the psychological development of the people in the twenty first century. As a consequence of globalization, the challenges of creating a viable identity are perhaps greater than they have been in the past. Identity in the age of Globalization is less influenced by prescribed social roles and based more on individual choices, on decisions that each person makes about what values to embrace and what paths to pursue in love and work. Some people reach this responsibility with identity confusion or seek refuge in a self-selected culture that offers more structure and takes over some decision. Anthony Giddens therefore observes, "When globalization alters and erodes traditional ways, identity has to be created and re-created on a more active basis than before."[6]

** ** **

In the light of the above discussion about psychological changes brought about by Globalization in the mental outlook of individuals, we can now turn our attention towards the impact of Globalization on Indian society in general and Hindu and Christian community in particular. To begin with, since concepts of national identity, and of family, job and tradition are changing rapidly and significantly, competitiveness introduced by Globalization is leading to more individualistic societies, where both Hindus and Christians are gradually forgetting their value of sacrificing individual pleasure for the sake of common good. Instead, the entire society is opting for consumerism. In a globalizing economy, multinational companies are taking the lead in establishing themselves and creating a major presence in almost every part of the world. Coca Cola, McDonalds, and Nike are examples of such growth and proliferation.

The media plays a major role in advertising the benefits of new products and services as being *better and superior* to what the local market has to offer. Slowly but steadily, the food that we eat, the clothes we wear and the life style we lead begins to change. This process becomes consumerism within a capitalistic culture. So people, as consumers, are being studied for their patterns and behaviours of spending. Consumerism has permeated and changed the fabric of contemporary Indian society. Western fashions are coming to India: the traditional Indian dress is increasingly being displaced by western dresses especially in urban areas. Indian MTV, soap television, and films set a stage for patterns of behaviour, dress codes and jargon.

An adverse impact of growing consumerism is the increasing lust for more and more money, leading, in turn, not only to corruption, social unrest and violence, but to effects on the health of the people, especially that of the urban youth, who fail to get regular jobs in government, banking, teaching, and nursing sectors, etc. To get money for satisfying their consuming urges, more and more young men and women in the cities are being attracted by the "Business Process Outsourcing" (BPO) industry which is generally symbolized by the Call Centres or Medical Transcription outlets. Their mushrooming growth all over the country is symptomatic of two things of the desire to earn a quick buck without any safeguards or security and secondly the way western business has begun to exploit the yuppie Indian without giving the latter the privileges and perks of living in countries like the United States.

Call Centres in India normally begin at 7.00 pm. just when the United States begins to get up and ends normally eight to ten hours later when business closes for the day there. The urban youth in metros like Bombay, Delhi, Calcutta, Bangalore or Madras, etc., constitute the "software" for these companies. He/she is fairly articulate, speaks English and perhaps will not even have to change his or her name. Call

Centres provide the right ambience for the growing youth. Lots of McDonald stuff and Cokes, sometimes even a disco; but then, when one is at a seat, one is glued to it and sometimes is not able to get up for ten to twelve hours. The salary is lucrative. A minimum start of Rs. 10,000–12,000, i.e. about $ 200 for a job that would pay in the United States at least $1,000 a month. Needless to add, these youth get this meagre amount only at the cost of developing irregular eating and sleeping habits, lack of commitment in relationships, and imbibing a culture, which has a negative social impact, stress related problems and so on.[7]

The growing consumerism and culture of Call Centres have, in turn, broken traditional family structures and values in India. Ostensibly, it may appear that Globalization has no significant impact on families and that our lives are 'normal' in most circumstances. The reality, however, is that growing consumerism affect people's identities and cultural values, which sometimes become altered significantly. Whether it is between generations, or intra-personal, new values can cause dissonance and conflict with existing deeper-rooted values; like, for example, Globalization's impact on children in a family. In the past, children were often regarded as the wealth of the family and one could see a great sense of joy and sharing in families that had three children or more. But, to provide modern consumer durables to their families, most middle class Hindus and Christians use family planning methods and restrict their number of children. This has of course several beneficial effects on the family, society and the nation as a whole.

Yet, as the joint family system weakens and there is less parental supervision and support (with both parents working), the youth seem more restless and insecure. Obedience, and very often blind, was regarded as "sacred" in families of yesteryears. Today, a little child is able to demand, cajole and even blackmail its parents. There are also reports of increased violent behaviour and aggression especially in urban areas and cities. Obviously, the aberrant behaviour of children is facilitated by the availability of modern gadgets that have become a "necessity" with the rapid advancement of science and technology. TV is a must and with it the cable connection with its 90 channels, a scooter or a car, a mobile phone, whatever. It has become common to find a child hooked either to the T.V. or to the computer (games, internet, and soft-porn) or even to the mobile phone. Parents often give their son or daughter a mobile phone so that they can keep in touch and know where they are. This is an extremely sad commentary on what Globalization is all about. While definitely not relegating the many uses and conveniences of a mobile phone, one needs to be aware that the underlying principle of "wanting to keep in touch" with the child by the parent and *vice-versa* very specially when one is living under the same roof, indicates (whether one would like to accept it or not), that there is some degree of fear, suspicion, etc. There is thus a tremendous urge and push towards consumerism which often tends to strike at the very root of what family life should be and is all about.

As regards the impact of Globalization on women, it has been a mixed blessing. One the one hand, it has allowed women to become a larger part of the workforce, with opportunities for higher pay raising their self-confidence and independence. Globalization has provided the power to uproot the distorted traditional views about women that have kept women economically poor and socially exploited. The growth of the computer and technology sector has provided middle class educated women with better wages, flexible timings, and the capacity to negotiate their role and status within the household and society. On the other hand, women continue to work in poorly paid, mentally and physically unhealthy, and insecure situations. For most women, their domestic responsibilities are not alleviated. Wage gaps have not showed any significant changes in most employment sectors other than information technology. Additionally, prostitution, abuse and dowry related suicides are on the increase. Undoubtedly, the materialistic greed for more and more is one of the main causes for atrocities on women.

** ** **

True, as indicated in the preceding section, Globalization has beneficial impact on our day-to-day life as well. Internet, for instance, has almost everything to offer: buying a ticket online or finding instant material for research. It helps people become more aware of the world they live in. It has been able to transcend boundaries and cultures, ethnic differences and strife. In other words, the IT revolution associated with Globalization has contributed to the explosion of knowledge. This in turn has facilitated democratization and questioning of feudal authorities.[8]

Globalization has also necessitated greater working together; that men and women find ways and means to respond to a problem in a corporate and cohesive manner. In the context of the institutional set-up, be it the Church or a Trust or a Society that belongs to it, there is also the mad race for knowledge to network, to communicate, to be aware of what is happening. This has made it extremely difficult for perpetuators of communal riots and violators of human rights and women's rights to escape global attention, condemnation and occasional action. Globalization and westernization has ignited the challenge of the feminist movement in India today. Global Hinduism, inspired by people such as Vivekananda and Ramakrishna, is developing. Within this movement, women's voices are beginning to be heard. The feminist magazine *Mansuhi* perpetuates the idea that men and women are equal.

Interestingly, elements of Hindu culture, such as *yoga*, *bhakti* (devotion), *gurus*, Hindu teachings, dance and music have been exported to the West, where they have gained great popularity and, as a consequence, gained popularity among urban Hindus in India. It appears as though the West in general and the US in particular is "exporting" Hindu culture to India in the era of globalization!

On the whole, however, the phenomenon of Globalization has more negative fall outs for society and culture in India. Fragmentation of the traditional family network facilitated by Globalization, for instance, is leading to an erosion of the available support within the immediate and extended family. Migration of younger generations from rural to urban areas and from one urban centre to another as well as trans-national migration has resulted in the elderly being left to fend for themselves at a time when family support becomes more crucial. With more women joining the workforce, the care for the aged within families has declined. For those who live within extended families, the elderly have to live in harmony with the younger generation that has to face a highly competitive world of Globalization. While the nuclear family system is increasingly becoming the norm, modern life-styles, changing professional and personal expectations are impacting relationships of marriage and commitment. While arranged marriages continue to be the general norm, in cities more and more young people have started to choose their own partners. Similarly, although divorce rates are increasing especially in cities, the concept of single parenthood has not yet caught on in the Indian culture. According to the India's Ministry of Health reports (1997), teenage pregnancies are reaching an all-time high. In the southern state of Kerala, teenage abortions rose by 20 per cent in a year, while the western state of Maharashtra, one-fifth of all abortion were with girls less than 15 years of age.

Finally, Globalization and marginalization go hand in hand in India. With millions of poor farmers, rural labourers, urban unemployed, slum-dwellers, 3 million refugees, 100 million street children, and the millions displaced by 'development' projects, poverty in the era of Globalization has assumed new dimensions. The question of "are the poor getting poorer?" relates to inequality both nationally and internationally. It is apparent that in order to ensure that the potential gains from Globalization are shared among all groups (rich and poor countries and between groups within a country) major reforms may be needed. As Amartya Sen states, "Even if the poor were to get just a little richer, this would not necessarily imply that the poor were getting a fair share of the potentially vast benefits of global economic interrelations."[9]

** ** **

Whatever might have been the adverse fall outs of globalization on Indian culture and society, it can not be wished away. One cannot turn back the wheels of history. Under the circumstances, the issue is not to search for an alternative to Globalization and IT revolution, but how to minimize its negative implications and maximize its advantages. Viewed thus, the most significant question facing Indian culture in general and Hinduism in particular is whether this belief system belongs to the world (universalization) and contributes to contemporary global culture, or is one that is exclusive, local and focussed on national identity of India. The friction between the Hindu, Muslim and Christian communities in India has evoked terrible violence. In order for Hinduism to move forward in to the future, this vexing problem must be addressed. Hinduism has within it the resources for peace and reconciliation, resources that may contribute to finding solution to the global problems that face humanity in the new millennium. The Hindu leaders and preachers must come forward to attack distortions like caste hatred, superstitious rituals, etc which have clouded the original humanitarian and universal values of Hinduism.

Christian Mission in India too should respond to the challenges of Globalization by collaborating with men and women of goodwill of our times, appreciating the values in Hindu faith and traditions. Both Christians and Hindus must come together and wage a joint war against all sorts of fundamentalism, extremism, terrorism and superstitions. A beginning in this direction can be made with dialogues between Hindu and Christian scholars for identifying differences and similarities in their approaches with a view to concentrate on areas where both and cooperate for the welfare of common people in this age of Globalization.

REFERENCES

1. Sen, Amartya, (2002), "Foreword," *Make Trade Fair* (Oxfam), *(Available at* http://www.maketradefair.com/)
2. Sundaram, V. *"Impact of Globalization on Indian Culture,"* (Available at http://www.boloji.com/perspective/223.htm)
3. *Ibid.*
4. Annett, Jeffrey, (2001), *Adolescence and Emerging Adulthood: A Cultural Approach,* Upper Saddle River, N.J. Prentice Hall. Also see his, "A Theory of Adulthood from the Late Teens through the Twenties," *American Psychologist*, vol. 55, pp. 469-80.
5. *Ibid.*
6. Giddens, Anthony, (2000), *Runaway World: How Globalization is Reshaping our Lives*, p. 65, London: Routledge.
7. Prakash, Fr. Cedric S.J. "Impact of Globalization on Christian Mission in India," (Available at http://bocs.hu/india/cp-globalization.htm)
8. See, for details, Nalini Kant Jha, (2003), *South Asia in 21st Century: India, Her Neighbours and Great Powers,* pp. ix-xi, New Delhi: South Asian Publishers.
9. Pai, Shobha, "*9*" (Available at www.bildungsmanagement.at/download/Konferenz%202006/Pais.pdf)

8

Socio-Political Analysis on the Rise of Fundamentalism in the Global World

S.M. MICHAEL

Introduction

Today's world is characterized by Post-modernism and Multi-culturalism on the one hand, and Globalization, Nationalism and Fundamentalism on the other. Our everyday life is challenged by these conflicting and contradicting forces of world history. In order to face these new challenges, we need a clear understanding of the socio-political and ideological make-up of the contemporary world. This chapter aims to provide this.

The chapter is divided into four parts. The first part deals with the historical development of the term 'Fundamentalism'. The second part analyzes the socio-political factors which have given rise to the phenomenon of fundamentalism. The third part suggests ways to meet the challenge of fundamentalism. Finally, some concluding remarks are given.

1. Towards an Understanding of 'What is Fundamentalism?'

Fundamentalism is often employed in contemporary journalistic as well as scholarly writings as a trendy substitute for communalism, or simply as a term of abuse. This is regrettable because there is a fair degree of consensus on the meaning of communalism. But fundamentalism, however, remains a rather vaguely defined omnibus word. All the same, because of the happenings in the world today, in spite of its ambiguity, the concept of fundamentalism is being used worldwide. Efforts are being made to sharpen the precision of the usage of this concept.

In the late-nineteenth and early twentieth centuries, a certain distrust of scientism and rationalism was voiced in certain quarters in England and the USA. The focus was on the implications of, first, certain trends in Biblical criticism and, second, materialistic philosophies and the social sciences. At the centre of the argument was the status of the Bible as scripture and some modernist textual interpretations with the objective of overcoming an apparent conflict between Biblical teaching and scientific knowledge, represented most challengingly by the Darwinian theory of evolution. Orthodox Christians saw the Bible as infallible or inerrant and as transparent, that is, not in need of interpretation. In other words, the authority, inerrancy and transparency of the Bible were unquestionable.

A series of twelve pamphlets, entitled *The Fundamentals*, published between 1910 and 1915 gave expression to the above-mentioned concerns. What was under attack in these tracts was modernism rather than science, but the conception of science that the pamphleteers entertained was that of Baconian induction. Their principal concern was to oppose modernist criticism of the Bible. In their nine-point statement of faith, they stressed above all else the notion of the inerrancy of scripture. A World Christian Fundamentals Association was formed and, by the mid-1920s, the term 'fundamentalist' was in use. Fundamentalists were now being asked to do "battle royal for the Fundamentals", which were chiefly doctrinal and intended to ward off 'the havoc' that 'rationalism' had unleashed (Marty 1986: 237).

In the 1960s and 1970s fundamentalists began to assert themselves in the context of the U.S. Supreme Court banning prayer in public schools (1963), and permitting abortion on demand (1973). This also brought to light the clash of religious and secular values. Following the second Vatican Council's efforts (1962-1965) at ecumenical reconciliation, and the perceived *compromise* of the Church with modernity, conservative Catholics also began to voice their concern about the fundamentals of the faith.

Similar attitudes developed among other major religions around the globe. For example, the Iranian Revolution of 1978-79 attained paradigmatic status as being fundamentalist in contemporary discussions.

The Iranian Revolution has its roots in the modernization process in Iran under Reza Shah Muhammad Pahlavi's reign after Second World War. This carried forward the beginnings made in the revolutionary changes that occurred in 1905-11. Secularization in Iran had been rapid and fairly wide-ranging, and yet it was partial. Most importantly, the civil code continued to be based on Islamic holy law (*Sharia*), and Shia *Ulema*, whose importance in Iranian public life dates back to the beginning of the sixteenth century, remained powerful. A reversal of modernization began to gain momentum around this time. It ultimately led Ayatollah Ruhollah Khomeini to seize power and he sought to destroy the 'modern' Iran that the Shah and the urban, propertied, ruling class had tried to build. It was, first, a bloody reaction to the present and, only then, a return to the past or the fundamentals of Islam. The idea of an autonomous secular state was rejected. The book *Fundamentals of Islamic Thought* (1985), authored by Khomeini's protégé, Ayatollah Mutahhari served as a manifesto of the revolution.

In recent times, the world has been shocked and horrified with images of hostages being beheaded by a group calling itself *Islamic State of Iraq and Syria*, or ISIS. Who are they? Why do these extremists target predominantly western/Caucasian people?

Within 20 years of Muhammad's ministry, he united almost all of Arabia under strict monotheist faith. Muhammad's first few successors, the Caliphs, defeated the mighty Persian and Byzantine Empires. To many in the Arab world, this is evidence of the greatness that Muslim Kingdoms (Caliphates) can achieve if Islam is strictly practiced.

This belief has two problems; firstly, Islam lacks a central authority to interpret the *Quran* and *Sunnah.* Essentially, every Muslim must live as he interprets the code. This leaves room for a wide variety of Islamic practices, from the mystic Sufi to the rigid Taliban. Secondly, the concept of Secularism, so proudly proclaimed by the West, is inconceivable to many Muslims. Every action of a Muslim is governed by Islam, a government is a public expression of this action. How can there be a Muslim government that is not Islamic? With the complex long political struggle between Communist Russia dominated by then Soviet Union, Capitalist United States and the Islamic militancy, the Islamic State of Iran and Syria (ISIS) has emerged. Any attempts at democratic process or withdrawal of Western armies, leads to an upsurge of extremists. This Islamic militancy and extremism have become worldwide in several countries in Asia and Africa through the organizations like Boko Haram.

Hindu fundamentalism has its roots in the nineteenth century Hindu revivalism and may be seen as awareness to the Christian challenge to its culture and tradition (Madan, 1997: 207). (For example, the Christian view of man as being created in the image of God endowed every human being with inherent dignity and helped to bring about reforms such as the abolition of *Sati* and child marriage). A striking feature of the revivalist movements was their concern with the identification of true scripture and with scriptural authority. These efforts reached their climax in the later writings of Dayanand Sarasvati. The Arya Samaj movement (1875) sowed the seeds of Hindu fundamentalism (Anderson and Damle, 1987; Jefferlot, 1996). The outcome of this ideology is *Hindutva* (Hinduness) (Michael, 1996:294-310). Through a long process of political mobilization, in 2014, the Bharatiya Janta Party (BJP) has come into power in India. Now, reports are emerging that the present Government is taking all steps to Hinduize the culture of India by bringing changes in the educational system. Violence against the minority religions is showing an increase today.

Thus, to the question 'what is fundamentalism' we may say that the concept of fundamentalism had its birth in the late nineteenth century West. What began as a laudatory term in the 1920s was pronounced a bad word by James Barr, a Biblical scholar, half a century later, suggestive of "narrowness, bigotry, obscurantism, and sectarianism" (1978:2). Following the Iranian Revolution of 1978-79 and the demolition of Babri Masjid in India in 1992, the terms "Islamic fundamentalism" and "Hindu fundamentalism" have attained paradigmatic status as being fundamentalist in contemporary discussions. It has a connotation of rigidity, intolerance, arrogance, hostility, divisiveness, prejudice and other negatives to describe narrowness, bigotry, obscurantism, and sectarianism (Barr, 1978:2). So, when one talks about fundamentalism, one is actually talking about experiences or situations which are ripe with political, cultural and religious conflicts and tensions.

3. Socio-Political and Ideological Analysis of Fundamentalism

(a) Fundamentalism is a Reaction to Modernism and Secularization

Modernism has its root in seventeenth century Enlightenment

philosophy. The Enlightenment was a period of remarkable intellectual development and activities within the field of philosophy. A number of traditional ideas and beliefs were overthrown and replaced by modern ones. Overall the Enlightenment was characterized by rationalism, scepticism about traditional doctrines, and supporting the empirical method in science. The proponents of the Enlightenment were critical of traditional authorities and discarded the idea of Biblical revelation as superstitious. They had supreme confidence in man as a rational being and believed in a rational, scientific approach to religious, social, political, and economic issues. They promoted a secular view of the world and a general sense of progress and perfectibility.

With supreme faith in rational man, they sought to discover and to act upon universally valid principles governing humanity, nature and society. In the light of these developments anthropologists began to study the social laws by which human society and culture was developing. They were interested in studying the progress of human culture and detected a grand law, something similar to the Darwinian principle of biological evolution. Anthropologists came up with the hypothesis that human culture was progressing from simple beginnings to complex stages of cultural growth. Thus, the first stage in the development of anthropology as a so-called science was characterized by facile schemes of unilinear evolutionism such as, broadly speaking, sexual communism leading to matriarchal societies, then to patriarchal ones and finally to more or less monogamous, bilateral ones, or again, in the domain of religion, animism giving way to polytheism and lastly to monotheism.

Such ideas of degrees of civilization dominated the thinking of the intellectual world during the nineteenth and early twentieth centuries. Science and technology were becoming increasingly powerful. The classical thinkers influenced by the Age of Reason or Enlightenment and the Darwinian Theory, emphasized a more positivist and evolutionary approach to understand religion. They held that the absurd doctrines of religion had come into existence because of ignorance and superstition and with the advance of the scientific method, such irrationalism would vanish. Marxian and Freudian views also undermined the authority of religion. The conflict between religious faith and rationalism was formative in the emergence of the modern ideology of secularization. Secularization was accepted as the natural and inevitable process in the development of human society. Influenced by this intellectual climate, many Biblical scholars began to interpret Biblical texts from a secular outlook. Certain hermeneutical principles of interpretations applied to the Bible led to trends in Biblical criticism which were not acceptable to orthodox Christians. As we pointed out early, at the centre of the argument was the status of the Bible as scripture and the admissibility or otherwise of modernist textual interpretations with the objective of overcoming the apparent conflict between Biblical teaching and scientific knowledge.

Thus, conflict between faith in the Bible and principles of rationalism was formative in the emergence and clarification of the fundamentals of Christianity in the West. Today, this trend has strengthened itself in the context of the apparent failures of science, technology and rationalism to deliver goods in solving human problems, especially the problem of *'meaning'* in human life.

Contemporary society has been experiencing both a crisis in religion as well as a global resurgence. This resurgence has taken place in all varieties of social systems—from the technologically most advanced to the traditional societies. The retreat from secularization and the revival of religion has taken place, according to social scientists, largely because science, technology and rationalism have failed to give meaning in both the personal and occupational lives of individuals and have failed to resolve some of the institutional problems of modern society. It has also failed to provide a guide to man's quest for ultimate meaning, accepting that man was by anthropological nature a religious animal. Individuals have been realizing the infinite fragmentation that modern developments have caused in their lives and are striving to put these fragments back together again into a meaningful whole (Wilson 1966, 1982, 1988; Beckford, 1986; Dawson, 1998; Giri, 1998).

(b) Challenges of Post-modernism and Multiculturalism

With the failure of modernism and with the rise of nation-states in Asia and Africa after Second World War, and the ever expanding communication system and migration of people from one cultural area to another have created a new situation leading to Post-modern and Multicultural societies.

Post-modernists question all types of grand theories and generalizations. A coherent, general understanding across cultural boundaries is seen as virtually impossible (Bhargava, 1999). Key analytic categories may not be as universally applicable as we had once imagined in modernism. Paul Heelas explains this by saying, "The cultural becomes disorganized; less black and white. The distinction between high and low fades away. The claim that one tradition should be adhered to because it, and it alone, is valid, is rendered invalid. And rather than authority and legitimacy resting with established orders of knowledge, authority comes to rest with the person" (1998:4-5). In the words of James Beckford, post-modernity consists in a "willingness to abandon the search for over-arching or triumphalist myths, narratives or frameworks of knowledge" (as quoted in Paul Heelas, *"Religion, Modernity and Post-modernity"*, Oxford: Blackwell, 1998:4). The Post-modern critique of "grand theory" has been one more argument in favour of multiculturalism and value relativism.

Thus, Post-modernism seems to be a fluid, multi-dimensional, transitory phenomenon. At any rate, if we accept the historical periodization of the pre-modern and the modern, then it follows that the post-modern comes after the modern and is in direct reaction to it. According to Bradbury, post-modernism is related to the concept of the post-industrial society. He notes that it is a paradoxical term since it holds that modernism is over and done with, and yet the movements that have taken over are not only dependent on the modern, but also in some degree in revolt against it. It is imbued with a sense of "collapsed signification and challenged humanism", but is at one and the same time for and against humanism and for and against high technology: It is amorphous, eclectic, pluri-cultural, ideologically and aesthetically not clear-cut, and, therefore, appears to be more than anything else's complex map of late twentieth century directions'.

A Pakistani anthropologist, Akbar S. Ahmed condenses and codifies the post-modern condition into four basic elements as follows: (1) *Eclectism* or the selection from various sources and styles of what, perhaps, are considered the best aspects. (2) *Syncretism* or the attempt at the reconciliation of different and even opposing principles and practices, and some would even say the attempt at reconciling the irreconcilable. (3) *Juxtaposition* or the placing of various elements close together or side by side. (4) And *irony* or the expression of a meaning that is often the direct opposite of the intended meaning (Ahmed, 1992).

Thus, Post-modernism seems to be a fluid, multi-dimensional or pluri-cultural and, therefore, transitory phenomenon. However, Jencks believes that it suggests that we have gone beyond modernism, but does not specify *where we are going*. Post-modernism is navigation in chaos. But if it does not specify where we are going does it mean that we must remain rudderless and just drift along with the low tides and the high tides? Or, and this seems to be more appropriate and relevant, must we seek for a guiding compass? If a guiding compass is a reasonable requirement, then postmodernism will not do. For, as Gertrude Himmelfarb, speaking in relation to trends in contemporary historiography, says, it derides the quest for truth and related values and under-writes nihilism.

So in what direction shall we look and what truths and values shall we endeavour to pursue in keeping with our higher interests and purposes? Modernism was essentially a reaction against something, whereas Post-modernism seems to be more fatalistic and resigned to the *status quo*.

The breakdown of traditional value complexes, without their replacement by a 'secularized' ethos, leads to moral ambiguity and value confusion. New religious movements represent a quest for new structures of meaning and values. Fundamentalism thrives in this situation.

(c) Challenges from Relativistic Orientations

Relativists stress the validity of all claims to truth and regard them as equal, since the world is moving in the direction of equality among men, cultures or nations, and also among genders. Therefore, to try and pursue a claim to any kind of unique truth is merely a cover for domination. The claim of Christianity as a unique and universal religion and its missionary efforts to convert the followers of other religions to its fold has led other religions to look into their claim for uniqueness. This has led to both the emergence of Religious Fundamentalism as well as Religious Relativism.

Today every religion is claiming to be very special and has a universal message for humanity. They are increasingly becoming missionary. One of the best examples is from India, while Indian religious leaders will state that all religions are equally valid and they are different means to the same goal. All the same, today they believe that "*Advaita*" is the most spiritual path and they would claim their mission to spiritualize the whole world with the spirituality of the "*Advaita*". The claim of every religion to be equally and universally valid paths for salvation has given rise to relativistic thinking in today's world. The rise of fundamentalism is a reaction to this relativistic thinking.

(d) Fundamentalism and the Clash of Civilization

According to Robertson, the expansion of the world religions of Islam and Christianity had an important role in the rise of religious fundamentalism. Lately, Hinduism has also joined the fold.

The expansion of Islam took place with the expansion of the Arab and Ottoman Empires from the twelfth to the fifteenth centuries. By the eighteenth century it had achieved a presence in diverse regions. Christianity had to wait for the military and colonial expansion of Europe in the sixteenth and seventeenth centuries to acquire a global presence. Prior to this period the globalizing consequence was the incorporation of tribal peasants into large scale political systems. These two universalistic religions of Christianity and Islam, both derivatives of the Abrahamic faith, became universalizing religions and most effective globalizers because of their claims that the world was created by a single God and that humanity was a common force of existence in relation to that God. It led to the argument that humanity constituted a single community that disvalued geographical localities and political territories, that there was a single value-reference for every person in the world and that this God proposed a single set of legal and moral laws.

By the sixteenth century, a newer and far more important globalizing religious force had emerged—Protestantism. Catholicism had blurred the relationship between State and Church so that a series of conflicts emerged between Kings and Popes. The Reformation resolved the dispute between State and Church by either subordinating the Church to the State (as in England), or by secularizing the State (as in U.S.A. and France). The State could now rely for its legitimization on the political process of nationalism rather than on religious legitimations.

The Secularization of the West in contrast to other parts of the world, the rise and fall of Socialist economies and the unprecedented triumph of Capitalistic economy (at least for the time being), and the increasing influence of Western materialistic, consumerist, impersonal, pleasure-seeking, market oriented globalization have brought about a clash of civilization. The culture this Capitalist economy through globalization creates seems destructive, possibly because of the competitive spirit fostered by capitalism. Society is increasingly becoming alien to the concern of the individual—society is no more in the mind of the individual. The personal has replaced the public and as a consequence problem of the self has become the most serious concern. The individual is more and more involved in seeking a solution to his own crisis so that he has become insensitive to the social good. This is in contrast to the Asian spirit and its culture.

The crisis of the individual is further deepened by the changes in the material life during the last few years. The character of the market has changed dramatically and globalization has opened up the possibility of unprecedented access to consumer goods. The transnational capital has created a new market and along with that a new culture which the individual imbibes not by his own choice; it is forced upon him. As in advanced capitalist societies, the market is becoming so irresistibly powerful that consumerism tends to be the ideology and the culture of the masses, creating material aspirations not commensurate with their real situation.

The Asian cultures and religions which stress the importance of family, community, traditions and social values find it extremely difficult to cope with the new developments. There is also the fear that their religious values will be either undermined or destroyed by the forces of Westernization and globalization. Anxieties generated in such a soil may also tend to spawn excessive religiosity, communalism and fundamentalism.

(e) Relationship between Nationalism and Fundamentalism

The last few centuries have been a very turbulent phase in the History of the World. On the one hand we have seen the power of colonialism and also the spirit of freedom in nationalistic movements which opened up much of Asia for nationalist and often communist revolution. In the 1940s there were several nationalist struggles which resulted in the formation of many nation states in Asia. To strengthen the identity of these nations, cultural, religious and ideological (communist) orientations are at work in Asia today.

An impression has been created that each country has its own religion and the Asian religions such as Hinduism, Buddhism and Islam are the religions of those countries in Asia where it is dominant. To strengthen the national identity and the dominance in the world, religion is made use of. Hence, there is a connection between nationalism and fundamentalism. Religion is used as a political tool to strengthen the national identity.

In the 1990s, scholars sensitive to the phenomenon of the emergence of religious groups who took political action leading even to national revolutions suggested a series of alternate terms to designate these conservative, neo-traditionalist and often militant religious groups. One such term favoured by writers such as Peter van der Veer and Mark Juergensmeyer was 'religious nationalism'. Juergensmeyer explained that when a religious perspective was fused with a political and social destiny of a nation, it was referred to as religious nationalism (1994). Religious nationalists were not just religious fanatics. For the most part they were political activists who were seriously attempting to reformulate the 'modern' language of politics in order to provide a new basis for the nation state. They were concerned not so much about the political structure of the nation state as about the political ideology underlying it (Juergensmeyer 1994: xiii). Nikkei Keddie who questioned whether nationalism was always the main focus of such efforts proposed the term "new religious politics".

In a famous Chicago study titled "Fundamentalisms Observed" (1994), Martin Marty and R. Scott Appleby, elaborately developed the characteristics of Fundamentalism. They explained Fundamentalism as a reaction against the invasive, intrusive and threatening features of modernity by the emerging nation-states of the non-western world. For example, Islamic Fundamentalism represented a delayed reaction to the hegemony of European colonial rule after they became Independent nation states. Religious identity was used as a protective shield against the onslaught of globalization, which was marked by the entry of integrated 'market systems' which came along with a variety of commodities, values, beliefs and styles of living. The fear of extinction and the threat to survival both as a people and as a culture and the loss of distinctiveness in the face of homogeneity resulted in the introduction of a comprehensive social system based upon religious principles which embraced law, policy, society, economy and culture. Thus, Fundamentalism tended to be totalitarian in its practice and encompassed all areas of private and public life. Religion was declared not just a faith but a way of life. Fundamentalism of this nature was not religious in the classical sense of the term, but was a variant of a secular faith couched in religious language.

They also observed that Fundamentalism was driven by the affinity-identity passions of ethnic communities and religious groups often thirsting for self-esteem and dignity. Fundamentalism as seen above was an effort to 'neutralize the other' and establish one's own identity. In other words, the question of 'cultural survival' was at the core of the issue of religious revivalism. This process could be observed in the East European countries that belonged to divergent cultural communities and ethnic groups after the demise of the Soviet Union. Their demand for economic autonomy and preservation of cultural identities resulted in ethnic conflicts between majority Muslim and Christian minority Serbs in Bosnia, between minority Christian Serbs and majority Muslims of Albanian origin in the Kosovo province of Yugoslavia. This process can also be observed in parts of Indonesia today. In India religious-cultural and ethnic clashes are being experienced in the efforts of those of the *Hindutva* ideology, the RSS or *"Sangh Parivar"*, to create a communal divide between the Hindu majority and the Muslim and Christian minority communities in India.

Religious and nationalist movements, it was further observed, often invoked authenticity and 'authentic culture' as a weapon against what was foreign and alien. However, this authenticity was questionable as it became difficult to prove what was authentic and what was not. The invoking of certain traditions and the denying of others required a reconstruction of history, if not its destruction. Historians took pains to demonstrate that historically intercultural exchange, trade and conquest had rendered any notion of authenticity highly problematic. Fundamentalist movements then relied a great deal on invented traditions (Marty and Appleby 1994: 814-37).

(f) Globalization, Problem of Identity and Fundamentalism

Globalization is a complex phenomenon. It connotes the interconnectedness of the world with contacts and linkages that the world is becoming a small world day by day. It is of a world where borders and boundaries have become increasingly porous, allowing more and more peoples and cultures to be cast into intense and immediate contact with each other.

The intensification of the communication network through satellite television, internet and email bring images quickly from screen to screen, providing people with resources from which to fashion new ways of being in the world. Thus, there is an increasing global standardization of cultural goods, tastes, and practices in clothes, food and music to architecture, film, and television cutting across national boundaries (Hall, 1996:619). All these bring disruptions in the traditional notions of society, religion and culture.

Globalization takes the whole world as a single economic unit and the market as its instrument. The economy in a globalized world is characterized by open, liberal, free market and free trade with less regulatory barriers. It is marked by international investment and instant capital flows. Due to this, multi-national companies move into different locations where labour is cheap. People from different national boundaries shift their places of work and residence exposing themselves to different cultural worlds. As a consequence, today we see peoples and cultures formerly located in different parts of the world now inhabiting the same physical area. All this creates a new global situation in which a fundamental restructuring of economic and political arrangements is taking place (See Michael & Jogdand, 2003).

Globalization, which promotes a secular and liberal culture, creates a troubled relationship between the native and the international. The claim of the emergence of a global culture is accompanied by cries of alarm that local values and nation-states are suffering a sense of threat to identity. This has given rise to ethnic revivals, struggles for indigenous rights, religious fundamentalism as defensive reactions to globalization. They have risen from a desire to defend and preserve valued ways of life against what are taken to be pernicious effects of foreign and global influences. As a result fundamentalist religious movements tend to emerge in order to strengthen the identity of nation and culture.

4. How do we meet the Challenge?

(a) To distinguish between 'The Fundamentals' (Foundation of Faith) and 'Fundamentalism' (Fanaticism—Religion based Extremism)

The rise of fundamentalism is related to the question of meaning, identity, power, dignity and self-esteem. It is religious politics. Fundamentalism is partly a reaction to the spread of the relativistic outlook and it asserts that faith must be taken seriously; if not, it ceases to grip the mind or to orient or guide the person. Hence, paying only lip-service to it is to defeat its potency and purpose. The fundamentalists, who today predominate in many parts of the world, accuse the relativists of diluting moral conviction and fervour and of thus weakening the moral fibre of man in his fundamental essence.

It is important to understand that the vast majority of those who lend their loyalty to a religious outlook are not fundamentalists, and this applies correspondingly to their moral orientation. This majority can be regarded as representing a methodological or philosophical point of view which is the very antithesis of the relativistic point of view. Hence, we need to distinguish between 'fundamentals' of a religion and 'fundamentalism'. When religion is used narrowly for selfish power, and to oppress people due to socio-political and other reasons, it may be named as fundamentalism (Barr, James 1978:2). On the other hand, a deep commitment to faith and the 'fundamentals' of a religion cannot be called fundamentalism.

Hence, we need to distinguish between "faith foundation", i.e. "fundamentals" of a religion and "fundamentalism" which connotes rigidity, intolerance, arrogance, hostility, divisiveness, prejudice and other negatives to describe narrowness, bigotry, obscurantism, and sectarianism (Barr, 1978:2). So, when one talks about fundamentalism, one is actually talking about experiences, situations, and an environment that does not promote harmony, tranquility and brotherhood, but encourages a context of growing hostile, divisive, separatist tendencies.

Clarifying the foundation of one's faith in terms of religious life in the complex and ever-changing and challenging world scenario of today cannot be called fundamentalism. On the other hand, using religion for the sake of narrow and selfish power games and economic interests is 'fundamentalism'. Fundamentalism in the negative sense is an aberration of religion. It is linked to political and economic interests of certain vested parties to maintain influence, power, wealth and status. It is invoking God for their inability to find a way out and to lead the people to light. Fundamentalism is one of the more dangerous tools of interested parties because it uses, or rather abuses religious beliefs which have an intrinsic mass appeal.

Hence, we need to be very careful to distinguish between "the fundamentals" or Foundation of Faith in a religion and "fundamentalism", which is a direct use of religion in politics for a narrow purpose leading to fanaticism.

(b) Going Beyond Ethnocentrism and Relativism

Evaluating other religions and cultures in the light of one's own is known as 'ethnocentrism'. This tends to foster claims of superiority *vis-à-vis* other religions. The other important attitude towards religion is 'relativism'. It is an intellectual position that holds that every religion is equally valid and we should not compare religions. The relativists stress the validity of all claims to truth and regard them as equal, since the world is moving in the direction of equality among men, cultures, nations, as well as genders. Therefore, to try and pursue a claim to any kind of unique truth is merely a cover for domination. It is the stand of the relativist that each religion has its own integrity, its own system of values. What is 'good', what is 'right' what is 'beautiful' do not exist by themselves. To hold that a given religion is intrinsically better than any other religion is considered to be somehow wrong, offensive, and narrow-minded. Hence, there should be no value judgment on religions.

A blind belief in the superiority of one's own culture or religion is ethnocentrism. Ethnocentrism leads to fundamentalism. Hence, we need to go beyond ethnocentrism. The relativistic worldview, on the other hand, making all cultural and religious values equally good is also impossible to hold. It is because this will justify some of the values such as human sacrifice (*sati*), female infanticide, headhunting, religious wars of aggression (*jihad*), religious murders, religious castes (*varna-dharma*), untouchability etc. present in certain religions. All these are justifiable according to a logic that stems from within the system itself. Relativism leaves us as separate islands of subjective being. The practical and effective alternatives are not ethnocentrism versus relativism, but rather rational norms with a potentiality for universal acceptance and realization. That means we must endorse some ultimate and absolute values. This presupposes a *normative* ethic.

(c) Priority of the Dignity of the Human Person and towards Intercultural Transformation

(d) In the last part Dignity of human person, you may add Dignity of human person and Cultures, and thus, if you modify some of your thoughts in this part synchronizing with the title, it may be good.

In the context of religious fundamentalism and relativism, we need to place the priority of human person over all other considerations. We need to safeguard the dignity of man/woman over all other considerations.

Today, religious fundamentalism in India manifests itself in the form of Cultural Nationalism. In fighting religious fundamentalism today, we need to ask ourselves what does nationalism mean for the poor, oppressed and marginalized. Are they able to experience a sense of common humanity in the Indian nationhood? Or is nationalism the luxury of the rich and the powerful? As Christians in India we need to be concerned about human dignity and the integration of all Indians. In the context of *Hindutva* and Hindu nationalism, we need to define nationalism in such a way that the poor and the downtrodden receive their due attention and care. As concerned citizens we need to ask what nationalism means for the poor; Dalits, tribals and other weaker sections. Behind the dreams and aspirations of these marginalized groups lingers the hope that a nation of fairness and justice will be realized; a nation, humane and inclusive.

5. Conclusion

By way of conclusion, we may say that fundamentalism is related to the new emerging socio-political and cultural patterns. It is an outcome of cultural crisis and a sense of loss. It is related to the question of meaning, identity, power, the dignity and self-esteem of human person. It is a revolt against cultural relativism. It is a response to a changing social order.

The wind of change due to globalization has gradually reached the whole world. The world has become small. Every aspect of human life is being affected by this process. Religion, culture and nation are challenged to reorient themselves to the newly emerging global order. Economic activities and power relationships are also adapting themselves to this process. Globalization is a double-edged sword. It has exciting possibilities but can also usher in unprecedented miseries. Globalization, which supports a secular and liberal culture also, creates a troubled relationship between the local and the international. The spread of a global culture is accompanied by cries of alarm that local values and nation-states will suffer a sense of threat to their identity. Fundamentalism feeds on this sense of a weakened identity and need for re-orientation in a complex world.

REFERENCES

Ahmed, Akbar S. (1992), *Post-modernism and Islam,* London: Psychology Press.

Anderson, Walter, K. and S.D. Damle (1987), *The Brotherhood in Saffron: The Rashtriya Swayamsevak Sangh and Hindu Revivalism*, New Delhi: Vistaar Publications.

Barr, James, 1978, *Fundamentalism,* Philadelphia: Westminster Press.

Beckford, J.A. (Ed.) 1986, *New Religious Movements and Rapid Social Change*, London: Sage Publications/UNESCO.

Bhargava, Rajeev (Ed.) (1999), *Multiculturalism, Liberalism and Democracy,* New Delhi: Oxford University Press.

Dawson, Christopher. (1949), *Religion and Culture,* London: Sheed & Ward.

Giri, A.K. (1988), *Global Transformations: Post-Modernity and Beyond,* Jaipur: Rawat Publications.

Hall, Stuart, *Question of Cultural Identity in Modernity: An Introduction to Modern Societies*, (Eds.) Stuart Hall and Paul du Gay, pp. 595-634 Cambridge (London): Sage Publications.

Hawley, J.S. 1999, "Fundamentalism" in (Ed.) Courtney Howland, *Religious Fundamentalism and the Human Rights of Women*, pp. 3-8, London: MacMillan Ltd.

Jaffrelot, C. (1996), *Hindu Nationalist Movement in India*, New York: Columbia University Press.

Juergensmeyer, M. (1994), *Religious Nationalism Confronts Secular State,* New Delhi: Oxford University Press.

Heelas, Paul (1998), *Religion, Modernity and Post-modernity,* Oxford: Blackwell Publishers.

Madan, T.N. (1997), *Modern Myths, Locked Minds,* New Delhi: Oxford University Press.

Marty, Martin E. (1986), *Modern American Religion, Vol. 1, The irony of it all, 1893-1919*, Chicago: University of Chicago Press.

Marty, Martin E. (1988), Fundamentalism as a Social Phenomenon, *Bulletin of the American Academy of Arts and Sciences,* Vol. 42: 15-29.

Marty Martin E. and R. Scott Appleby (Eds.) (1994), *Accounting for Fundamentalisms*, Chicago: University of Chicago Press.

Michael, S.M. (1996), "The Cultural Context of the Rise of Hindutva and Dalit Forces" in *Vidyajyoti*, No. 5, pp. 294-310.

Michael, S.M. and P.G. Jogdand (Eds.), (2003), *Globalization and Social Movements: Struggle for a Humane Society,* New Delhi: Rawat Publications.

Pereira, Kenneth Mario (1997), *Inter-Religious Dialogue Vis-à-vis The Absolute Claims of Christianity,* Rome: Gregorian Pontifical University (M.Th. Dissertation).

Veer Van der P. (1996), *Religious Nationalism, Hindus and Muslims in India,* New Delhi: Oxford University Press.

Vivekananda, Swami (1957), *The Complete Works of Swami Vivekananda,* Calcutta: Advaita Ashram.

Wilson, B. (1966), *Religion in a Secular Society,* England: Penguin Books.

Wilson, B. (1982), *Religion in Sociological Perspective*, New York: Oxford University Press.

Wilson, B. (1988), "Secularization: Religion in the Modern World" in S. Sutherland *et al.* (Eds.) *The World's Religions*, pp. 953-956, London: Routledge.

9

Inflationary Trends after Globalization and its Impact on Indian Economy

P. NATARAJA MURTHY

The term inflation is most conveniently associated with a substantial and persistent rise in the general level of prices or a rate of expansion of money income greater than the rate of growth of real output. Inflation is not confined to any specific country, not it is unique to the developing country. After globalization, inflation had attained a new dimension in the world economy, since not only the capitalist, but also the mixed and the socialist economies of the world have been suffering from the vicious problem of inflation.

The present chapter is an empirical study going into the precise nature of inter-relationship among money, output and prices in India during 1993-2012, which covers the period of three five year plans. One can observe two phases, in the context of Whole Sale Price Index base years. The first period starts from 1993-94 to 2004-05 (Period I) and the second one from 2004-05 to 2011-12 (Period II). It is obvious that in accordance with the policy shifts, the macro-fundamentals of the system, respond to the emerging situation. Hence, it is necessary to probe into this issue, in the light of policy changes. Further, this issue is at the core of monetary economics and has remained an area of controversy, despite years of research.[1] From the days of Adam Smith, the main focus of macro-economic thinkers and policy-makers has been one of achieving macro-economic stability. The macro-economic stabilization needs the achievement of acceptable inflation rate, optimal growth of output, respectable value of currency and favourable balance of payments. From the early days of Quantity Theory of Money to the contemporary discussions on Rational

Expectations hypothesis, economists have been debating on how changes in money, ultimately influence the economic system. In spite of a decade of research and analysis, there is yet no unanimity on how and to what extent, changes in money supply affect the real variables in the system. Depending on the assumptions made a wide variety of conclusions have been drawn.

There are many versions provided by different schools of thought to explain the relationship among money supply, prices, interest rate and output in the economy. Earliest among them is the classical school explaining that changes in prices, which is the most important target variable in achieving stabilization, is basically due to the changes in money supply. The Quantity Theory of Money, which is the corner-stone of the classical monetary theory, holds that the impact of changes in the supply of money on output is negligible. They result only in proportion to changes in the aggregate price level. It is assumed here, that labour markets operate under full employment, so that, the impact of changes in money is on the price level.

Until the time of Great Depression, for almost two centuries, this version of Quantity Theory became the dominant macro-economic policy and was therefore dictated by the need to control the money supply in order to achieve the desired rate of price change. But this view of proportionality between money supply and the price level was rejected by the Keynesians, due to its inability in explaining the causes and remedies for the great economic debacle.[2] In the case of the Keynesian model of income determination, with its assumption of no changes in prices, the full impact of money supply is seen only on output. An increase in the quantity of money leads to a fall in the real interest rate, which stimulates investments. This in turn, through the multiplier process, increases income and output in the economy. The Keynesian analysis assumes that the price level is relatively sticky in the short run, while the commodity market is cleared by variations in the level of output and the money market by changes in the rate of interest.

Perhaps the real world lies somewhere in between these two extreme poles, represented by the Quantity theory and the Keynesian analysis. When money is injected into the system, a dichotomy arises due to nominal money balances. This causes the price level to rise so that the nominal stock is brought in equilibrium with real demand. The original quantity theory implied that changes in money stock had no effect on output. Nevertheless, some of the most ardent supporters of the quantity theory of money now do not assume this extreme position. In fact, there is an attempt, to view the quantity theory of money and the Keynesian demand function for money as belonging to the same group, the difference arising from what asset is being considered as an alternative to money.[3] While the Keynesian theory works through changes in interest rate, treating money as substitute for financial assets, the reformulated quantity theory of money regards money as a substitute not only for financial assets, but also for real goods. It is now generally accepted that the impact of changes in the quantity of money will partly be on price level and partly on output.

As almost all the economies suffered from high inflation rates due to cheap monetary policy adopted during in the Second World War, monetarists criticized the Keynesian ideas, which led to the emergence of a new theory called Monetarism. The Monetarists' view on the effect of changes in money supply on economic activity is found in the writings of eminent economists like Friedman[4] (1959), Laider[5] (1966), Anderson and Jordon[6] (1968). This view asserts that central bankers should concentrate on quantity of money and this has to be exogenously determined, rather than through the operation of the interest rates. The Monetarists view of treating inflation as a monetary phenomenon, is also supported by the new classical school, known widely as Rational Expectations School. Broadly, the disagreement between monetarists and Keynesians relates to the transmission mechanism, among the four-policy and output. But the real business cycle school, which is otherwise called the New Classical Macro-economics,[7] treats money supply as endogenous, and concludes that monetary policy is irrelevant.

One view of the Banking school is that money is an endogenous variable, which can be used to analyse changes in price level and output. Money supply and output determine the price level. The price level and output affect the government budget. The latter is influenced among other factors, by changes in real money supply acting as a proxy for real credit. Besides, the extent of inflation will depend upon the various elasticities, quantifying the relationships among money output and prices.

Real Bills doctrine of the Banking school believed that there exists a reverse causation running from prices to money supply. This argues that when provided the Bank regulated its note issue, by discounting only good quality short term commercial chapter (known as real bills) the quantity of money in circulation would be consequence and not the cause of Prices.[8]

Of late, increasing attention has been devoted to the question of causality between money output and prices.[9] As against the conventional position that money stock influences output and/or prices, it has been argued that causation runs in the opposite direction, i.e., that money stock simply accommodates prices changes (induces typically, by non-monetary factors). Intermediate positions have also been favoured, emphasizing the possibility of 'bi-directional' causation, especially between money and prices.

From the foregoing discussion, one learns that the causality between money supply and general price level is a subject matter of controversy in macro-monetary economics.[10] The monetarists and non-monetarists disagree as to the efficacy of money supply as the basic instrument for controlling inflation. More recently, writers go into the question, whether the price level reflects the causal effect of money supply on price, or the relationship is the other way round, that prices affect money supply.

In summary, one may state that the issue remains unresolved, whether or not there exists a relationship among money supply, price level and output. Hence the researcher plans to study the causal relationship between money-output, money-price, output-prices, and the inter-relation among money, output and prices in India, during the plan era, covering the entire period of eight five year plans (1951-1997).

Casual observations reveal that it is macro not so in reality and that state-level variations in prices are determined by regional demand and supply factors, apart from the impact of aggregate price level[11] (Bhattacharya *et al.*).

Firstly under liberalization and globalization wherein full play of the market forces are envisaged, an increase in competition is expected to put downward pressure on prices and underlying factor costs Binayani and Razin (2007).[12]

The Consumer Price Index presently compiled relate to different base years and cater to specific segments of the population again, the procedures for compilation of price indices do not systematically incorporate new products and adjust for quality improvements (Sreenivasan, T.N., 2008; Angus Deaton, 2008);[13] Patnaik, Amaresh Samantaraya (2006).[14] Their periodization of pre-and-post liberalization is not decided on any scientific basis and is also based on any single indicator. Hence to determine the periodization we re-examine the trends in inflation using a scientific test-baiperon test-to identify the structural breaks.

C.B. Sharma (2011)[15] argues that Indian policy-makers often acted beyond the norms of theoretical discipline in terms of money supply. Government and the corporate world often compromise with high inflation for a higher growth and argue that there is a trade-off between inflation and growth, to achieve higher growth, country has to suffer high inflation. Thakur and Bharadwaj (2011)[16] say that the serious effect of inflation will disrupt the smooth working of the price and it loses the flexibility, which leads to the reduction of mobilization of productive resources. Singh (2012)[17] is highly critical about the existing measures used; it has no all-purpose, all-inclusive and universally valid index yet now. Growth rate of money, output and prices are used to assess the behaviour of respective variable over years.

Table 9.1: Behaviour of Money, Output and Prices in India (Period I)

Year	*Money*	*Output*	*Prices*
1994-95	7.29	13.57	16.00
1995-96	7.97	16.16	7.76
1996-97	4.30	18.01	11.20
1997-98	6.68	19.44	12.23
1998-99	7.59	14.60	1.28
1999-00	4.30	16.82	3.16
2000-01	5.52	14.10	3.07
2001-02	3.99	14.66	3.57
2002-03	8.06	16.75	4.02
2003-04	6.97	11.97	3.87
Average	**6.27**	**15.61**	**6.62**

Source: Computed.

Table 9.1 shows the annual growth rate of money output and price for Period-I. In this period, price increased at a low rate of 6.62 per cent per annum, with an average rate of growth of money rising at 6.27 per cent and real GDP, at 15.61 per cent. In the years 1995-1996 and 1996-1997 the money dropped to 4.30 per cent from 7.97 per cent, the inflation rate rose to 11.2 per cent from 7.76 per cent with an improvement in the output growth from 16.16 per cent to 18.01 per cent. The growth of money increased from 4.30 per cent to 5.52 per cent in the years 1999-2000 and 2001-2002, the growth rate fell by 2.62, and the inflation rate dropped marginally. In the years

2002-2003 and 2003-2004, the growth of money dropped from 8.06 per cent to 6.97 per cent, the growth in output plummeted to 11.97 per cent from 16.75 per cent; the inflation rate also fell marginally by 0.15 per cent.

Table 9.2: Behaviour of Money, Output and Prices in India (Period II)

Year	*Money*	*Output*	*Prices*
2005-06	9.48	21.10	4.50
2006-07	9.57	21.72	9.47
2007-08	9.32	21.38	1.92
2008-09	6.72	19.34	8.06
2009-10	8.39	16.85	3.81
2010-11	8.39	16.01	9.56
2011-12	6.88	12.99	8.93

Source: Computed.

Annual growth rate of money, output and prices of Period-II is shown in Table 9.2. The price increased at a lower rate with 6.61 per cent per annum, with the average rate of growth of money rising at 8.39 per cent and real GDP at 18.48 per cent. In the years 2007-2008 and 2008-2009, rate of growth of money fell from 9.32 per cent to 6.72 per cent and growth rate fell by 2.04 per cent, whereas the inflation rate rose to 8.06 per cent from 1.92 per cent. Whereas in the years 2010-2011 and 2011-2012 the growth rate of money dropped from 8.39 per cent to 6.88 per cent, output from 16.01 per cent to 12.99 per cent, the inflation rate fell marginally by 0.63 per cent.

Table 9.3: Correlation between variables (Period I and Period II)

	Period I	*Period II*
Output Prices	0.11	–0.41
Money Prices	0.31	–0.39
Output Money	–0.16	0.69

Source: Computed.

Correlation is used to assess the relation between respective variables over the years.

In Period–I, Output Prices, Money Prices has direct relation where as in period–I, these has inverse relation, while the relation between output and money in vice versa. Except output and money relation in Period–II, all have low correlation.

Table 9.4: Variations in Money, Output and Prices

Variables		*Min*	*Max*	*Difference (Max–Min.)*	*Mean*	*Variance*
Money	Period-I	3.99	8.06	4.07	6.27	2.56
	Period-II	6.57	9.57	3.00	8.39	1.42
Output	Period-I	11.97	19.44	7.47	15.61	5.01
	Period-II	12.99	21.72	8.73	18.48	10.90
Prices	Period-I	1.28	16.00	14.72	6.62	24.27
	Period-II	1.92	9.56	7.62	6.61	9.78

Calculated variance for money, output and Prices for Period–I and Period–II is revealed in Table 9.4. The highest range (maximum minus minimum) and also the highest variance is found with the variable price while it is output in Period–II.

It is inferred that in Period–I, the price has high volatile fluctuation and it is stabilized in Period–II. The average growth rate of money is high in Period–I compared to Period–II which accompanied with the high growth of output in Period–II lowered the inflation rate.

REFERENCES

1. Jadhav, Narendra (1994), *Monetary Economics for India,* p. 121, Bombay: MacMillan India Ltd.
2. Paul, Thomas and Bhanumurthy, N.R. Money supply, Output and Price level Relationship in India in *Indian Economic Journal*, Vol. 47 (1), July 1999, pp. 42-50.
3. Rajan, Ranga, C. 1985, *Money, Output and Prices,* Chapter presented at the Dr. S.K. Murenjan Memorial Lectures, *Reserve Bank of India*, December, pp. 1037-1044.
4. Friedman, 1959, The Demand for Money: Some Theoretical and Empirical Results in *Journal of Political Economy*, Vol. 67, pp. 111-140.
5. Laider, David. 1966, Some Evidence on Demand for Money, in *Journal of Political Economy,* Vol. 74, pp. 55-68.
6. Anderson and Jordon (1968) Monetary and Fiscal Actions: A Test of their Relative Importance in Economic Stabilization in *Federal Reserve Bank of St. Louis Review,* Vol. 50, pp. 11-24.

7. Das, Purna Chandra, 2000, Does Money Matter in the Indian Context? Evidence from Vector Auto Regressions in *Prajnan, Journal of Social and Management Sciences,* Vol. 29, Issue 1, pp. 143-163.
8. Laider, David, 1989, "The Quantity Theory is Always and Everywhere Controversial—Why?," *Centre for International Economic Studies*, University of Adelaide, Australia, pp. 89-103.
9. Jadhav, Narendra, Himanshu Joshi and Partha Roy, 1992, Money, Output and Prices: Causality, Issues and Evidence in the *Indian Economic Journal*, Vol. 40 (1), pp. 18-35.
10. Bhattacharya and Sharma, 1984, Inflation and Structural Changes in the Causal Relationship between Money and Price: Indian Experience, 1960-83, *Working Chapter, Reserve Bank of India.*
11. Bhattacharya, *et al.*, Forecasting State Domestic Product and Inflation: Econometric Model for Andhra Pradesh, Karnataka and Uttar Pradesh, in *Economic and Political Weekly*, July 31, 2004.
12. Binyamin and Razin, Flattened Inflation Output Trade off and Enhanced Anti-inflation Policy as an Equilibrium Outcome of Globalization, *HKMIR Working Chapter No. 23, 2007*, Hong Kong Institute for Monitory Research.
13. Angus, Deaton. Price Trends in India and Their Implications for Measuring Poverty, in *Economic and Political Weekly*, February 2008.
14. Patnaik, R.K., and Smataraya, Amaresh, Indian Experience of Inflation: A Review of Evolving Process, in *Economic and Political Weekly*, January 28, 2006.
15. Sharma, C.B. (2011) "Inflation in India: A Result to the Excess Supply of Money", in (Eds.) Aparna Bharadwaj and Rajesh Kumar, *Inflation Trends in India,* p. 64, New Delhi: Regal Publications.
16. Thakur and Bharadwaj, *Inflation Trends in India* in *op. cit.*, p. 74.
17. Singh, Shrawan Kumar, *Inflation in India: An Analysis*, in n.15, p. 94.

10

Analysis of the Relationship between Economic Growth and FDI Inflows in India

N. PRASANNA

Introduction

India, since Independence, like several other developing countries, pursued a policy of import substitution and foreign capital restriction, with the public sector playing an important role in the economy. The government managed the Balance of Payments (BoP) through import controls; with exports and Foreign Direct Investments playing a very small role. Strains first occurred in the BoP in the 1980s and a mild reform was undertaken in the trade policy which led to an increase in the exports and the inflow of FDI. But, the BoP position kept on deteriorating. This problem further worsened by a combination of many other factors such as increase in the burden of debt repayment, stagnation in tourism earnings, collapse of the largest trading partner of India (the former Soviet Union) and increase in the crude oil prices due to the Gulf War.

This resulted in a severe economic crisis at the beginning of the 1990s. The crisis had its root in the persistent deficits in the BoP in the previous several years. The Gulf War of 1990 added to the problem as it resulted in the shooting up of oil prices which required enhanced spending in terms of foreign exchange. By March 1991, current account deficit in the BoP reached a record level of about 10 billion US dollars or over 3 per cent of Gross Domestic Product. Exports were declining and foreign debt to foreign exchange ratio was very high at about 147 per cent. This led to the depletion of foreign exchange reserves and India did not possess sufficient reserves to meet the next few weeks of imports. A default on payments for the first time in history became a distinct possibility in June 1991. Foreign capital was flying away from India and the international community was not willing to give any loans. The severe economic crisis forced the Indian policy-makers to make drastic reforms in the economic policy regime of India as part of the conditionality of International Monitory Fund and World Bank structural adjustment programmes (UNCTAD, 1999).

But, as mentioned earlier, an important issue in India regarding the development policy has been whether the economic growth should be promoted by adopting planning and controls or through free market system in which private sector and foreign investors are permitted to play an important role. Prior to 1991 the issue was resolved in favour of planning and controls. However, such policies were not giving the desired results of rapid economic growth and development. In fact in the 1980s, these policies led to slowdown in economic growth, large fiscal deficits, high inflation rates and huge deficits in the BoP resulting in heavy indebtedness.

To overcome these problems some economists such as I.M.D. Little, Jagdish Bhagwati, Bela Balassa, etc. (see for example Balassa, 1985; Bhagwati, 1993; Joshi and Little, 1996) who had been advisors to the World Bank and IMF argued for the adoption of economic Liberalization by developing countries to promote economic growth, bring down fiscal deficit, check inflation and solve the problem of BoP. Here, it is imperative to mention the Washington Consensus which was also framed by the World Bank and IMF and moved in the direction of reforms for developing countries (Kumar, 2000). In the Indian context economists like Jagdish Bhagwati, T.N. Srinivasan and Kirit Parikh are associated with pressing for economic reforms in 1991 (this subject has been addressed in more detail by Bhagwati, 1994; Bhagwati and Srinivasan, 1993; Desai, 1993; EPW Research Foundation, 1994; Ghosh, 1994; Hanumantha Rao, 1994; Rao, 1994; Wadhva, 1994; Parikh, 1999). So, a paradigm shift in the economic policy of India took place when the economic reforms were ushered into the Indian economy.

Coming to the context of FDI, the issue of liberalizing the inflow of FDI was part and parcel of the economic reforms programme. But, as observed by Rao (1994) the specific reason behind the encouragement of liberal FDI policies has been the desire to attain 7-

8 per cent annual growth in GDP (now the desire is in double digits) which requires higher investment rates and ICORs. In the presence of a sizable gap between the savings and investment rates which has always been around the 3-4 per cent mark since liberalization, a 7-8 per cent economic growth would be impossible considering FDI Steering Committee Report's (2002) observation that for attaining 7-8 per cent annual growth in GDP, 32 per cent gross investment rate and an ICOR of 4.5 would be required. There was thus, a great need to raise domestic savings and at the same time ensure larger FDI inflows. However, given the low 20-22 per cent savings rate, India's only alternative was to aggressively seek FDI as it is a non-debt creating and reasonably stable source of external finance in the face of IMF and World Bank advising India not to opt for Fiscal Deficit and External Commercial Borrowings (ECBs).

In this direction, a series of policy reforms have been initiated since 1991 regarding liberalizing approval procedures, investment restrictions, and limitation on foreign equity participation, restrictions on acquisitions and take-over by foreign investors, local content requirement, restrictions on remittance of funds abroad and special incentives to foreign investors. All these initiatives have resulted in phenomenal rise in FDI inflow into India. The economic growth in terms of growth rate of GDP in the last 17 years has improved and in the recent past 7-8 per cent growth in GDP has been achieved. But, in real terms, it needs to be seen if the increased FDI inflows have led to higher economic growth or is it the other way round.

FDI and Economic Growth

Foreign direct investment can play an important role in the development process (De Mello and Luiz, 1997). However, the objectives of Multi-National Corporations and Trans National Corporations differ from those of the host governments: governments seek to spur national development, while MNCs and TNCs seek to enhance their own competitiveness in an international context. There can be considerable overlap between the two, but there are also differences. These differences created much suspicion about FDI in the past in developing countries, especially in India. However, perceptions have changed greatly in recent years. [(It would be interesting to note that United Nations Conference on Trade and Development (UNCTAD, 1999) puts that liberalization of FDI (and trade) policy is often part of the conditionality in IMF and World Bank adjustment programmes, and is promoted by many leading aid donors rather than the independent choice of the concerned country]. The ways in which MNCs and TNCs operate and organise themselves globally have also changed. Both are in response to the new global context: rapid technical progress, shrinking of economic space, improved communication, intensification of competition, new forms of market rivalry, increasingly mobile capital, widespread policy liberalization and more vocal (and influential) stakeholders.

Hence, most developing countries today consider FDI an important resource for development. However, the economic effects of FDI on various measures of economic performance are almost impossible to measure with precision as it represents a complex package of attributes that vary from one host country to another. These are difficult to separate and quantify. Where its entry has large (non-marginal) effects, measurement is even more difficult. There is no precise method of specifying a counter-factual-what would have happened if FDI had not entered into the host country.

Many long period cross-section studies that include FDI as a variable tend to find some positive relationship between FDI and growth. One study reported a significant relationship between inflows of FDI as a percentage of GDP and the growth of per capita real GDP across all developed countries for the period 1960-1985 (Blomstrom *et al.*, 1994). It was suggested that although the gap in technology and productivity between foreign-owned firms and locally owned ones is larger in poorer countries than in richer ones, that does not necessarily mean that the poorer countries gain the most from inward FDI. It was argued that "the least developed countries may learn little from the multinationals, because local firms are too far behind in their technological levels to be either imitators or suppliers to the multinationals". And it found, in confirmation of this supposition, that inflows of FDI were significant as determinants of growth for the upper half of the distribution of developing countries, by per capita income, but not in the lower half.

A similar conclusion was reached in a study for 69 developing countries of growth in per capita real GDP from 1970 to 1989 (Borensztein *et al.*, 1995). FDI itself was a marginally significant positive influence on growth, but FDI interacting with a measure of average educational attainment was a stronger and more consistent influence. The higher the level of education of the labour force, the greater the gain in growth from a given inflow of FDI. (Borensztein, 1998). This view is also supported by Barro and Martin (1999), and Helpman and Grossman (1991) who use endogenous growth theory in explaining the long-run growth rate of the economy by using endogenous variables like technology and human capital. An interaction between FDI and education was also found in a chapter on FDI in China that concluded that "Education becomes even more effective when it is associated with foreign knowledge... the interaction between school enrolment rates and foreign investment is significantly positive, suggesting mutual reinforcement between domestic human capital and foreign knowledge that accompanies the investment" (Mody and Wang, 1997). Whereas another study by Lensink and Morrissey (2001) concludes that there is a consistent finding that FDI has a positive effect on growth and that the positive effect of FDI is not sensitive to the level of human capital (as found in some previous studies).

Another mechanism through which the influence of FDI can take effect is through the impact of inward FDI on domestic capital formation. FDI appears to increase investment in a one-to-one ratio or encourages capital formation by domestic firms, so that, a one-dollar increase in the net inflow of FDI is associated with an increase in total investment in the host economy of more than one dollar (Borensztein *et al.*, 1995). This does not mean that cases of FDI crowding-out local capital formation can be ruled out.

A few long period cross section studies have included a measure of FDI as a potential source of growth (Blomstrom *et al.*, 1994; and Borensztein *et al.*, 1995). Reflecting this, a comprehensive review of variables used in such studies did not include FDI (Levine and Renelt, 1992). However, some of the variables identified in these studies as factors of growth are typically under the influence of FDI. Like, relatively "robust" relations were found between investment ratios (investment/GDP) and growth and between investment ratios and trade ratios. But, both investment ratios and trade ratios could be affected by FDI flows, and thus, indirectly form a channel for an effect of FDI on growth. Another study refers to the effects on growth of knowledge spill-over (Eaton and Kortum, 1994 and 1995 and Coe and Helpman, 1995). FDI is also a plausible vehicle for these knowledge spill overs, by itself (through Research and Development), imitation, competition, etc.) and through its relation to the intensity of trade (Lensink and Morrissey, 2001 and Sjöholm, 1999).

The relation of FDI to trade is more generally a possible connection that may blur the relationship of FDI to growth in quantitative studies including both variables. There is evidence that foreign-owned firms in most countries not only trade more with their parent countries, but also trade more in general than locally-owned firms. This is partly explained by their being concentrated in trade-intensive sectors, and partly because their trading propensity in any given sector tends to be greater than that of local or domestic firms (Dunning, 1993). It is likely, therefore, that high foreign ownership, or a large inflow of FDI, will increase the importance of trade for a host country, thus affecting growth indirectly.

Time series studies focused initially on the impact of FDI on domestic investors. An early study made on Canada, showed that "$1.00 of direct investment led to $3.00 of capital formation" (Lubitz, 1966). A later study of FDI into Canada found a positive direct effect on capital formation greater than the amount of the FDI (Van Loo, 1977). That is, there was some complementary effect on fixed investment by domestic firms. However, when indirect effects through impacts on other variables such as exports, imports, and consumption, operating through the accelerator, were added, the addition to total capital formation was much smaller.

Long-period analyses of growth face endogeneity problems, particularly uncertainty about the direction of causation between growth and investment ratios. In an attempt to avoid some of these problems, in one analysis, the period since 1970 was broken into five year sub-periods (Blomstrom *et al.*, 1994). The main conclusion was that there was more evidence that high growth led to high subsequent investment ratios than for the opposite relationship. In analyses using previous period investment, FDI appeared as a positive and significant influence on a country's rate of growth. The study suggested that FDI in one period may have affected host country capital formation in the following period.

The results by Borensztein *et al.* (1998) and Carkovic and Levine (2002) found a little support for FDI having an exogenous positive effect on economic growth. These results are robust to the inclusion of other growth determinants such as human capital measures, domestic financial development, and institutional quality along with the use of lagged values of FDI.

Time series as well as panel data estimation conducted by De Mello (1999) for a sample covering 15 developed and 17 developing countries for the period 1970-90 to understand the relationships between FDI, capital accumulation, output and productivity growth, reveal mixed results. The time series estimations suggest that the effect of FDI on growth or on capital accumulation and total factor productivity (TFP) varies greatly across countries. The panel data estimation suggests a positive impact of FDI on output growth for developed and developing country sub-samples. However, the effect of FDI on capital accumulation and TFP growth varies across developed (technological leaders) and developing countries (technological followers). FDI has a positive effect on TFP growth in developed countries, but a negative effect in developing countries but the pattern is reversed in the case of effect on capital accumulation. De Mello infers from these findings that the extent to which FDI is growth-enhancing depends on the degree of complementarity between FDI and domestic investment. The degree of substitutability between foreign and domestic capital stocks appears to be greater in technologically advanced countries than in developing countries. Developing countries may have difficulty in using and diffusing new technologies of Multi-National Enterprises. Findings of Xu (2000) for US FDI in 40 countries for the period 1966-94 also corroborate the finding of De Mello that technology transfer from FDI contributes to productivity growth in developed countries, but not in developing countries, which he attributes to lack of adequate human capital.

The coefficient of the FDI-GDP ratio turned out to be negative, though not significant in a fixed effects model based on pooled data for five South Asian host countries, among which India figures prominently in the period 1965-1996 (Agrawal, 2005). Similar results, but significant, were found in a study comprising 73 developing countries (Singh, 1988), and another of 41 developing countries (Hein, 1992). Another pooled time series cross section macro model with 16 developing countries and the period 1966-88 concluded FDI to be having an immiserizing growth effect on the host countries (Fry, 1992). However, these approaches ignored that FDI is endogenous. Similar qualifications apply to Pradhan (2002) who estimated a Cobb–Douglas production function with FDI stocks as additional input variable. FDI stocks had no significant impact when considering the whole period of observation (1969-1997) In an earlier study, Pradhan (2001) found a significant positive effect of lagged FDI inflows on growth rates only for Latin American countries in a panel data estimation covering 1975-95 period for 71 developing countries. The effect of FDI was not significantly different from zero for the overall sample and for other regions.

The Granger causation test provides another measure to corroborate the positive relation between FDI inflows and growth. Using aggregate data for 1974-96 Chakraborty and Basu (2002) explored the two–way link between FDI and growth. It suggested that FDI plays no significant role in the short–run adjustment process of GDP, though it is positively related to GDP and openness to trade in the long-run. In an earlier study, Dua and Rashid (1998) report that FDI inflows do not granger cause industrial output. Kumar and Pradhan (2002) in a cross section study of 107 developing countries consider the FDI-growth relationship to be Granger neutral in the case of India as the direction of causation was not pronounced, and Sahoo and Mathiyazhagan (2002) corroborate these results.

Thus, conclusions of the empirical analyses of FDI and economic growth remain unclear, especially as regards the causality within the relationship. While some (Rodan, 1961; Chenery and Strout, 1966; Caves, 1974; Kokko, 1994; Markusen, 1995; Caves, 1996; Sahoo *et al.*, 2001) show a positive impact of FDI on economic growth, others (Singer, 1950; Griffin, 1970; Weisskof, 1972; Fry, 1992; Dua and Rashid, 1998; Agosin and Mayer, 2000) a negative impact; yet others have found growth to be a determinant of FDI rather than the other way round (Kasibhatla and Sawhney, 1996; Chakraborty and Basu, 2002). Since growth depends on many factors whose effects are difficult to disentangle, and since FDI itself affects several of these factors, an indeterminate conclusion is probably the most sensible. But, there is little doubt that fast growth and large FDI go hand in hand in many instances.

Conceptual Framework

Economic growth in any country depends upon the sustained growth of productive capacity, supported by savings and investment. Low levels of savings and investment, particularly in developing countries like India results in a low level of capital stock and economic growth. The earlier growth models by Harrod (1939) and Domar (1946) explain that capital formation raises the standard of living, which in turn results in higher growth. Criticising the growth models proposed by Harrod and Domar on the ground of the fixed proportion of factors of production and substitutability between labour and capital, Solow

(1956) argues that capital formation increases labour productivity in a dynamic process of investment growth. Some of the recent growth theories such as those by Lucas (1988) and Rebelo (1991) broaden the definition of capital to include human capital and the accumulation of knowledge. Similarly, Romer (1986, 1990) and Helpman and Grossman (1991) incorporate knowledge capital gained through research and development to explain growth along with other variables. Overall theoretical growth literature demonstrates the role of capital or changes in the definition of capital (knowledge capital or human capital) in enhancing economic growth.

The recognition of the role of knowledge capital in economic growth creates a basis for analysing the role of FDI, which brings new technology and knowledge along with capital. In recent years, the need for FDI inflows has increased as MNCs and TNCs have assumed significant importance as a source of economic growth and development (Bajpai and Sachs, 2000). Since, FDI may help developing India by providing new knowledge and complementing domestic investment, it is important to analyse the empirical relationship between FDI and economic growth in a growth accounting framework.

Further, the phenomenon of economic growth is complex, and the lines of causation frequently go both from supposed causes to growth and from growth to the supposed causes. So, the causality between FDI inflows and economic growth needs to be seen before proceeding to probe the impact of FDI on the economic growth of India. Furthermore, the various factors that are thought to explain growth are themselves interrelated. These problems face all studies attempting to throw light on whether, in what way, and to what extent a particular factor or group of factors affect growth. They similarly apply to the study of the impact of FDI on growth.

Analytical Framework

We now deal with empirically testing whether the impact of FDI inflows on the economic growth of India is significantly positive or it is the other way round, i.e. economic growth in India is leading to higher inflows of FDI. The Neo-Classical growth accounting framework has been employed for the analysis through the Vector Auto-Regressive model (VAR).

Economic growth in the Neo-Classical framework is influenced by parameters such as capital, labour and human capital. Similarly, FDI enters into a country based on many criteria; some of them which can be incorporated in the Neo-Classical framework are past-economic growth record, investment climate for the operation of private sector, the resource base (mainly labour) and the level of skill of the host country. Considering this, it would be much appropriate to analyse the relationship between economic growth and FDI in this framework rather than relating the two variables in the absence of other influences.

The use of a Neo-Classical framework through the VAR to probe into the relationship between FDI and economic growth would give more correct and true results than many tests reviewed in the past literature using Granger causality test (see for example, Blomstrom, *et al.*; 1994; Dua and Rashid, 1998). The Granger causality test can be used only with two variables. It removes the possibility of testing the relationship between two variables in the presence other variables affecting both these variables. Then the Multiple Linear Regression (MLR) results of the VAR model are used to probe into the details of the impact of FDI inflows on economic growth.

Hence, this study first develops a structure of the Neo-Classical framework to understand the two-way causality between economic growth and FDI. This would help in establishing whether the causality is unidirectional from FDI to growth or unidirectional from growth to FDI or it is bidirectional. If the relationship is unidirectional from FDI to growth or bidirectional further exploring would be needed to understand the relationship more fully.

To develop a structural model for empirical analysis, this study takes the standard Neo-Classical growth accounting framework through the Cobb-Douglas production function. Here, the total capital stock is assumed to comprise two components, viz., domestic and foreign owned capital stock. Further, three variations are made in the model; the first is based on an augmented Solow production function that makes output a function of stocks of capital, labour, human capital and productivity (Mankiw *et al.* 1992; Benhabib and Spiegel 1994; Kumar and Pradhan 2002; among others); the second and third are based on the review of literature in this study emphasizing that current growth is a function of the past growth (UNCTAD, 1999) and that growth is a function of exports due to the export oriented growth strategy (Wen, 2002). The growth model is algebraically put as follows:

$$Y_t = \beta_1 + \beta_2 Y_{t-1} + \beta_3 I_t + \beta_4 F_t + \beta_5 E_t + \beta_6 L_t + \beta_7 H_t + u_t \quad \ldots (1)$$

where, following the established practice in the literature (Blomstrom, Lipsey, and Zejan 1994; Bosworth and Collins 1996; Balasubramanyam *et al.* 1996; Hu and Khan 1997; Athukorala and Chand 2000; Wen 2002), the dependent variable is taken as Growth in Per Capita Real GDP (1993-94 prices). The domestic capital stock is proxied by Gross Domestic Investment—GDP-ratio (1993-94 prices) and the foreign capital stock is proxied by FDI inflows GDP (deflated to 1993-94 prices) ratio. Exports (deflated to 1993-94 prices) are taken as the Rate of Growth of Exports, labour is taken as the Growth in the Labour Force Participation Rate and human capital is taken as the growth in Growth in the Total Secondary School Enrolment Rate. (All the variables have been taken in their logarithmic form for the analysis.) The growth model would now be algebraically put as follows:

$$GPRG_t = \beta_1 + \beta_2 GPRG_{t-1} + \beta_3 DINV_t + \beta_4 FDI_t + \beta_5 ROGX_t + \beta_6 LPR_t + \beta_7 SER_t + u_t \quad \ldots (2)$$

where, GPRG is the Growth in Per Capita Real GDP, DINV is the Gross Domestic Investment—GDP ratio, FDI is the FDI–GDP ratio, ROGX is the Rate of Growth of Exports, LPR is the Growth in the Labour Force Participation Rate and SER is the Growth in the Total Secondary School Enrolment Rate. The subscript ‘t’ stands for the time period, β_1 is the regression constant denoting total factor productivity, β_2, β_3, β_4, β_5, β_6 and β_7 are the coefficients of the respective regressors and u denotes the standard error.

In the above Equation (2), there may arise a difficulty of two-way interaction between the dependent variable GPRG and independent variables DINV and FDI, i.e. high growth rates may induce high investment rates at least as much as high investment rates induce high rates of Growth in Per Capita Real GDP. To reduce such ambiguities (although without the expectation of completely eliminating them) the above mentioned independent variables are taken in lagged form. That is, only observations for period ‘t-1’ and ‘t-2’ enter the equations for growth in period ‘t’. The optimal lag structure would be determined with the help of information criteria AIC, SIC and HQC. Therefore, the final form of the equation is written as follows:

$$GPRG_t = \beta_1 + \beta_2 GPRG_{t-1} + \beta_3 GPRG_{t-2} + \beta_4 DINV_{t-1} + \beta_5 DINV_{t-2} + \beta_6 FDI_{t-1} + \beta_7 FDI_{t-2} + \beta_8 ROGX_t + \beta_9 LPR_t + \beta_{10} SER_t + u_t \quad \dots (3)$$

This set of variables may influence investors' choice of country for investing directly as much as they would influence economic growth. Hence, the equation with FDI as a dependent variable would be:

$$FDI_t = \beta_1 + \beta_2 GPRG_{t-1} + \beta_3 GPRG_{t-2} + \beta_4 DINV_{t-1} + \beta_5 DINV_{t-2} + \beta_6 FDI_{t-1} + \beta_7 FDI_{t-2} + \beta_8 ROGX_t + \beta_9 LPR_t + \beta_{10} SER_t + u_t \quad \dots (4)$$

In the above Equation (3), the only change from the Equation (4) is the dependent variable, i.e., FDI_t instead of $GPRG_t$. All the independent variables are the same.

The main source of data for the present study is the online database of the Reserve Bank of India (RBI) from which the data on the total FDI inflows, GDP, Gross Domestic Investment, Population, Manufacturing Sector and Exports have been acquired. The data on Sector-wise and Country-wise FDI inflows have been gathered from the Secretariat of Industrial Assistance's (SIA) online data base. The data on the Labour Force Participation Rate and Total Secondary School Enrolment Rate have been compiled from various sources which are the online database of the NSSO, the online database of the World Bank, the website of the Indian Planning Commission and the website of the Economic Survey. The data relating to GDP and Gross Domestic Investment have been taken at 1993-94 prices while the data relating to FDI and exports have been deflated to 1993-94 prices.

For ensuring the consistency of data, the present study uses the Augmented Dickey Fuller Test (ADF) to check for the presence of a unit root so as to confirm that the data sequence of a variable is stationary. The results of the ADF tests (Table 10.1) show that all the variables do not have the presence of a unit root and are stationary in their original form. Hence, all the variables are taken in their original

Table 10.1: ADF Test Results for Equations (4.1 and 4.2)

Variables	*Actual*	
	T	*P-Value*
GPRG	–2.572*	0.098
DINV	–3.027*	0.100
FDI	–5.137***	0.000
ROGX	–2.690*	0.075
LPR	–4.817***	0.000
SER	–3.323***	0.013

*** and * Significance at 1 per cent and 10 per cent level respectively.
P – Values based on MacKinnon (JAE, 1996).

form for the analysis. Further, this study has used the Akaike Information Criterion (AIC), Schwartz Information Criterion (SIC) and Hannan-Quinn Criterion (HQC) to select the appropriate lag length for the VAR model.

Results and Discussions

To understand the causality within the relationship between FDI and economic growth and to arrive at a possible conclusion in the Indian context, first the two-way causality is tested. FDI would be considered to cause a change in the Growth in Per Capita Real GDP which has been taken as an indicator of economic growth, only if the lagged values of FDI significantly contribute to the explanation of current growth in the presence of other influencing parameters and the Growth in Per Capita Real GDP would be considered to cause FDI only if the lagged values of GPRG significantly contribute to the explanation of current FDI inflows in the presence of other influencing parameters. Therefore, this test essentially looks at the predictive performance between variables to determine the existence or direction of causality between them in the presence of other parameters. Given the fact that it takes into account the effect of lagged values of the causing variable on the current value of the dependent variable along with current and lagged values of other variables, it takes care of the dynamic nature of FDI's effect on economic growth.

The optimal lag length for the VAR model has been decided based on the three information criteria as mentioned earlier. The results of the lag selection criteria are displayed in Table 10.2. The lag length

Table 10.2: Lag Selection for VAR

Lag Length	*AIC*	*SIC*	*HQC*
1.	0.918	1.614	0.775
2.	–1.651*	–0.782*	–1.830*

* Lower values indicate better significance.

with the lowest values of the criteria would be selected. This clearly shows that a two year lag length is optimal for the model. Hence, a model with a lag length of two years is selected for VAR estimations. The VAR analysis is made with the inclusion of robust standard errors so as to give more correct results. The results of the two-way causality test are presented in Table 10.3.

From the results of the two-way causality test on FDI inflows and the indicator of economic growth (Table 10.3), it is made clear that the causality is unidirectional in India from FDI inflows to economic growth during the study period 1991-92 to 2006-07. As this test has been performed in a growth accounting framework with the inclusion of other parameters that influence both these variables, it may be considered to give better results than two-way causality tests such as 'Granger causality'.

But, the unidirectional causality may not be taken as an end in itself. It just reveals the direction of causality between FDI inflows and economic growth. For further probing into the effect of FDI on economic growth, the MLR results are seen (Table 10.4). The MLR results from the growth equation suggest that the lag order one FDI variable has a negative impact on growth with a coefficient of—0.768. However, the lag order two FDI variable contributes positively and to a larger extent to the Growth in Per Capita Real GDP in India with a coefficient of 1.246. So, when the net effect of both the lags of FDI is put together it may be said that a one unit change in the past FDI

Table 10.3: VAR Model: Two-way Causality Test on FDI and GPRG

Independent Variables	*All Lags of FDI on GPRG*	*All Lags of GPRG on FDI*
F-Value	152.36***	1.212
P-value	0.001	0.411

Dependent Variable in Equation 1 : Growth in Per Capita Real GDP
Dependent Variable in Equation 2 : FDI
*** Significance at 1 per cent level.

Table 10.4: MLR Model: The Impact of FDI on Economic Growth

Independent Variables	*Beta (β)*	*T*	*P-Value*
(Constant)	–8.916	–1.404	0.255
GPRGt-1	–0.464*	–2.580	0.082
GPRGt-2	0.153*	2.346	0.100
FDIt-1	–0.768***	–16.235	0.000
FDIt-2	1.246***	6.059	0.009
DINVt-1	2.116**	4.425	0.021
DINVt-2	2.468	2.070	0.130
ROGX	–0.120**	–3.723	0.034
LPRt	–4.880***	–6.177	0.008
SERt	–0.406***	–6.559	0.007
R-square		0.860	
F-statistic		431.161	
P Value		0.000	

Dependent Variable: Growth in Per Capita Real GDP.

***, ** and * Significance at 1 per cent, 5 per cent and 10 per cent level respectively.

inflows would lead to a half unit change in economic growth in the current year in the same direction.

The other variables in the growth accounting framework, viz., past Growth in Per Capita Real GDP, Gross Domestic Investment ratio, Rate of Growth of Exports, Growth in Labour Force Participation Rate and the Growth in Total Secondary School Enrolment Rate register a significant relationship with the current period's Growth in Per Capita Real GDP. But, the point to be noted here is that all these variables put together have a net negative effect on the Growth in Per Capita Real GDP.

Comparing the average annual Growth Rate of Per Capita Real GDP during the study period would help in knowing the effect of FDI on economic growth. The average annual Growth Rate of Per Capita Real GDP was 2.3 per cent in the early 1990s which has increased to 4.5 per cent during the period 1996 to 2005. This proof is sufficient enough to suggest that FDI inflows is one of the influencing factors that has significantly contributed to promoting economic growth in India during the reform era.

It may be seen from the results of the MLR analysis of the growth framework that the net effect of past Growth in Per Capita Real GDP on its current period is negative. This is due to the fact that the Growth in Per Capita Real GDP has an uneven trend (Prasanna, 2006). In many instances a higher growth is followed by a fall in the Growth of Per Capita Real GDP. This is further corroborated by UNCTAD (1999) that in general, in developing countries a higher Growth Rate of Per Capita Real GDP seem to be associated with lower growth in the following period, an indication that the past-growth coefficients reflect cyclical swings rather than long-term influences.

The results of the past investment ratios in the growth framework, with coefficient values 2.116 and 2.468 for the one and two year lags respectively, suggest that past investment have a positive relationship with the current Growth in Per Capita Real GDP. But, the lag order two Domestic Investment variable's significance is lower than the 10 per cent level. This needs some discussion. To explain the cause for the lower significance of the two year lagged Domestic Investment ratio, the results from a study made by Prasanna (2010) would be helpful. The study suggests that the net effect of the past FDI inflows in India is crowding-out of the Domestic Investment in the long-term. This implies that the FDI inflows rather than complementing Domestic Investment are competing with it. This may provide some explanation for the lower significance of the two year lagged Domestic Investment variable.

The Rate of Growth of Exports has been contributing (though not very effectively as its coefficient is only 0.120) negatively to economic growth. The reason for this may be seen form a study made by Prasanna (2011) on the impact of FDI on the Export Performance of India. The study reveals that Per Capita FDI as well as Per Capita Manufacturing Value Added do not effectively contribute to Per Capita Total and Per Capita High-Technology Manufactured Exports as their coefficients are very low. This implies that growth in the manufactured exports is not sufficient in India for attaining the objective of the export-led growth strategy.

An astounding revelation of this study is relating to the results of the Growth in Labour Force Participation Rate and Growth in Total Secondary School Enrolment Rate. Both these parameters which are taken to be granted as positive contributors to economic growth in many studies show high negative influence on the Growth in Per Capita Real GDP. The coefficient of Growth in Labour Force Participation Rate is the highest in the equation at—4.880 while the coefficient of Growth in Total School Enrolment Rate is—0.406. The reason for the huge negative impact of these two factors may be attributed to low social expenditure on the part of the Government of India.

Policy Implications

With the objective of becoming more efficient in the global environment, a number of countries adopted market oriented reforms. This resulted in a surge of FDI inflows in these countries. India, a late comer on the scene of economic reforms, started liberalising its FDI policy and introduced new institutions for facilitating FDI following a macro-economic crisis in 1991. Subsequently, India has been experiencing increased FDI inflows. This study examines whether this increased inflow of FDI has proved beneficial for India in promoting economic growth, enhancing investment opportunities and improving export performance. Based on the results and discussions in the previous chapter, this chapter spells out some policy suggestions for enhancing FDI's positive impact and minimising its negative impact on the Indian economy. The chapter later provides the scope for further research in this area.

From the results and discussions it can be seen that the effect of FDI on economic growth and domestic investment is negative in the first year, whereas it is positive in the second year. Considering that the second year's positive effect is able to offset the first year's negative effect, the economic performance of India in the short-term may increase many folds if this offset is to a larger extent. This could be done by attracting more FDI in all areas.

(i) One such way of doing this could be increasing the source of FDI, country-wise. The present scenario shows FDI flowing mainly from U.S.A. and Mauritius contributing to around 45 per cent of the total FDI inflows into India which means that rest of the 112 countries contribute only a meagre share of FDI flows into India. This may be seen as an opportunity by the Government of India and more FDI may be attracted from the remaining countries through Bilateral and Multilateral MoUs.

(ii) Secondly, FDI inflows may be attracted from what are called 'footloose industries.' 'Footloose industries' imply those TNCs that operate only to indulge in the production and export of commodities. Such TNCs just require infrastructural facilities to enter a host country. Hence, attracting such TNCs may lead to increase in FDI as well as exports without causing any damage to the Indian economy.

(iii) Furthermore, the following sector specific policy suggestions related to private sector banking, insurance, airlines, telecommunications, infrastructure, print media, broadcasting, and services may be taken into consideration for increasing FDI inflows into India.

Although FDI has a positive effect on economic growth, its negative impact on domestic investment reduces the effect of domestic investment on economic growth. This leads to a combined reduced effect of both these investments put together on economic growth. It would be much better if FDI had a positive impact on domestic investment so that both FDI and domestic investment added together could cause a larger positive impact on economic growth. The way for achieving this is to have a crowding-in effect of FDI on domestic investment. This could be done in the following ways:

(i) By encouraging more FDI into the infrastructure sectors like telecommunications and transportation through either by relaxing the sectoral cap on the investing companies in infrastructure which is currently at 49 per cent to at least 74 per cent in the first phase and then to 100 per cent or by allowing for full capital account convertibility.

(ii) By decentralising FDI inflows into India instead of concentrating on few metropolitan cities which may lead to the establishment of foreign industries in the areas where there is less scope which would ultimately lead to crowding-in new domestic entrepreneurs.

(iii) By starting backward linkage programmes with TNCs which means starting a dialogue process by the Government of India with the TNCs to train and disseminate knowledge and technology to local manufacturers who would provide a supply chain for the TNCs. In return, the Government of India may offer better incentives for such TNCs.

(iv) By identifying gaps in the domestic manufactures. This could be done by examining the imports of finished goods and analysing whether such goods could be produced domestically just with the help of technology and capital. If so, FDI may be sought in that industry. This may lead to the establishment of a new industrial base which would in turn lead to complementing domestic investment.

These measures may lead to increase the complementary effect of FDI on domestic investment and may ultimately lead to higher economic growth. Simultaneously, these measures may also cause an increase in the inflows of FDI.

FDI as well as domestic investment would give better effect to economic growth if labour force participation rate and secondary school enrolment rate contribute positively to economic growth. But in the Indian case, it can be seen from the results that labour force participation rate and secondary school enrolment rate contribute negatively to economic growth. So, steps may be taken to make labour force participation rate and secondary school enrolment rate to contribute positively to economic growth. This requires labour force participation rate and secondary school enrolment rate to have an increasing trend. Considering that social expenditure on the part of the Government of India has been declining, a Public Private Participation (PPP) may be adopted for improving the labour force participation rate and secondary school enrolment rate. Viewing the knowledge spill over capability of FDI, it may be encouraged in this participation, which may make both the government and private sector more accountable.

Much FDI into India has come seeking the immense size of the domestic market. FDI inflows may be welcome into the Indian domestic market subject to non-displacement of domestic investment in India. Considering that India has the most liberal M&A policy among South/Southeast Asian countries, FDI coming into the Indian domestic market may displace domestic investment. Not only the increase in the quantity of FDI is important, but also its quality. So, a reassessment of the M&A policy in India may be considered.

So, if the Government of India desires to continue on the FDI-led growth strategy and benefit from it in the long-run, it may need to concentrate more on domestic efforts to expand investment opportunities and manufacturing in line with the FDI policy framework. Hence, it is necessary to revise and amend the investment and manufacturing policy framework. Most importantly, the Government of India should recognise that FDI is not a panacea for achieving the national objectives, it can only complement domestic efforts to meet the development objectives. Hence, to achieve faster economic growth and develop India sustainably and dynamically, FDI policies may not be pursued in isolation. Instead, they may be linked with policies in core areas of the economy.

REFERENCES

Agosin, M.R. and Ricardo Mayer, 2000, Foreign Investment in Developing Countries: Does it Crowd in Domestic Investment? *UNCTAD Discussion Chapter No.* 146, (Geneva: UNCTAD).

Agrawal, P. Foreign Direct Investment in South Asia: Impact on Economic Growth and Local Investment, in E.M. Graham (2005), (Ed.) *Multinationals and Foreign Investment in Economic Development.* (Basingstoke Palgrave MacMillan): 94-118.

Athukorala, P. and S. Chand, 2000, Trade Orientation and Productivity Gains from International Production: A Study of Overseas Operation of United States TNCs. *Transnational Corporations*, 9(2), pp. 1-27.

Bajpai, N. and Jeffrey, D. Sachs, 2000, *Foreign Direct Investment in India: Issues and Problems,* Harvard Institute of International Development, DDP No. 759, March.

Balasubramanyam, V.N., Salisu, M. and D. Sapsford, 1996, Foreign Direct Investment and Growth in EP and IS Countries, *The Economic Journal*, 106 (434), pp. 92-105.

Barro, R. and Salai-I-Martin, (1999), *Economic Growth,* Cambridge: MIT Press.

Benhabib, Jess and Mark M. Spiegel (1994), The Role of Human Capital in Economic Development Evidence from Aggregate Cross-Country Data, *Journal of Monetary Economics*, 34, pp. 143-73.

Bhagwati, J.N. and Srinivasan, T.N. (1993) *India's Economic Reforms.* Ministry of Finance, Government of India, New Delhi.

Bhagwati, J.N. (1993), *India in Transition: Freeing the Economy,* Oxford: Clarendon Press.

Bhagwati, J.N. (1994), *India in Transition: Freeing the Economy,* New Delhi: Oxford University Press.

Blomstrom, Magnus, Robert E. Lipsey and Mario Zejan, 1994, What Explains Developing Country Growth? *Cambridge, MA, National Bureau of Economic Research*, Working Chapter.

Borensztein, E., J. De Gregorio and J.W. Lee (1995, 1998) How Does Foreign Direct Investment Affect Economic Growth, *Journal of International Economics*, 45:115-135.

Bosworth, Barry P. and Susan, M. Collins (1996), Economic Growth in East Asia: Accumulation *versus* Assimilation in Borrkings, ed., *Chapters on Economic Activity*, 1, pp. 135-203.

Carkovic, M. and R. Levine (2002) Does not Foreign Direct Investment Accelerate Economic Growth? *University of Minnesota Working Chapter, 6,* Minnesota, Edward).

Caves, R. (1974), Multinational Firms, Competition and Productivity in the Host Country, *Economica*, 41, pp. 176-193.

Caves, R. (1996), *Multinational Enterprise and Economic Analysis,* Cambridge: Cambridge University Press.

Chakraborty, C. and P. Basu, 2002, Foreign Direct Investment and growth in India: A Co-Integration Approach, *Applied Economics*, 34(9), pp. 1061-1073.

Chenery, H.B. and A.M. Strout, 1996, Foreign Assistance and Economic Development, *American Economic Review*, 56, pp. 679-733.

Coe, David T. and Elhanan Helpman, (1995), International R&D Spillovers, NBER Working chapter No. 4444, Cambridge: MA National Bureau of Economic Research.

De Mello, Jr. and R. Luiz, 1997, Foreign Direct Investment in Developing Countries and Growth: A Selective Survey. *Journal of Development Studies,* 34(1), pp. 1-34.

De Mello. Jr. (1999), Foreign Direct Investment-led Growth: Evidence from Time Series and Panel Data, *Oxford Economic Chapters*, 51, pp. 133-54.

Desai, Ashok (1993), *My Economic Affair,* New Delhi: Eastern.

Domar, E.D. (1946), Capital Expansion, Rate of Growth and Employment, *Econometrica,* 14, pp. 137-147.

Dua, P. and A.I. Rashid. (1998), FDI and Economic Activity in India. *Indian Economic Review*, 33(2), pp. 153-168.

Dunning John, H. (1993), *The Globalization of Business* (London and New York: Routledge.

Eaton, Jonathan and Samuel Kortum (1995), Engines of Growth: Domestic and Foreign Sources of Innovation, *Working Chapter*, 5207 (Cambridge: MA National Bureau of Economic Research).

EPW Research Foundation, What Has Gone Wrong with the Economic Reforms? *Economic and Political Weekly*, 29(18): April 30, 1994, pp. 1049-1053.

Fry, Maxwell J. 1992, Foreign Direct Investment in a Macro-economic Framework: Finance, Efficiency, Incentives and Distortions. *PRE Working Chapter,* 7, Washington, DC: The World Bank.

Ghosh, Arun 1994-95 Budget: A Total Surrender, in *Economic and Political Weekly*, 29 (16 and 17), April 16-23, 1994, pp. 889-892.

Government of India, Economic Survey 2005-2006, New Delhi, Available at http://www.indiabudget.nic.in.

Government of India, Planning Commission, http://www.planning commission.nic.in).

Government of India, Secretariat of Industrial Assistance, Directorate of Industrial Policy Promotion, Online Database. (Available at http://www.dipp.gov.in/fdi_statistics).

Granger, C. and P. Newbold (1974), Spurious Regressions in Econometrics, *Journal of Econometrics*, 2, pp. 111-20.

Griffin, K.B. (1970), Foreign Capital, Domestic Savings and Development. *Oxford Bulletin of Economics and Statistics*, 32, pp. 99-112.

Harrod, R.F. (1939), An Essay in Dynamic Theory in *The Economic Journal,* 49, pp. 14-33.

Hein, Simeon. 1992, Trade Strategy and the Dependency Hypothesis: A Comparison of Policy, Foreign Investment, and Economic Growth in Latin America, *Economic Development and Cultural Change*, 40(3), pp. 4895-521.

Helpman, E. and G.M. Grossman, (1991), *Innovation and Growth in the Global Economy*, Cambridge: MA MIT Press.

Hu, Z.F. and M.S. Khan, 1997, Why Is China Growing So Fast? *IMF Staff Chapters*, 44(1), pp. 103-131.

Indian Planning Commission, *Report of the Steering Group on Foreign Direct Investment*, New Delhi (2002): Academic Foundation.

Joshi, V. and Little, I. (1996), India's Economic Reforms, 1991-2001. Oxford and New York: Oxford University Press, Clarendon Press.

Kashibhatla, K. and B. Sawhney, (1996), FDI and Economic Growth in the US: Evidence from Co-integration and Granger Causality Test. *RivistaInternazioriale di SceinzeEconomiche e Commerciali*, 43, pp. 411-420.

Kokko, A. (1994), Technology, Market Characteristics and Spillovers. *Journal of Development of Economics*, 43, pp. 279-93.

Kumar, N., and J.P. Pradhan, 2002, Foreign Direct Investment, Externalities and Economic Growth in Developing Countries: Some Empirical Explorations and Implications for WTO Negotiations on Investment. *Research and Information System for the Non-Aligned and Other Developing Countries (RIS) Discussion Chapters,* 27, (New Delhi: RIS).

Kumar, N. 2003, Liberalization, FDI Flows and Economic Development: An Indian Experience in the 1990s. *RIS Discussion Chapters,* 65 (New Delhi: RIS).

Lensink, Robert and Ooliuver Morrissey, 2001, Foreign Direct Investment: Flows, Volatility and Growth, *DESG, University of Nottingham*, April 5-7.

Levine, Ross and David Renelt, 1992, Sensitivity Analysis of Cross-Country Growth Regressions, *American Economic Review*, 82(4), pp. 942-963.

Lucas, R.E.J., 1988, On the Mechanics of Economic Development, *Journal of Monetary Economics,* 22, pp. 3-42.

Mankiw, N. Gregory, David Romer, and David N. Weil (1992), A Contribution to the Empirics of Economic Growth, *Quarterly Journal of Economics*, 107(2):407-437.

Markusen, J.R. (1995), The Boundaries of Multinational Enterprises and the Theory of International Trade, *Journal of Economic Perspectives*, 9, pp. 169-89.

Mody, Ashoka and Fung-Yi Wang, 1997, Explaining Industrial Growth in Coastal China: Economic reforms... and what else? *World Bank Economic Review*, 11(2) May, pp. 293-325.

National Sample Survey Organisation (NSSO), India, (Available at http://www.mospi.nic.in/nsso_test1.html)

Parikh, Kirit (Ed.) (1999), *India Development Report, 1999-2000*, New Delhi: Oxford University Press.

Pradhan, J.P. 2002, Foreign Direct Investment and Economic Growth in India: A Production Function Analysis, *Indian Journal of Economics*, 82 (327), pp. 582-586.

Rao, C. Hanumantha, 1994, Reforming Agriculture in the New Context, *Economic and Political Weekly*, 29 (16 and 17), April, 16-23, pp. 1005-1010.

Rao, V.M., 1994, Agriculture and Liberalization: Some Implications for Development Policies, *Economic and Political Weekly*, 29 (16 and 17), April, 16-23, pp. 999-1003.

Reserve Bank of India (RBI), Online Database, (http://www.rbi.org.in)

Rebelo, S., 1991, Long-run Policy Analysis and Long-run Growth, *Journal of Political Economy*, 99, pp. 500-521.

Rodan, R.P.N., 1961, International Aid for Underdeveloped Countries, *Review of Economics and Statistics*, 43, pp. 107-138.

Romer, P. (1986), Increasing Returns and Long-term Growth, *Journal of Political Economy*, 94, pp. 1002-1037.

Romer, P. 1990, Endogenous Technological Change, *Journal of Political Economy*, 98, pp. S71-S102.

Sahoo, D., and M.K. Mathiyazhagan, 2002, Economic Growth in India: Does Foreign Direct Investment Inflow Matter? *Singapore Economic Review*, 48(2), pp. 151-171.

Singer, H., 1950, The Distributions of Gains between Investing and Borrowing Countries, *American Economic Review*, 9, pp. 473-485.

Singh, R.D., 1988, The Multinationals' Economic Penetration, Growth, Industrial Output, and Domestic Savings in Developing Countries: Another Look, *The Journal of Development Studies*, 25(1), pp. 55-82.

Sjöholm, Fredrik (1999), Technology Gap, Competition and Spillovers from Direct Foreign Investment: Evidence from Establishment Data, *The Journal of Development Studies*, 36(1), pp. 53-73.

Solow, R. (1956), A Contribution to the Theory of Economic Growth, *Quarterly Journal of Economics*, 70, pp. 65-94.

United Nations Conference on Trade and Development (UNCTAD), World Investment Report 1999: *Foreign Direct Investment and The Challenge of Development,* New York and Geneva: United Nations.

Van Loo Land, Frances, 1977, The Effects of Foreign Direct Investment on Investment in Canada, *Review of Economics and Statistics*, L9(4), November, pp. 474-481.

Wadhwa, Charan D. (1994), *Economic Reforms in India and the Market Economy,* New Delhi: Allied Publishers for Economic and Scientific Research Foundation.

Weisskof, T.E., 1972, The Impact of Foreign Capital Inflow on Domestic Savings in Underdeveloped Countries, *Journal of International Economics*, 2, pp. 25-38.

Wen, Mei, 2002, Foreign Direct Investment, Regional Geographical and Market Conditions, and Regional Development: A Panel Study on China, *Australian Economic Review,* 25(1), pp. 10-28.

World Bank (1991/1994), World Development Report, (Washington, D.C.: The World Bank).

World Bank Online Database. (http://www.worldbank/data).

11

Towards a Spiritual Ecology of Global Modernity

A Rudimentary Outline

ASEEM SRIVASTAVA

> "In their dealings with the countryside and its people, the promoters of the so-called global economy are following a set of principles that can be stated as follows. They believe that a farm or a forest is or ought to be the same as a factory; that care is only minimally necessary in the use of the land; that affection is not necessary at all; that for all practical purposes a machine is as good as a human; that the industrial standards of production, efficiency, and profitability are the only standards that are necessary; that the topsoil is lifeless and inert; that soil biology is safely replaceable by soil chemistry; that the nature or ecology of any given place is irrelevant to the use of it; that there is no value in human community and neighbourhood; and that technological innovation will produce only benign results."
>
> —*Wendell Berry*[1]

"Civilization has turned into a vast catering establishment. It maintains constant feasts for a whole population of gluttons. The intemperance which could have been tolerated in a few has spread to the multitude. The resulting universal greed is the cause of the meanness, cruelty and lies in politics and commerce that vitiate the whole human atmosphere. A civilization with an unnatural appetite must feed on numberless victims, and these are being

> sought in the parts of the world where human flesh is cheap. The happiness of entire peoples in Asia and Africa is being sacrificed to provide fastidious fashion with an endless train of respectable rubbish…Mother Earth has enough for the healthy appetites of her children and something extra for rare cases of abnormality. But she has not nearly enough for the sudden growth of a whole world of spoilt and pampered children."
>
> —*Rabindranath Tagore*[2]

The destabilization of the natural world is the overwhelming fact of our time. Gasping for breath, one of the astronauts who sent a message *via* film to the COP 21 leaders in Paris last year, says:

> "Suppose I can transfer the experience which I have, to you. Then you would go out and see the earth. And when you have, let's say, the spirit and the insight, and the attitude of an astronaut, you start to love the earth. And if you really love something, you do not want to lose it. Our earth has cancer. I have cancer too."[3]

Everything that follows in this short essay rests on the premise of humanity in crisis and an earth ailing on account of it. If one bears in mind the facts of element aryecology, it follows that the miseries of humanity are compounded further by the deteriorating condition of the earth. If in earlier times humanity had to be protected from nature, now it is nature that needs protection from humanity, or else the elements unleashed will not spare humanity either. We have yet to find a way to conduct a respectful, yet fearless, dialogue with nature, for that would require us to re-learn the art of listening to her. How best to think today about our relationship with the natural world?

Spiritual Ecology and Global Modernity

At the outset, it may be helpful to broadly clarify the key terms in the title of this essay and the context to which they belong. For this, it is first necessary to speak a little about globalization and its history.

Globalization, many have argued, is centuries old, having "contributed to the progress of the world through travel, trade, migration, spread of cultural influences, and dissemination of knowledge and understanding."[4]

This is not the view taken in this essay. I take the perspective I have defended at length elsewhere, whereby there *is*, infact something terribly new about globalization, especially since the end of the Cold War with the fall of Berlin Wall in 1989. The partisans of globalization fail to note the ecological, ideological, geo-political, military, and, not to forget religious implications of the ubiquitous global economic integration we have seen during the last generation or so. They fail to perceive the unique character of the recent–corporate, state-led–form of globalization which has let loose historic changes, not merely on the Subcontinent but on the planet as a whole, jeopardizing the viability of civilization and life on earth as we know it. What we are seeing is a historically unprecedented kind of globalization, happening at an accelerating pace, thanks in good measure to the most powerful advanced technologies ever known to humanity.

"Contemporary globalization is rooted in the world of business, trade, finance, media and technology. It originated in the West and was embraced by Indian and other ruling elites. It has far-reaching consequences for Indian society as much as for that elsewhere. Today's globalization is a definitive prescription not just for certain arrangement of economic affairs, but for a way of life, at the root of which is the thinly concealed perpetual quest for control and dominance by the elites of the world."[5]

The speed and scale of the impact of globalization across the earth during the last few decades has been such that one would be justified in claiming, as the old saying goes, the more thing change, the more they remain the same. For, at the bottom, what appears to have matured with the consolidation of this form of corporate and financial globalization is the project of global modernity itself. What originated in the West has now come to be inflicted upon (or adopted by) virtually the entire world as the way of life.[6]

One feature of this way of life is, as indicated before, the overwhelming dominance of finance in the economy, and of the economy over human society itself. Such has been the speed at which this has happened that it is necessary to say, in consonance with the view propounded by the Economic Anthropologist Karl Polanyi in the 1940s, that the economy has all but eclipsed human society itself, subjugating it to its own commercial ends.[7]

In the era of aggressive corporate nationalism, economic growth has become the overriding objective of governments, no less than of giant corporations, the two together arbitrating on the widest range of human affairs, from military defence to health, education, family and child welfare. "Global financial markets impose their laws and precepts on the planet", writes Zygmunt Bauman.[8] The cloud-elites run the whole world.

Not surprisingly, emerging in parallel with this rise to hegemonic dominance of global finance is the planetary ecological crisis. As some have pointed out, climate change defines the very time in which we live.[9] Given the rapidly worsening situation and the likely consequences, *climate stability* must be the overriding goal of humanity today. It should be seen as much more important, for instance, than achieving high economic growth. It is dangerous to see climate change—more appropriately, climate chaos—as one more environmental problem 'out there', a nuisance in the way of our other plans. On the contrary, given the global obsession with economic growth, it is the overwhelming planetary ecological context for all the other problems and crises humanity faces today, including 'other' environmental problems such as air pollution or de-forestation. But nobody objects too much if the burden of the problem is placed upon the poor, upon unborn generations, or upon other species and ecosystems remote from our everyday experience. Nobody complains either if each one has to bear their little share of the difficulty (of hotter summers or uneven rainfall). It is clear that some suffer much more than others, but nothing changes unless those who suffer are politically or economically influential and cannot remedy the damage to them through their own private resources.

Climate chaos and uncertainty are not problems to be tackled after we have sorted out problems in other domains; economic, political or cultural. They are to be addressed centrally while facing challenges in these latter domains. Thinking properly, we should not be willing to accept a 'solution' to an economic problem like unemployment, for instance, if it involves making the climate more unstable (there are other ways of tackling unemployment). The reason is that, in the end, the lesser goal will be defeated by a greater negligence. However, needless to say, this is not happening anywhere today.

One is required to face the ecological imperative today. It is in this context that one thinks of healing the terribly strained human relationship to the natural world. One way to think about this is 'spiritual ecology'. While there is a wide range of perspectives which inform spiritual ecology, my focus here is on the restoration of 'wholeness' to the human condition. Our cognition, no less than the man-made world around us, is today fraught with fragmentation and disintegration. One has to think of ways of healing at least five disturbed ecologies: the relationship of an individual to himself (inclusive, most significantly, of his relationship to the divine and the unknown), the relationship of the individual to his community, the relationship between individuals within communities, the relationship of communities with respect to each other (as communities), and the relationship between humanity as a species, and the rest of the natural world. At all these levels, relationships have come under great strain from the very rapid technological and commercial developments of the last century, especially of the last quarter-century, which we associate with the era of globalization.

In particular, the rapid growth in information and mobility—of people, no less than of goods, services, investment and capital—during the global age may have contributed in no small measure, given the physical and psychological dislocations involved, to the attrition and erosion of human communities, in turn giving rise to insecurities which could account in part for the many movements for religious revival in so many parts of the last several decades. It appears that underlying tissues of belief and practice that have held communities together for so long have been torn by the advances of the last several decades.

One must therefore imagine ways of thinking and feeling, living and being that restore to all forms of life the dignity due to them. This requires us to move beyond the ubiquitous materialism of our time and reach for reserves to replenish the spirit in order to face the challenges before us. In this short essay, I can do no more than touch upon a few questions raised by the fundamental changes—in human reality as well as in human perception—that have come about in the global age. This will hopefully contribute to a better understanding of our shared predicament, without which no clear path ahead can emerge.

Places and Spaces

The most fundamental level at which change is called for today is at human cognition sphere. Subtle, but enormously powerful, changes have been brought upon human cognition in the global age at the hands of advanced media and communication technologies. One major result is that aspects of real geography, especially local geography, have faded into the barely visible backwaters of cartography and forgotten maps. With them have also receded into insignificance, specific places, towns and villages, meadows and forests, rivers and mountains, deserts and oceans. All these unique aspects of actual nature and the real human world have been overtaken and foregrounded by a colonising network of multiple, abstract inter-related man-made grids, fed by the productive edifice of technology and commerce. These are the two variables, in league with power politics, which seem to determine all human cognition now. These inter-locking grids entail everything from air routes in aerospace, shipping networks over water, and road and rail networks on land to mobile networks over cellular space or information networks in cyberspace. IBM screams in every other commercial: "let's build a smarter planet." And this is what it consists of.

In sum, our experience of actual places has been so heavily overlaid with such developments as to make us all but admit that we no longer live in this or that place. We occupy this or that *space*, much like businesses competing for markets. In fact, the screen-savvy young are all too comfortable with such an understanding. Places are being converted into spaces at such a pace as to render them not merely homogenous but, for all practical purposes, interchangeable and exchangeable with each other. It does not bear reminder that we have now come to live in an economy; no longer in a human society as traditionally understood. Only rooted rural communities can still lay claim to living in a human society, properly speaking.

We now live in highly processed man-made environments, at a very great distance from the natural world. In the global age there is a global hardware (of expressways, airports, and shopping malls), and a global software (of mobile, computer, and television screens), to help us navigate our lives or, more exactly, our business. Human society is more programmed and mobile than ever before. It may be our illusion that we still retain an element of volitional autonomy through all this. What then is our experience of the imperilled natural world? How much do we experience the damage we are bringing upon nature and thus upon our own future?

This damage is sustained by the earth in no small measure precisely to ensure the construction and maintenance of the global artifice of modernity just referred to. Do we experience, for instance, the dying of rivers or the perishing of a rainforest on account of the mining that is done to run and grow the industrial edifice that regulates consumer society? In a remote-controlled world, wherein decisions are made at great distances from ground zero, where they have their impact, it is usually not the case. Indigenous, rooted communities are usually the ones who have stories of loss to tell. We ourselves are insulated by ephemeral green bubbles from the consequences of policies that benefit us—for the time being. Increasingly, even this ceases to be true as problems like metropolitan air pollution and garbage disposal proliferate.

In sum, our experience of the natural world, and what we are doing to it, has grown thinner with every advance made in the world of technology. It would be no exaggeration to say that our distance from raw nature has all along constituted to the very definition of "progress" in modern times. Technology itself has taken the place that nature might have held for generations past, and now comes to us as fate. The belief is quite widespread that one day the techno sphere may actually replace in full the biosphere itself! It is with such a background belief that few object to the deployment of a technology if it emerges in the sphere of the doable.

Our ecological alienation today is such that we learn of the consequences of policies designed to grow the economy, if at all, *via* periodic disasters and catastrophes, news of which filters through to us from our television screens. Needless to add, responsibility for the choices and actions of leaders, both political and corporate, not to mention the rest of us, is rendered suitably opaque.

Are places all destined to become abstract spaces? Or is there room for human responsibility, an 'anthropo-responsiveness' distinct from anthropo-centrism, to act in the interests of species' survival and freedom?

The Re-sacralization of Nature

If the answer to the latter question above is a 'yes', what view are we, as a species, to take of the natural world? The enormous ecological failures of a grossly utilitarian view of the world are present today in abundant evidence. It has been imagined throughout modern times that humanity is somehow morally entitled to help itself to everything in the natural world and, in the end, to the planet itself. (What is to prevent, ultimately, the planet helping itself to us, as a species?) Behind this is the ancient belief that "man is the measure of all things". Could this be a misplaced belief ?

Throughout modern history, the advance of industrial society, especially in this era of high technology, has often meant the relentless secularization of societies and their public realms across the world.

This secularization has accompanied, importantly, the now steady, now rapid de-sacralization of the natural world. It accounts in significant measure for some of the disturbed ecologies named above. The human experience of the natural world has been denuded of the sacred altogether—to the point where we have arrived at the threshold of destroying even things of commercial or technical value.

How do we view this entire phenomenon in such a way as to evolve a radically fresh spiritual ecology for the challenges that face us today—as individuals, as communities, as an imperilled species? Can India—given its gifts of diversity and resilience of multiple traditions—be an ecological pioneer for the world? Can we think in terms of ecological and cultural renewal in India, instead of adopting the rhetoric of sustainability, in such a way that we can contribute to facing the challenges of the ecological *cul-de-sac* in which so much of the world lives today?

These questions boil down to asking fundamental questions about practices and beliefs, especially of beliefs about life itself, involving the unknown and the mysterious (thus, often spiritual, if not religious).

Could the human relationship to the natural world—at each level: individual, collective and species—be a basis for the sort of global inter-faith dialogue one needs today? Could a new spiritual ecology, some variant of pantheism, be conceived as a universal faith of futuristic moment? Is it possible that "diversity is divine", as was once declared by the Bengali mystic-saint Ramakrishna Paramahansa?

This chapter has merely offered a rudimentary outline of some questions that need to be faced in the quest for a spiritual ecology appropriate and necessary to the global modernity of the twenty first century. The old has all but perished, without clear signs of the new era to dawn. A radical spiritual ecology, appropriate and necessary for our times and which constitutes a delicate cusp of history, is the need of the day.

NOTES & REFERENCES

1. Berry, Wendell. (1995), *Another Turn of the Crank*, Counterpoint, Washington DC, p. 13.

2. Tagore, Rabindranath. (2007), The Robbery of the Soil, in *Tagore on Books*, New Delhi: Rupa & Co.
3. A pioneering Astronaut's final speech on the sickness (and salvation) of our Planet, quoted in *Solar Plaza Blog*, January 7, 2015. (Available at http://blog-solarplaza.com/2015/1/7/a-dying-astronauts-final-speech-on-the-sickness-of-our-planet). WubboOckles died the day after the interview was filmed. The film can be watched at https://www.youtube.com/watch?v=NN1eSMXI_6Y.
4. Among them, Amartya Sen, 2002. "How to judge globalism?" *The American Prospect*, January 4, (Available at http://prospect.org/article/how-judge-globalism)
5. See Srivastava, Aseem and Ashish Kothari, (2014), *Churning the Earth: The Making of Global India*, pp. 15-16, New Delhi: Penguin.
6. For a clear argument to this effect, see Christian Comeliau, (2002), *The Impasse of Modernity,* London: Zed Books Ltd.
7. See Karl Polanyi, (1957), *The Great Transformation*, Boston: Beacon Press.
8. Zygmunt Bauman, (1998), *Globalization: The Human Consequences*, p. 66, Oxford: Blackwell.
9. See, for instance, Amitav Ghosh, 2015, India seems to be home of lost causes in *The Times of India*, December 2, (Available at http://timesofindia.indiatimes.com/home/environment/global-warming/Amitav-Ghosh-India-seems-to-be-home-of-lost-causes/articleshow/50005108.cms)

12

Impact of Globalization on Indian Women

VASUNDHARA MOHAN

Globalization is a complex process in which political, economic, social, and cultural relationships no longer remain restricted to territorial boundaries or state actors. It is the expansion of the geographical domain of the global, i.e., the increase in the scale and volume of global flows, and increasing impact of global forces on local life. It also implies the spread of ideas that have originated in one part of the globe, affecting the customs, institutions, and attitudes. At present these being usually western in origin, globalization has come to be reckoned largely to mean or largely equivalent to Westernization. This is especially so with global economic institutions like the IMF, World Bank etc., being considered to have shaped and programmed the concept of Globalization with the support of Western economic, cultural and political norms and advocating them to the rest of the world. Blind faith in such institutions and adopting their advice has resulted in catastrophic results in a number of countries. The erstwhile Soviet Union is one such example.

The term Globalization is believed to have been used for the first time by Theodore Levitt, a Harvard Business School Marketing Professor in 1983.[1] The concept became popular following his article in the Harvard Business Review entitled "The Globalization of Markets"? However, the term Globalization in the present times has its origin in the Washington Consensus (1990) developed by the US Government and international financial institutions, to deal with the debt crisis that the Latin American countries were facing at that time. They believed that the following 10 policies were necessary elements of "first stage policy reform" that all countries should adopt to increase economic growth.

- Fiscal discipline.
- A redirection of public expenditure priorities toward fields offering both high economic returns and the potential to improve income distribution, such as primary health care, primary education, and infrastructure.
- Tax reform (to lower marginal rates and broaden the tax base).
- Interest rate liberalization.
- A competitive exchange rate.
- Trade liberalization.
- Liberalization of inflows of foreign direct investment.
- Privatization.
- Deregulation (to abolish barriers to entry and exit).
- Secure property rights.

Although controversial, the above policies were forced on the "needy nations" under the guidance of IMF and World Bank. John Williamson, Chief Economist at the World Bank says: "Audiences the world over seem to believe that this signifies a set of neo liberal policies that have been imposed on hapless countries by the Washington-based international financial institutions and have led them to crisis and misery. There are people who cannot utter the term without foaming at the mouth."[2] According to Amartya Sen, Nobel-Prize winning economist, globalization "has enriched the world scientifically and culturally, and benefited many people economically as well". The United Nations has even predicted that the forces of globalization may have the power to eradicate poverty in the twenty first century.[3]

But there are several others who disagree that Globalization is the right prescription. They allege that globalization has perpetuated inequality in the world rather than reducing it. Even the IMF admitted in 2007 that inequality levels may have been increased by the introduction of new technology and the investment of foreign capital in developing countries. The Washington Consensus did not necessarily reject the use of social policy, but its focus mainly on efficiency and fiscal discipline often led to cuts in social spending. The adverse impact of the WC policies on those in, or on the borders of, poverty was highlighted by a growing literature which documented the human costs of the crisis and showed that poverty was rising in the "adjusting" countries, and demonstrated the tendency of the adjustment costs to fall on the most vulnerable. The WC stood accused of being at least oblivious to the disproportionate burden on the poor arising from the processes of adjustment and stabilization.[4]

In view of the criticism, the Washington Consensus was revisited after evaluating the performance of Latin America. In the Washington Consensus II that followed (2003), two specific prescriptions viz., Social Safety Nets and Targeted Poverty Reduction were included.[5] Thus, it was left to the governments adopting the Washington Consensus to keep in mind the need to pay special attention to these two aspects and while continuing to stress the virtues of the reforms suggested, the IMF blamed the poor countries for their own failures.

Impact of Globalization on Women

Women constitute one of the vulnerable sections of any society. Globalization has contradictory effects on women; both positive and negative. With the International Monetary Fund and the World Bank encouraging developing countries to use export-led growth to expand their economies, the globalized economies demanded a large work force, which necessarily had to include women.

Thus, on the positive side, over the last 20 years, global development of capitalism has depended almost everywhere on women pouring into the formal workforce. But, the Washington-Consensus-generated employment opportunities did not achieve the expected results. For, in spite of the opportunities for employment, a wide gender gap continued to exist, attributed to the prevailing socio-cultural factors of each country. According to the Millennium Development Goals Report, globally, only 40 per cent of women held wage earning jobs in the non-agricultural sector. Whether in the public or private sphere, from the highest levels of government decision-making to households, women continue to be denied equal opportunity with men to participate in decisions that affect their lives.[6]

Proponents of globalization foresaw that economic growth facilitated by policies to liberalize investment, trade, and financial flows as well as privatization would reduce public sector deficits and will have a beneficial effect on gender equality. Competitive pressures in a globalized economy, it was argued, will make women an attractive source of labour. Women have surely emerged as an attractive source of labour but it however remains that the real reason for this is on account of the fact that women workers have provided the cheap labour from which super-profits have been extracted. This feminization of the formal workforce has been a contradictory experience for most women. Wage structure apart, on the positive side, there is no doubt that women living in traditionally conservative countries have been able for the first time to find employment opportunities, become economically independent and to have a choice in their personal lives. By bringing women into the workforce, globalization has given women a power they lacked in the past; the power to end the system that bred poverty, exploitation and oppression.

With globalization and privatization increasing the demand for educated and technically qualified workforce, private sector entered the field with investment in education from the mid-1980s. Over the last one decade or more, India has seen a huge growth of educational institutions in the private sector, especially those offering higher and technical education, which is available for those who can afford the fees. The role of private sector is likely to increase in future considering the substantial investments required in the sector. In fact, by 2006, the share of private institutions went up to 63.2 per cent and their student share to 51.5 per cent.[7] Graduating from such institutions, girls now have a wider choice of employment in well-paying jobs and become economically independent. The IT industry has, especially, opened immense scope for women's educational progress. A large number of women have acquired the necessary qualifications to join the IT sector, which has given them a new identity, financial independence, freedom of expression and a remarkable social status.

According to a NASSCOM (National Association of Software and Services Companies) report, women now account for close to 30 per cent of the total workforce in the Indian IT industry and this was expected to go up to 45 per cent by 2010. What is significant is the steady rise of the figures. According to the Registrar General of India, from 19.7 per cent in 1981, this figure rose to 22.7 per cent in 1991, and 25.7 per cent in 2001. Going by the trend, NASSCOM claimed that the percentage of women workers in the IT and ITES sectors in India was rising by almost 18 per cent annually. The number of women technicians was expected to rise to 50 per cent by 2010.[8]

A NASSCOM study of June 2005 on women professionals in the IT industry in India reveals that most women in this sector are self-confident, determined and immensely talented professionals and have managed to make their mark within their organizations on account of their hard work and skills. In 2005, the men to women ratio in the IT industry was 76:24. The number of women employed in the IT industry rose from 4,21,460 in 2006 to 6,70,984 in 2008.[9]

Irrespective of globalization-generated demand, there are just not enough women in the labour force in India. The difference in the male and female labour participation rate in India is over 50 percentage points, one of the highest among G-20 nations, according to World Bank data. In fact, the most dynamic economies over the past few decades have a far higher proportion of women at work. A study by the McKinsey Global Institute estimates that India's gross domestic product (GDP) in 2025 can be higher by as much as 60 per cent if women's participation in the economy were on par with that of men.[10]

Negative Aspects

However, the negative aspects of the impact of globalization on women outweigh the positive aspects. It is true that by becoming economically independent women have acquired access to more choices about what they wish to do with their lives. With private sector taking care of higher education, the government was required to concentrate on elementary and higher secondary education. But, this did not happen. The absence of adequate number of such schools and the deplorable conditions in the existing schools has not only affected girls' education but has also narrowed down the feeder cadre for the higher educational institutions.

Critics of globalization also allege that women are often disadvantaged in an economic process founded on liberalized trade, investment, and financial flows. This is related to the fact that the state's role is often reduced under such a policy regime, partly because the mobility of capital puts downward pressure on public spending, making it difficult to fund social spending and safety nets. Further, there is evidence that women's employment is increasingly insecure, and women are often slotted for jobs with least security and stereotyped. Finally, investment mobility is greatest in labour-intensive industries, where women are concentrated. Women are disadvantaged in efforts to bargain for higher wages, since firms can credibly threaten to relocate in such cases.[11]

Similarly, the 'double burden' faced by working women who do not forget their traditional role in the family makes their lives fiendishly difficult as they try to reconcile work and family life. If working outside the home and being economically independent means that they do not have to answer to any man, work outside the homes entails long hours at low wages and makes caring for children very difficult, especially in countries where working women have no immediate access to crèches or child care centres. If for some women joining the global workforce even circumscribes their right to have children, for others it means neglecting the children they are working to feed. But everywhere, an overwhelming majority of women going out to work say that they would not dream of going back to the home.[12]

The demand for child-care facilities of working women was felt in India long ago; but for different reasons. First it was the need for child welfare and education, and later by a more inclusive view of child development. Till globalization and liberalization drew increasing number of women into the workforce, the setting up of child-care facilities for working women did not attract the required attention. A time had come when working women and child care could not be seen in isolation or independent of each other. With joint family system crumbling leaving no care-givers at home, working women with children needed child-care centres close to their work place. A National Crèche Fund was set-up by Government of India in 1994 with the objective to meet the growing demand for crèches and to provide day care facilities to the children in the age group of 0-5 years. But the attempt to make the availability of crèches mandatory at all work places was shelved in 2006. But, a survey conducted by six states across the country revealed that 96.8 per cent of the mothers said that there were no childcare facilities at the worksite.[13]

Broken Homes

Everything comes with a price; including globalization. India had one of the lowest divorce rates in the world, with about 13 out of 1,000 marriages collapsing annually as against 500/1000 in the US.[14] But there has been an increase in the divorce rates in India and with the government proposing to make divorce easier and faster, in line with other countries, there are chances of divorces increasing further. A marriage counsellor form Gurgaon observes that there's been a 100 per cent increase in divorce rates in the past five years alone.

Increasing number of divorces is observed in the IT industry. Financial freedom, lack of time at home, erratic working hours, work pressure, financial security and stress are being seen as the main reasons for the increasing number of divorces in the IT industry. Couples no longer want to put more efforts into a relationship to fix the issues as they concentrate more on their careers and less on their personal lives. According to an Advocate handling divorce cases, couples from the IT sector do not even try to reconcile and are in a hurry to end the marriage. Financial stability is a major problem as the couples feel that they can lead a life without each other as both are financially stable.

It is reported that in Bangalore, a major hub of IT industry, the number of divorce cases pertaining to those in the IT sector has seen a steady rise since 2003. Statistics reveal that in 2003, the number of divorces in the IT sector was 283 (out of a total of 1,280) rising to 526 (out of 1,240) in 2004, 946 (out of 1,860) in 2005 and 1,246 (out of 2,493) in 2006. In 2007 till June 2007 the number of divorce cases from the IT sector is 828 already.[15]

Similar picture comes to the fore from Kerala. In 2009-10, out of 11,600 divorces, a majority has been from the IT industry. A senior legal practitioner opined that most couples who work in the IT industry break up within two to three years of marriage, attributing it to the odd working hours, high stress of the job, and an egoistic attitude.

It may be pertinent to recall what liberalization and globalization did to Russian women. Under conditions of liberalization, Russian women entered fields that were demeaning to women. Besides a profusion of pornographic films, travel and tour operators started offering the company of young Russian and Ukrainian women the dollar-rich tourists. Having taken a decision to enter the modern world, the government pleaded its inability to curb these developments, for, the moment the government tries to step in, "voices are immediately heard accusing dictation, censorship and the suppression of pluralism."[16] Thanks to liberalization and globalization, similar trend is also observed in India, with educated women offering "escort services" through advertisements in the news chapters and websites. Social media like Facebook, Twitter, LinkedIn etc., are being abused for advertising such services; a phenomenon that was unheard of before liberalization and globalization.

Rural Women

Globalization has affected both the quantity and the quality of work available to the majority of women in India. The traditional role of women in agriculture, livestock and animal husbandry, Khadi and village industries including handicrafts, handlooms, fisheries etc. is being undermined. Mechanization and automation which are becoming the mainstay of the market-based economy, have adversely affected the village based traditional economy. If privatization means setting up industries in urban areas, reduction of public sector involvement coupled with the neglect of irrigation projects has been reducing the regular employment opportunities for women in the rural areas. With male migration on the increase from the rural to urban areas, women are compelled to bear the triple burden of caring, farming and paid employment in the rural sector. In the neo-liberal work practices, women find it difficult to cope with their multiple responsibilities, especially with the disappearance of social and financial safety nets and government subsidy, poverty alleviation programmes, universal education, and woman-oriented health programmes. Education and training of rural women are affected owing to privatization. When poverty calls for readjustment of budget, the female children end up being the main casualty because most of the resources are spent to educate the male children. A non-supportive rural life makes women to migrate to urban centres in search of employment; alone or along with their males. Such migration of women often gives rise to exploitation and trafficking in women at the local, regional and global levels.

Whether rural or urban, when the open market economy leads to price rise in food and other basic necessities, it is the women who directly deal with family subsistence have to cope with such changes. Basically, liberalization and globalization of the economy have marginalised a majority of women in India due to reduction of employment opportunities, reduction of wages, casualization of jobs and women workers, and their exclusion from the modernized production process due to lack of education and training.[17]

While Indian economy experiences the existence of both traditional handicrafts and modern mechanised production, industrial capitalism has brought in machine-based mass production. Indian handicrafts industry still shows its importance and constitutes a significant segment of the economy and provides employment to millions of artisans belonging to the weaker sections of society such as SCs, STs and the women. However, since the onset of liberalization and flooding of markets with cheaper substitutes, artisans, including women have started shifting to non-traditional occupations in areas away from their homes. Even kites are imported from China!

A July 2004 report on the impact of globalization of textile industry on rural women in the handloom sector of Orissa states[18]:

> "The impact of the entry of global competitors and allied economic reform in industry sector on rural handloom industry is widely realised. The handloom sector, both co-operative society and private sector, with its vast rural work forces especially women of weaver communities is confronted the challenge of competitive economic environment. The handloom industry has dwindled steadily over the last decade, rendering thousands of weavers unemployed, forcing large scale migration to other states and closure of hundreds of co-operative societies and production centres. As a result, the socio-economic status of the rural women particularly engaged in traditional weaving activities has critically been affected".

The study has reported a gradual decline in the food intake, health care and children's education of the weaver-families.

Pradeep Kumar Jena refers to reports which suggest that all over the Northeast, forces of globalization and privatization, backed by hegemony of the state machinery are ousting the indigenous women's markets and production centres.[19] According to another report, the silk weaving industry in the North-East states has been facing keen competition with silk produced in other South and South-East Asian countries besides lacking innovation, lack of training and poor educational status of the women weavers. This has an adverse effect on the female labour engaged in the silk industry. "Negative sociological features specifically in relation to gender disparity, child labour poor working conditions are increasing."[20]

We may also refer to displacement of villagers and tribals due to the establishment of large-scale projects by industrialists, both Indian and foreign. A Tribal woman, especially, had greater control over the family economy than in caste societies. Her greater decision making power in the family as well as her relatively high status depended on the abundance of the natural resources and the control she exercised over them, particularly over land and forests. Displacement deprives the community of these resources that are the source of nutrition and other survival needs of the family, besides robbing the women of the control they exercised over the resources.[21]

Conclusion

Under the onslaught of globalization, Indian society and economy have changed enormously, opening up the economy, scrapping the 'license *raj*' and reducing the number of areas reserved for the public sector, and ushering in privatization. The liberalization of the domestic economy and the increasing integration of India with the global economy have helped step up the Gross Domestic Product (GDP) growth rates.

It is true that globalization has indeed promoted ideas and norms of equality in women and bringing in them awareness and has acted as a catalyst in their struggle for equitable rights and opportunities. But, it has also exacerbated gender inequality in a patriarchal society, especially in the developing world. Globalization has led to further marginalization of women in the informal sector and impoverishment through loss of traditional sources of income. Entry into the market of goods produced in a mass scale and cheap through mechanization has spelt a death-knell to handicrafts. Global economic institutions have pushed western norms, ignoring and marginalizing women's indigenous movements in the Global South. It is contended that neo-liberalism prioritizes on economic growth, efficiency, and profit making over other values such as the promotion of economic justice and democracy and good governance.[22]

According to a UN Development Fund for Women's report (1997),[23] over the past two decades, globalization has contributed to widening inequality within and among countries, coupled with economic and social collapse in parts of Sub-Saharan Africa and countries in transition like in Eastern Europe. While reviewing the progress made since the 1995 UN Conference on women, the Beijing+5 Document, 2000 has noted that while globalization has presented opportunities to some women, it has also led to marginalization of many others. Though globalization has created new opportunities for women in economic and social spheres, the change in the status of women is not great.

The chief objective of the private sector being profit, it has ignored its social obligations. While the Washington Consensus had called for more market oriented policies with least government intervention, through misinterpretation of the essence of privatization, governments have ignored their social obligations and redirected public spending on social sector initiatives like education, health care and infrastructure. Structural Adjustment Policies (SAPs) have led to cuts in public expenditure, reductions in public sector employment, higher prices for food and other crops, and reductions in the role of government intervention in the economy. Many poor countries borrowing money from IMF, World Bank etc., have been forced to cut down expenditure of publicly-funded health and educational services etc., which have a direct effect on women, in the form of increased maternal mortality, non-availability of affordable education to poor families etc.

Globalization is also linked to momentous political changes in the form of the rise of identity politics, transnational civil society, and new forms of governance and universalization of human rights. Accepting World Trade Organization regulations, states have allowed free entry of foreign corporations, extended more incentives to big businesses, and lifted import controls on agricultural products. These changes have resulted in further marginalization of rural and indigenous women.

There is also economic exploitation of women by Transnational Corporations with the blessing, if not collusion, of governments. Trade liberalization policies having led to the decline of small-scale and subsistence farming, and pushing out female farmers from agriculture and forcing them to migrate to urban areas in search of jobs or seek employment in export processing zones, at lower wages than their male counterparts in their countries.

The labour demand pattern under Globalization inherently favours short-term, temporary employment. This has led to an increase in the short-term contracted labour migration with distinct gender differentiated consequences. Migrant women from developing countries are increasingly victims of trafficking. In the absence of effective international mechanisms that regulate and protect the rights of labour moving across national borders, the migrants have become vulnerable to human rights abuses.

Despite the positive effects of globalization on women, globalization has a darker and more sinister side. "India has one of the lowest female labour force participation rates. At 33 per cent at the national level, India is far below 50 per cent at the global level and 63 per cent in East Asia. Out of the total 397 million workers in India, 123.9 million are women and of these women 96 per cent of female workers are in the unorganized sector.[24] Thus, although more women are now seeking paid employment, a vast majority of them obtain only poorly paid, unskilled jobs in the informal sector, without any job security or social security. Additionally, subjected to intense exploitation, working women are exposed to more risks that cause health hazards and are forced to endure greater levels of physical and mental stress. Thus it would appear that globalization has made many international corporations richer by the billions at the expense of women who are suffering enormously due to this expansion of corporate empires".[25]

Female labour force participation has been on a declining trend in India, in contrast to most other regions, particularly since 2004/05. Drawing more women into the labour force, along with other important structural reforms that could create more jobs would be a source of future growth for India as it aims to reap the "demographic dividend" from its large and youthful labour force.[26]

Finally, globalization and neo-liberalism have not resulted in increased political influence of women. This is more so at the level of global politics because global economic institutions are not adequately representative. At the policy level, the impact of globalization on women and gender relations continues to be neglected nationally and internationally. More remains to be done to integrate gender equality dimensions in their normative, policy and operational work so as to ensure the continuing leadership of the system in promoting gender equality, development and peace within the context of globalization.

In conclusion, the answer to the question whether a particular social group of a country has derived any advantage of globalization depends on the economic status, political privilege and other advantages it already enjoys. For, globalization has benefitted people who are already wealthy, socially and politically privileged. But those who are poor, and socially and politically disadvantaged face tremendous difficulties, and find themselves much worse off than before since they are compelled to operate in a more aggressive competitive economic environment, but without the government/public supports that they once relied on.[27] As productive and reproductive labour in their families, women make significant contribution towards the overall community cohesion and welfare, and maintain the social fabric. In view of the deep-rooted differences in gender roles and socio-cultural expectations, the impacts of economic globalization are felt quite differently by women and men. Structural adjustment policies and the elimination of public subsidies for health, education and other social services has resulted in the transference of the "welfare" function of the state onto families, and by extension onto girls and women. This trend became entrenched as the World Bank and IMF are primarily concerned with the developing nations spending money in repayment of loans and creating profits for corporations rather than on healthcare, education, and other "quality of life" improvement projects. Consequently, the developing nations continue to cut back on social spending, thus increasing the burden on the families. The socio-cultural differences and the effect of unrestricted liberalization on women and poor families was lost sight of under Washington Consensus. It was only later, in the Washington Consensus-II, that specific prescriptions viz., Social Safety Nets and Targeted Poverty Reduction were included. But, the States that adopted the original Consensus ignored the need to keep in mind the social security nets in their enthusiasm to transform their economies; and the damage was done.

Globalization is here to stay. In view of the glamour and advantages attached to globalization, neither the governments nor the public want to go back to the pre-globalization days. However, it is for the governments to implement a judicious mix of globalization with pro-poor schemes and pro-women policies so that the poor and women enjoy the benefits of globalization. Also it is for the women to take advantage of the opportunities offered by Globalization in a judicious manner.

NOTES & REFERENCES

1. Globalization: Origin of the Word, in *Mr Globalization*, 21 July, 2010. (Available athttp://www.mrglobalization.com/globalization/252-globalization—origin-of-the-word)
2. *Global Trade Negotiations Home Page*, Centre for International Development at Harvard University. (Available at http://www.cid.harvard.edu/cidtrade/issues/washington.html)
3. When did Globalization Start? In *the Economist,* London, 23 September, 2013. (Available at http://www.economist.com/blogs/freeexchange/2013/09/economic-history-1)
4. Saad-Filho, Alfredo, *Growth, Poverty and Inequality: From Washington Consensus to Inclusive Growth,* In United Nations, Department of Economic and Social Affairs, DESA Working chapter No. 100, November 2010.

5. Fischer, Stanley, The Washington Consensus, *Peterson Institute of International Economics,* Available athttp://www.piie.com/publications/chapters_preview/6628/02iie6628.pdf).
6. United Nations, New York, *Millennium Development Goals*, 2013. (Available at http://www.un.org/millenniumgoals/pdf/report-2013/mdg-report-2013-english.pdf)
7. Sudarshan, Anand and Sandhya Subramanian, Private Sector's Role in Indian Higher Education, *India Infrastructure Report 2012*, IDFC Foundation, (Available at http://www.idfc.com/pdf/report/2012/Chapter_16.pdf)
8. Women on Top, NASSCOM (Available at http://www.nasscom.in/women-top)
9. Vijaya, K. (2014) The impact of Globalization on the Role of Women in the Economy: A Case Study of India with special Focus on Tamil Nadu, in *Proceedings of the 4th International Symposium,* August 2014, South Eastern University of Sri Lanka, Oluvil. (Available athttp://www.seu.ac.lk/researchandpublications/symposium/4thinternational/socilascienceshumanities/The%20Impact%20of%20Globalization.pdf)
10. Why India needs more working women? In *livemint.com*, 29 September, 2015. (Available at http://www.livemint.com/Opinion/hfaRh6PsbtrUlpcGOP9AxL/Why-India-needs-more-working-women.html)
11. Seguino, Stephanie, 2006, The Great Equalizer?: Globalization Effects on Gender Equality in Latin America and the Caribbean, *Munich Personal RePEcArchive Chapter No. 6509* posted 8. January, 2008 UTC. (Available at https://mpra.ub.uni-muenchen.de/6509/2/MPRA_chapter_6509.pdf)
12. Horgan, Goretti, (2001), How does Globalization affect women? In *International Socialism Journal*, Issue 92; Autumn 2001. (Available at http://pubs.socialistreviewindex.org.uk/isj92/horgan.htm).
13. Government of India, Ministry of Women and Child Development, Report: *Need Assessment for Crèches and Child Care Services*, December 2013, p. 120) (Available athttp://www.cwds.ac.in/Publications/ChildCareReport.pdf)
14. Apoorva Dutt in *Hindustan Times*, January, 4, 2015.
15. The rising divorce rate in the IT Sector (August 2, 2007. Rediff.com. (Available at http://www.rediff.com/news/2007/aug/02divorce.htm)
16. Dzasokhov, A.S., Member of the CPSU Politburo in an interview with Pravda on February 8, 1991 (in Russian), quoted in this author's Russian Women Through Transition, in *Gender and Development: Theory, History, Policy and Cases,* (Eds.) B.N. Ghosh and Parvesh K. Chopra, Leeds (2002), Wisdom House Publications, p. 215.
17. Dasgupta, Kalpana, *Globalization and Indian Women: Problems,*

Possibilities and Information needs—An Overview World Library and Information Congress: 69th IFLA General Conference and Council, 31 July, 2003. (Available at http://webdoc.sub.gwdg.de/ebook/aw/2003/ifla/vortraege/iv/ifla69/chapters/600-Dasgupta.pdf)

18. Sahoo, Narayan, (2004) Project Director in Foreword to the Report by Development Innovators, Bhubaneswar, July 2004. The study was sponsored by Government of India, Ministry of Women and Chid Development, New Delhi. (Available at http://ncw.nic.in/pdfreports/IMPACT%20OF%20GLOBALIZATION%20OF%20TEXTILE%20INDUSTRY%20ON%20ORISSA.pdf)
19. Jena, Pradeep Kumar, (2010), *Indian Handicrafts in Globalization Times: An Analysis of Global-Local Dynamics,* in Interdisciplinary Description of Complex Systems 8(2), 119-137, 2010. (Available at http://www.indecs.eu/2010/indecs2010-pp119-137.pdf)
20. Goswami, Kishor, *Impact of Globalization of Silk industry in Northeast India An Assessment from the Gender Perspectives.* (Available at https://faculty.washington.edu/karyiu/confer/beijing06/chapters/goswami.pdf)
21. Fernandes, Walter and Indrani Choudhury, 1997, Liberalization, the Environment and Impact on Women, in *Women's Link*, October-December 1997, p. 27.
22. Feminist Perspectives on Globalization, in *Stanford Encyclopaedia of Philosophy,* May 6, 2014. (Available at http://plato.stanford.edu/entries/feminism-globalization/)
23. Globalization and its impact on women: A critical assessment, in *Mainstream*, Vol. XL, VII. No. 21, May 9, 2009) (Available at http://www.mainstreamweekly.net/article1351.html)
24. Subhalakshmi, G. (2012), Impact of globalization on women workers in India, in *International Models Project on Women's Rights* (IMPOWER.Org) June 6, 2012. (Available at http://www.impowr.org/journal/impact-globalization-women-workers-india)
25. *Ibid.*
26. Das, Sonali, *et al.*, *IMF Working Chapter No. 15/55*, March 2015, IMF. (Available at www.imf.org/external/pubs/ft/wp/2015/wp1555.pdf)
27. Guttal, Shalmali (2000), Women and Globalization—Some Key Issues, Chapter presented at the Conference on *Strategies of the Thai Women's Movement in the 21st. Century,* Bangkok, March 28-29, 2000.

13

Impact of Globalization on Women in India

A Critical Assessment

ARCHANA SINHA

Introduction

According to the US Agency for International Development and the World Bank, 57 per cent of the 72 million primary school aged children who do not attend school are females at the global level. Additionally, girls are four percent less likely than boys to complete primary school (Gender Statistics, 2010). In particular, care for women during maternity is still lacking in many parts of the world. Approximately 5,29,000 women die annually during pregnancy and childbirth (Gender statistics, 2010). Countries with the lowest maternal mortality rate include Estonia (2), Singapore (3) and Greece (3), while the highest maternal mortality rates can be found in Chad (1,100), Somalia (1,000) and Sierra Leone (890) (CIA World Fact book). To help remedy worldwide gender disparities, the UN Millennium Development Goals prioritize gender equality and empowerment of women. In particular, the MDG-3 is meant to "promote gender inequality and empower women." As part of the Millennium Goals, the international community, especially the UN, will monitor several indicators of gender equality including the levels of female enrolment at school, participation in the workplace, and representation in decision-making positions and political institutions. However, progress on these goals has been uneven.

There is a need to examine the effects of globalization on women worldwide; on their participation in the economy, representation in the political process, education, and health. It is also necessary to consider globalization's ability to benefit women in the internationalization of the movement for gender equality, and the legal structures that support this goal and recognize women's rights as basic human rights.

A gender-wage gap exists all over the world, largely due to the type of work that women choose to go into (or, for many women, the type of work that is available for them) (Rampell, 2013). What accounts for these differences within gendered relations? In many cases, cultural barriers within households and communities impede increased economic participation, or undermine the quality of such participation. For example, even working women face differential treatment such as wage gaps and segregation into traditionally female industries. Women have historically borne the burden of non-monetized labour like child-care and domestic work. Economies demand women in the monetized as well as non-monetized sectors of work. In fact, globalization has the potential to improve women's economic achievement. Increased employment opportunities for women in non-traditional sectors might enable them to earn and control income, thus providing a source of empowerment and enhancing women's capacity to negotiate their role and status within the household and society. Though globalization may have increased women's vulnerability and dependency, there is still hope that prioritizing women's issues has yielded progress and will continue to do so. As the UN has stated, "Women have entered the labour force in unprecedented numbers, increasing the potential for their ability to participate in economic decision making at various levels, starting with the household" (United Nations, 2007). Significant changes in the underlying factors threatening to suppress this potential are necessary before serious progress can be made.

Education

While many gains have been made, and more children than ever are now attending primary school (King, 2013), there is still not world-wide gender parity in education. In every income bracket there are more female children than male children who do not attend schools. Girls in the poorest 20 per cent of households have the lowest chance of getting education (Jensen, 2010). The MDG Report 2010 finds that in places of extreme poverty or extremely rural areas, females are less likely to complete any type of schooling (Jensen, 2010). Poverty remains the most important factor in education inequality. According to a Demographic and Health Survey study of 24 low-income countries, only 34 per cent of girls in the poorest-quintile households complete primary school, compared to 72 per cent of girls in the richest-quintile households (King, 2013).

Human Right in the Universal Declaration on Human Rights, the World Education Forum produced the "Education for All" targets, which include ending inequality between males and females in education. The Forum recommended that governments and organizations implement integrated strategies for gender equality in education that recognize the need for changes in attitudes, values, and practices. Several of the world's poorest countries, located in Sub-Saharan Africa, West Asia, and the Arab states, will fail to reach "Education for All" targets, especially gender equality, by the agreed date of 2015. UNESCO's monitoring team found that norms and values hold females back as much or more than policy. The education of girls is not valued in many societies because they are expected to contribute more at home, while boys should gain skills to work outside the home.

There are region-specific hazards for girls, as well. For example, in South America, the further a school is from a household, the less likely girls are to attend, because travel introduces an increased risk of assault and rape. In parts of the Middle East and North Africa, the public life of a female is so limited that exposure to anything outside the home is deemed unnecessary.

Health

One of the common hazards faced by the working class in the era of globalization is the increasing threat to job security, which in turn negatively impacts the health of female workers. Among the workers in the informal sector a large number of them are women, who have no job security. They are often unskilled workers who receive low wages. Availability of work is irregular; and when work is available, women must work long hours. The uncertainties of obtaining work and the dire need to retain a position in the midst of intense competition cause mental tension, strained social relationships, psychological problems and chronic fatigue, all of which are difficult to prove as work-related.

Everyone in the developing world remains more susceptible to poor health because of lack of services, or lack of access to services, and lack of education and information about health issues. Women have additional vulnerabilities, especially malnutrition, sexually transmitted diseases, pregnancy complications, cervical and breast cancer, domestic violence, sexual abuse, and genital mutilation. In many cultures, women are the first to take care of the vulnerable, sick, and dying and the last to receive preventative or lifesaving treatment. Statistically, one in sixty-one women die during pregnancy or childbirth in developing countries, while in the least developed ones one in seventeen die (Gender Statistics, 2010). To alleviate these problems, the World Bank emphasizes public education programmes that promote healthy lifestyles, eliminate gender discrimination in education and access to services, and prioritize help for young girls. According to the Bank, investments that improve women's health and nutrition are justified on both economic and humanitarian grounds, because they serve to alleviate poverty and develop human resources. Maternal health is one of the most important elements in these efforts. The Millennium Development Goals have charged the UN Children's Education Fund (UNICEF) and the World Health Organization (WHO) with promoting and monitoring a reduction in maternal mortality by three quarters between 1990 and 2015. Thanks to these efforts, maternal mortality decreased by 47 per cent between 1990 and 2010 (Gender dimension of Millennium Development Goals Report, 2013).

Sub-Saharan Africa has the largest problem with maternal mortality, with 1,100 maternal deaths per 1,00,000 live births, a figure more than twice as high as in any other region. Sadly, the vast majority of maternal deaths are preventable with proper care and intervention. Reasons for maternal mortality include delays in seeking medical help, transporting pregnant women to health centres and receiving medical assistance, and may also be attributed to social, cultural, religious, and economic factors. For example, a woman may not alter her lifestyle or workload inside and outside the home, because she cannot afford to and because the expectant father does not alter his, burdening her physically and leaving no time for medical attention, which often requires time and travel to obtain. A sensitive issue for women's global health is the role of reproductive rights. The Platform for Action takes a definitive stance in defence of such rights, including abortion. Empirical evidence shows that, in all world regions, household size contributes directly to poverty and to the workload borne by women. The percentage of poor women decreases with a corresponding decrease in fertility rate. In addition to being a cause of higher welfare for women, lower fertility rates are also shown to be an effect of other positive indicators of development, especially higher education rates and well-functioning markets for labour and credit.

Work

Globalization also means that a new international division of labour has emerged. Economic globalization, deep economic restructuring across countries and neo-liberal economic policies have led to informalised and decentralized processes of production that have transformed labour markets and the world of work in industrialised and developing countries. In the process, social security and legal protection to workers have been undone. Globalization is riding on the back of millions of poor women and child workers in the margins of the economy. The relationship between the formal sector and the decentralized sector is a dependent relationship. The formal sector has control over capital and markets, and the 'informal' sector works as an outranked. In India, more than 90 per cent of women work in the decentralised sector, which has a high degree of labour dismissal and undesirability. These women have almost no control over their work and no chance for upward mobility because of the temporary and repetitive nature of the work. The number of girls working in the informal/unorganized sector for precarious wages has also increased. Using girl-child labourers is the cheapest way to increase the profit margin. The shift from a stable/organized labour force to a flexible workforce has meant hiring women part-time, and the substitution of better-paid male labour by cheap female labour.

Studies have shown that the burden of poverty falls more heavily on women than on men. The inequality in income and consumption levels between women and men has also been documented. At least 11 per cent of households in India are supported solely by women's income. In other words, they are "female-headed households" (FHH), that is, households run by widows, single women, deserted or divorced women. FHH are usually the poorest of the poor. The combined effects on these households of the new economic policies, which translate into (among other effects) reduced PDS (Public Distribution System) quotas, drop in healthcare facilities and educational facilities are serious. Children of FHHs suffer more due to nutritional deficiency, inadequate primary healthcare facilities, and cuts in expenditure for the education sector. In the National Perspective Plan (NPP) for Women (1988-2000), the government responded quite positively to demands from for State support to FHH. But the SAP works against the objectives of the NPP.

Sociological research studies have been by and large critical of the effects of economic globalization on developing countries. However, greater world-wide economic integration may have created new employment opportunities for women. There is a twin view concerning the impact of globalization on women; it is felt that the status of women will improve in some respects but not others, they are also possibly to see greater social disruption, struggle to make a living, violence, exploitation and need to move to from home to support their family. The globalized world is one where there are more cultural, economic and social connections between people, and although this has created more opportunities, it has also created some significant hardship for women.

Globalization has reduced the ability of women to find paid work that offers security and dignity (Desai 2002). Although women's roles in the labour force have changed from traditional agricultural and domestic roles, to manufacturing and production, the overall effect of globalization has been negative. There are empirical claims of women gaining more autonomy over their own wages and a feeling of independence from traditional gender roles in society—especially in marriage and childrearing. Women are also becoming the breadwinners in most households because of the lack of male responsibility in the household. Young daughters are financially supporting their parents and siblings, while mothers are seeking informal work to provide for their children.

Globalization has changed the intra-household responsibilities for males and females, where females are given more responsibility over the survival of the family. The limited advance of women in the formal sector shows a great disregard for their social and economic responsibilities within developing nations. Female labour is not rewarded in relation to the impact they have on society. Therefore, women's work continues to be stigmatized as inferior, in comparison to males work, regardless of their increased responsibilities in society. However, the establishment of various NGOs around the globe and the collaborative efforts of these organizations have improved the lives of women in developing nations.

Gender Issues

Religion, tradition and culture are often used to justify women's subordinate position in society. In all the world's major religions, religious texts have been interpreted to reinforce the power of men in society. Their attitudes towards gender issues include: a belief that women's proper place is in the home; and her disapproval to reproductive rights. In most religions, women are the majority of believers, but it is men who claim to hold the positions of authority and have the rights, including the authority to interpret religious texts. In many religions, women have historically not held leadership positions, and, in some where women have held leadership positions in the past, they are now denied the same leadership position today. Some religions still bar women from holding leadership positions. For millions of women around the world, religion is a source of identity, belonging, and comfort in times of hardship, but ironically, it is often a force, which encourages them to accept violence and subjugation as part of life, and depresses possibly positive social change. Beyond exclusion from religious leadership, women are often excluded from other aspects of religious life and worship.

Culture is a complex phenomenon, in terms of which people both form and express their sense of identity. Although religion and culture are two separate concepts, there is a great deal of over-lap between them. Traditional cultural practices have often found their way into religious systems, while religious beliefs influence the cultural life of communities. Within a human rights framework, the right to culture as a human right, as with freedom of religion, is balanced against other universal rights such as the rights to equality and dignity.

The economic policies and structural adjustments associated with globalization create the most negative impact on women in the developing world. The denial of social and economic rights is the most inhumane aspect associated with the formal and informal sectors. Economists and policy-makers who implement these adjustments need to consider the impact of the current policies on women's lives and the inequalities that exist between men and women. Enabling the advancement of female opportunities and guaranteeing female workers more rights will increase the quality of life and create a more sustainable living standard for women and their families in the developing world. Without these changes, women will continue to suffer in their subordinate positions within the economic market.

Impact of Religion on Women in Development Process

Globalization is a process of accumulative inter-dependence, inter-connectedness and integration of economies and societies to an extent that an incident in one part of the globe affects people in other parts of world. Globalization means the diminishing importance of geographic, political, economic and cultural limits. Information Technology has played a key role in reducing these boundaries. Nevertheless, there is a fear that easier communication can become a source of cultural homogeneity. The new global village provides a world-wide cultural awareness, but may lead to less diversity. But, as this process is not consistent throughout the world, it leads to clash, conflict and fragmentation.

In the Indian context the impact of globalization has been uneven for women. While a small layer has gained work opportunity in the newly emerging forms of employment, especially in the IT, service and food-processing sectors, the semi-/unskilled women have lost control over their natural resources (land, water, forest, etc.), as well as in traditional industries, resulting in the loss of traditional livelihood and sustainability. Gender is not a homogeneous category, but is intersected by class, caste, community and ethnicity.

Religion has a profound influence across cultures and societies. Understanding the role and impact of religion on women sheds light on important components of a society that fundamentally shapes its population. This reality is often not captured in data and is therefore misunderstood, particularly as it relates to women, since their contribution is often unremunerated. Globalization raises larger questions about the role of women in the production and distribution of wealth, and in the preservation of cultural and religious identities of future generations that go unnoticed in most cases around the world. Throughout history, women have been denied basic human rights, in the name of religiously imposed restrictions or economically designed exploitation and influence of their position in family and in society. Even more threatening to women is the manner in which religious ideologies are used to perpetuate injustices to women in male-dominated societies. Religion and culture as powerful institutions within the society play a major role in shaping gender roles and perpetuating gender inequality and are powerful institutions within society. Further, gender relations within the religious and cultural communities are a reflection of gender relations within broader society. However, it is difficult to make the link between women's position in religion and culture, and women's position in society.

For example, in religion as in the workplace, men dominate in decision making positions and women are found in supportive and caring roles. While there are exceptions to this, the challenge to ensure gender equality in religion and culture remains a big one. Religion has an extremely powerful influence over people's lives. In particular, it impacts on gender relations and consequently on how women are treated in society and at home. Religion is often used to deny women their fundamental human rights. Some religions do not allow women to occupy decision-making positions, with the result that women are unable to participate in and influence civil and political life.

Positive Effects

The positive effect of globalization is that it has opened up wider communication lines and enticed more corporations as well as different organizations into India. This provides prospects for not only working men, but also women, who are becoming a greater part of the workforce. Globalization has contributed to bring about welcome changes in the lives of women who have been able to avail of the opportunities, which have opened up in the various sectors of development. These are:

- Prospects of higher and quality education have become feasible for those women who can afford them, economically and socially;
- Employment in technological and other advanced sectors, which have global bearing, has opened up for suitably qualified women;
- With new jobs for women, there are opportunities for higher wage/salary, which increases self-confidence and brings about the power of self-determination. This, in turn, promotes equality between the sexes, something that Indian

women have been struggling for their entire lives. Globalization has the power to relocate the traditional treatment towards women to afford them an equal bearing in society;

- With changing attitude towards women, especially in the urban areas, women enjoy more egalitarian set of gender relationship;
- Augmentation of women's movements through exposures at the international level helps to bring about major changes in the economic, social and political lives of women;
- Reduction in gender inequalities will have positive effect on women's empowerment in the socio-economic context;
- Attitudinal changes towards women's role in the family due to good education, benefits of family planning and health care, child care, good job opportunities etc. help in the development of more confident and healthy women;
- Positive approach to economic and cultural migration facilitates women to be exposed to better prospects at the international level;
- It has also brought great freedom to women, especially those living in traditionally conservative societies, where women are able for the first time to be economically independent of men and to have at least some choice in their personal lives. Eventually, by bringing women into the workforce, globalization has given women a power they lacked in the past, that is, the power to end the system that rears poverty, exploitation and oppression; and
- When it comes to building associations within a social group or tribe, women are likely to do better, and throughout history one can find many examples supporting this.

Within the past decades, globalization has produced a remarkable impact on the lives of women in developing nations. It affects the social, economic, and cultural situation of women. Gender differentiation has undertaken new dimensions with globalization. The economic impact on women has widened from its domestic field to global economic scene. There is no doubt that the economic empowerment of women has a direct relationship to the employment opportunities that the globalization offers to women, though, changes in agricultural technology have led to marginalization of women.

Paradoxically, globalization has had the largest gender impact at the domestic level. As women got more jobs and bigger incomes, the power-balance within the home gets shifted. Globalization did help women. By raising income levels throughout the economy, it helped both men and women. Things certainly differ enormously from country to country and from city to village, but on the whole globalization made people richer. It has not really promoted gender parity, that is, to end, or at least reduce discrimination.

Negative Effects

In spite of the positive effects of globalization through increased employment opportunities for women, it has a darker, more disturbing side. Although women hold a unique position in every society, they still belong to a deprived section of the society due to various social and cultural barriers and inhibitions. Women are customarily most exploited and least privileged members of households and are treated, primarily, as caregivers; they are often overburdened with domestic work. Notwithstanding their second-class status in several societies, women's issues have acquired growing importance globally with the surfacing of the impact on gender discrimination in the cultural, social, economic, and employment arenas.

- Although humiliation, harassment and exploitation of women are common throughout history, they have become more pervasive with globalization;
- Out of the total 397 million workers in India, 123.9 million are women and of these, 96 per cent female workers are in the unorganized sector. Accordingly, although more women are now seeking paid employment, a vast majority of them obtain only poorly paid, unskilled jobs in the informal sector, without any job security or social security. Additionally working women in India are more likely to be subjected to intense exploitation; they are exposed to more and more risks that cause health hazards and are forced to endure greater levels of physical and mental stress. Thus, it would appear that globalization has made many international corporations richer by the billions at the expense of women who are suffering enormously due to expansion of corporate empires;

- In the era of globalization, women do two thirds of the world's work, receive ten percent of world's income and own one percent of the means of production;
- Globalization has contradictory effects on women. Those who assign male gender to globalization hasten to point out as how women's role in reproduction and the family has suffered from the effects of the neo-liberal agenda;
- In the context of development, women's leadership and agency in social change have been controls for women's empowerment within communities. Women's rights worldwide are a significant indicator to understanding global well-being;
- Unemployment, underemployment and temporary work are more common among women than among men. This subset of workers does not have any social security or health care benefits. Consequently, work-related illnesses, which they suffer from, remain hidden. Furthermore, long-term unemployment constitutes a serious risk for the worker's emotional stability, because it leads to poverty and affects their self-image and self-esteem.

This feminization of the formal workforce has been a contradictory experience for most women. While on the one hand becoming economically independent has led women everywhere to having more choices about what they do with their lives, the 'double burden' faced by women because of their role in the family means that the lives of women workers are everywhere inhumanly challenging as they try to reconcile work and family life. Working outside the home and being economically independent, the 'race to the bottom' on which the growth of global capital is being built means that, typically, this work entails long hours at low wages and makes caring for children very difficult. Wherever women are working they usually earn less than men, sometimes less than men who are doing exactly the same work.

Problems encountered by Indian women over the ages include patriarchy and social pressures, caste-based discrimination and social restrictions, inadequate access to productive resources, poverty, insufficient advancement facilities, and powerlessness. These basic problems have afflicted the lives of Indian women with little relief. But the new circumstances created by Structural Adjustment

Programme (SAP) for globalization are varied and include all aspects of women's lives in India. They have affected both the quantity and the quality of work available to the majority of women. The traditional role of women in agriculture, livestock and animal husbandry, handlooms, etc., is being challenged because mechanization and mechanization is becoming predominant in the market-based economy which unfavourably affects the village-based traditional economy.

- Privatization and reduction of public services will reduce regular employment opportunities for women. Globalization has increased the number of low paid, part-time and exploitative jobs. This will tend to result in worse working condition, lower pay and inferior career opportunities. Curtailment of state provisions in child care, community care and social security, will increase the dual burden of employment and family responsibilities for women in general. With male migration on the increase from the rural to urban sectors, women have to bear the triple burden of caring, farming and paid employment in the rural sector;
- The neo-liberal work practices make it very difficult for women to cope with their multiple responsibilities. With the disappearing social and financial safety nets and government subsidy, the poverty alleviation programmes, universal education, and woman oriented health programmes will be adversely affected;
- Trade Liberalization allowing MNCS to enter into food processing and other feminised industries will lead to reduction in low skilled women labour;
- Privatization of education and training will increase the cost of education. When family budgets are readjusted, the female children will be the main casualty because most of the resources will be spent to educate the male children;
- Migration of women especially for economic reasons often gives rise to exploitation and trafficking in women at the local, regional and global levels;
- Open market economy leads to price rise in food and other basic necessities. Women who have to directly deal with family subsistence have to cope with such changes;
- Basically, Liberalization and globalization of the economy will marginalize majority of women in India due to reduction

of employment opportunities, reduction of wages, casualization of jobs and women workers, exclusion from the modernized production process due to lack of education and training;

- Globalization has also had contradictory effects when it comes to questions of sexual freedom and reproductive rights, in particular a woman's right to choose if and when to have children. While the mass invasion of women into the workforce has resulted in a real shift in attitudes to sexual activity, the 'race to the bottom' has seen global capitalism unwilling to provide even minimal protection for the important role played by women in bearing the next generation of workers. Changes in women's relationship to production can lead to changes in their family relationships and attitudes to family life, sex and sexuality and the extent to which this is happening in India should not surprise us. Women who are now economically independent means that women are progressively more unwilling to remain in relationships that are abusive or not supportive; and
- Among the distinct groups of society upon whom globalization's impact has been most influential, women clearly stand out. Women have entered the workforce in large numbers in states that have embraced liberal economic policies. This has resulted in further marginalization of rural and indigenous women. Globalization has also increased women's unpaid work as social services are privatized.

Globalization has had adverse effects on women especially in the developing countries. As consumers, women are increasingly facing a consumer culture which reduces them to commodities and as producers; women are exposed to work exploitation and occupational hazards. Owing to their several roles, as would-be mothers, as mothers responsible for the health of their children and families, as working women at home and outside they are major consumers of healthcare products. As producers also women have to suffer exploitation in terms of low wages, poor working environment, instability of employment, and denial of right to representation.

Propositions

Globalization can be a major force for prosperity only if it is backed by adequate national policies and a conducive social and economic environment. This chapter gives an overview of what the forces of globalization have in store for the women of India. A large group of working women of India is in the rural and unorganised sectors. Socially, a majority of Indian women is still tradition-bound and is in a disadvantageous position. Since, globalization is opening up the Indian economy suddenly at a very high speed, without the required economic and social policies to provide the much required safety net, women who have been involved with production in the traditional ways, have to cope with numerous problems and yet try to avail of the opportunities which an open economy promises.

Well-being is generally described as the state of being happy, healthy or prosperous. The researchers used the UN Human Development Index as an indicator of quality of life. It offers a realistic perspective of the national levels of well-being of 130 countries, covering almost 90 per cent of the world's population. The Index also takes into account non-income dimensions such as education and health. It shows that globalization has brought higher levels of development to more countries than was the case 30 years ago. At the same time, medium developed nations, such as India, are caught up with advanced economies. However, the intensity by which well-being has increased differs across countries. In the last 30 years women have come a long way. The contradictions women face has never been more bruising than they are now. Overall, income inequality across countries has only been reduced by less than ten per cent.

- Alongside advances in independence for women and changes in family life, goes the "double burden"—the struggle to do the second shift at home, cooking, cleaning and, crucially, caring for children. This is part of the "race to the bottom". The worst aspect of it is the choice many women face between feeding their children and looking after them. This choice starts in some countries as soon as women give birth—where there is no national right to paid maternity leave, some women have no choice but to resume work very soon after giving birth. This helps explain why it is an issue for women workers.
- This calls for networking among women and other groups affected by globalization and undertaking joint campaigns on common concerns. Women's movements have to fight for change at all levels. Women have to work for self-

> empowerment at multiple levels. It has had a mixed impact on women's rights. On the one hand, it has led to increasing violations of women's economic, political, and cultural rights in a large measure due to withering away of the welfare state, feminization of poverty, expansion of religious fundamentalism, and new forms of militarism and conflict. On the other hand, aspects of globalization have provided women with increasing opportunities to work in solidarity at regional, national and international levels to demand their rights. Their objective is to help promote mechanisms that strengthen the positive aspects and consequences of globalization, especially with respect to women's rights and gender equality.

It is seen that the situation facing the majority of the Indian women is far from positive. Both the government and NGOs seem to be aware of the fact that the globalization process requires proper focus on rural development, education, health and child care and gainful employment for the underprivileged at the initial stages. Since poverty alleviation programmes are the main responsibility of the Government, there are direct and sector-wise schemes. These include—Public Distribution System, work security, health schemes and services, child care, credit and insurance schemes.

The key aim of women's' empowerment is to bring them within the purview of the mainstream development process. Enabling women address their capacities and capabilities and addressing their own development has been the main focus of NGOs and women's organizations. Innovative approaches for poverty alleviation such as savings, credit, and asset creation for poor women have evolved in India. These trials have been able to organize poor women to strengthen their capacity to survive; meet their social needs; enter into income generating activities; increase their savings; utilise the savings along with available credit; improve their socio-economic conditions and that of their families through sustained process.

Being at the lowest rung of the socio-economic ladder, women should become one of the most important beneficiaries of information meant to reduce their socio-economic gap. Information needs of women in the new globalized environment are as diverse as the socio-economic scenario. Treating women as a uniform and monolithic group will streamline their information needs. Within women's group itself, globalization has created the haves and the have-nots, which means, those who are in a beneficial position due to globalization and those downgraded further into disadvantaged position under the new economic policy. The information needs will also differ accordingly. It is only through complete understanding of the plight of women in the Globalization process can the government, NGOs and decision makers prepare proper strategies to empower women and bring them into the mainstream developmental process.

Conclusion

Globalization presents opportunities to some women, but leads to marginalization of many others and thus calls for mainstreaming in order to accomplish gender equality. Globalization affects different groups of women in different places in different ways. On the one hand it may create new opportunities for women to be harbingers in economic and social progress. Women workers suffer the worst working conditions, poorest pay and have to care for children and other dependents. With the initiation of global communication networks and cross-cultural exchange there seems to be a change in the status of women, although not to a very large extent. However, globalization has certainly endorsed ideas and norms of equality for women and has brought about awareness and acted as a catalyst in their struggle for equitable rights and opportunities. On the other hand, it may aggravate gender inequality in a patriarchal society, especially in the developing world. In the economic realm it may lead to further marginalization of women in the informal labour sector or impoverishment through loss of traditional sources of income. Gender equality is critical to the development process. The process of globalization may have resulted in new possibilities of growth, but due to unequal distribution of its benefits women have been unfavourably affected in many cases. It calls for creating opportunities for women to be part of this development process. Just enacting legislation will not help; what is vital is its proper implementation. The main concern is of state's withdrawal from social responsibility and its impact on women. The process of globalization must be redesigned so that it is more people-centred instead of profit-centred and more accountable to women. Globalization offers women unprecedented opportunities, but equally new and unique challenges. Gender inequality springs from many sources, and it is often difficult to determine which forms of inequality are being eliminated by the effects of globalization, and which are aggravated. Progress toward eliminating gender inequality in the future depends on finding ways where the global approach strengthens women's security and welfare, and fighting the issues, mostly in the economic realm, where women are made worse off by the new global system.

NOTES & REFERENCES

1. Rajput, Pam, (Ed.) (1994), *Globalization and Women,* New Delhi: Ashish Publications.
2. Goswami, P.R. (2002), Literacy, Information, and Governance in the Digital Era: An Indian Scenario, in *The International Information and Library Review*, Vol. 34, Issue 3, September 2002, pp. 255-270.
3. Siwal, B.R. (1998), Structural Adjustment: Macro-Perspective, in *Social Welfare*, Vol. 45, No. 1, April 1998, pp. 48.
4. Sood, A.D., 2001, How to wire Rural India: Problems and Possibilities of Digital Development, in *Economic and Political Weekly,* Vol. 36, Issue No. 43, 27 October, pp. 4134-41.

14

Globalization, Women and Religion

MOLY KURUVILLA

Introduction

Globalization is the new buzzword that has dominated the world since the 90's of the last century. Globalization is no longer just an economic phenomenon. It is accompanied by cultural, social and political changes as well. It has dramatically changed the lives of both men and women in all spheres of life over the world. Rapid social changes, consumerist culture, stiffer competitions, disruption of families, increasing violence, loss of tolerance, increased individualism and selfishness are features of the present globalized society.

Because of the deep rooted differences in gender roles and socio-cultural expectations (Kuruvilla, 2010), the impact of globalization is felt differently by men and women and by women belonging to different class, race and culture. Globalization offers both blessings and curses to women all over the world. By bringing them into workforce, globalization has given women the power to question the system that breeds poverty, exploitation and oppression. Globalization has led to a new identity, financial independence, freedom of expression as well as a remarkable social status for women. At the same time, globalization has pressurized women by putting a double burden of maintaining a balance between home and work front. In a study on the role conflict of women managers in higher education (Kuruvilla & Seema, 2016), a majority of the respondents reported facing severe role conflict and practices saying prayers and visiting holy places as the major strategy for coping up with the conflicts. They faced no restrictions and required no special permission in doing these two things. Thus in the globalized society women turn out to be more religious in search of peace and happiness. At the same time they are confused about the pulls and pushes exerted by religions. A study on contraceptive usage (Kuruvilla and Aswathi, 2014) reveals how religious teachings very often pull back women from availing the new reproductive technologies that enable them to have better control over their bodies.

In an era of stiff competition, stress has become a part and parcel of everybody's life. The fear of new forms of gender-based violence like cybercrimes, pornography and trafficking has been added to the stress of girls and women. The rising trend of individualism and selfishness has developed fear and helplessness among large masses of people. This in turn has nurtured the formulation of different identities based on caste, religion and political affiliations. Religiosity rather than spirituality is adopted as a strategy for survival in the globalized society. At a time when the political identity is questioned, religious identity is projected as a safeguard. But when these two identities get mixed up, it ends up in communal feelings that threaten the very fabric of harmony and peaceful coexistence in secular India. In this context women are often projected as symbols of religious identities with undue emphasis on their dress codes and rituals. At the same time religions fail to support women's emancipation or gender justice.

India is a tradition bound society where women have been socially, economically, physically, psychologically and sexually exploited from times immemorial; sometimes in the name of religion, sometimes on the pretext of writings in the scriptures and sometimes by social sanctions. Very often as part of cultural tradition the gender bias is transmitted from generation to generation without being questioned by anybody and religions serve to perpetuate this bias that have negative implications more for girls and women than boys and men.

According to the First Report on Religion Data, 2001 (quoted in Kuruvilla, 2011), there is considerable difference in child sex-ratios among various religious communities, as given in Table 14.1.

Table 14.1 shows that the child sex-ratio and overall sex-ratio vary considerably with the religious communities. There are 931 Hindu women for every 1000 Hindu men, which is less than the national average of 933 women for every 1000 men. The figure among Muslim community is 936 per 1000. Christians have the highest sex-ratio of 1009 females per 1000 males and Sikhs record the lowest

Table 14.1: Sex-Ratio among various Religious Communities

Religious Communities	*Child Sex-Ratio*	*Overall Sex Ratio*
Hindus	925	931
Muslims	950	936
Jains	870	940
Sikhs	786	836
Christians	964	1009
Buddhists	942	953
Others	976	992
All	927	933

Source: First Report on Religion Data (2001), Registrar General and Census Commissioners, India.

overall sex-ratio of 839 per 1000. With regard to child sex-ratio, it was the worst among Sikhs, followed by Jains, Hindus and Buddhists, while that of Muslims and Christians was better.

Female foeticide which is considered to be a major reason for the imbalance in sex-ratio was once assumed to be prevalent among Hindus because of their custom requiring male progeny to perform cremation rites. But today it is found to be equally rampant among Sikhs, Muslims and Christians. A study by Kuruvilla (2012) among male and female parents endorses such an association between religion and son preference.

Religion appears to be an important factor in creating the social knowledge and discourse which constructs the individual's view of gender and the role and place of gender in the society. Cultural and religious customs reinforce traditional gender roles, especially those regarding women's responsibilities in the home and family. The rituals, ceremonies and beliefs of all religions are gender-stereotypic. Religion provides certain rules for different gender roles in a community (Bakombo, 2013; Morin & Guelke, 2007). Some among them are, regulations regarding clothing (Kelly, 2010; Khan, 1997), marriage that is predominately controlled by caste and religion (Saha & Dey, 2014), the exclusion of women from positions of leadership in the religious community (Sullins, 2006; Kuruvilla, 2012) etc. Besides this, during menstrual periods generally girls/women have high restrictions in entering places of worship (Guterman, Mehta & Gibbs, 2013). Son-preference is evident in all religions and men are considered as superior and women as inferior, impure and sinful.

Religious dogmas are misinterpreted by the religious leaders and practitioners who are all men so as to keep women secondary. The influence of religion on women's gender role attitudes is well documented in the social science literature (Bartkowski, 1999, 2003; Sherkat, 2000).

The findings of several studies highlight the influence of religion on the mind-sets and thought patterns of men and women of different age groups in the Indian context. The study on gender role perception among teacher trainees (Kuruvilla, 2013) conducted on a sample of 632 students including boys and girls from 20 B. Ed. colleges of Kerala has revealed religion rather than education as a major factor in influencing the gender role perceptions of youngsters. There was a significant difference in the gender role perception between Hindu and Muslim students with the former having progressive and the latter having traditional perceptions. Similarly significant difference exists in the gender role perception between Christian and Muslim students with Christian students having progressive and Muslim students having traditional perceptions about women's roles in the society. No significant difference in gender role perception was seen between Hindu and Christian students. The findings reveal the role of religion in shaping gender role perception of the sample.

Study by Kuruvilla and Nisha (2015) also reveal a significant difference in the gender role perception of adolescent girls belonging to different religions.

Table 14.2 shows that there is a significant difference in the gender role perceptions of adolescent girls belonging to the three major religious groups. As indicated by the mean scores, Hindu girls have more progressive gender role perception than the Muslim girls.

Table 14.2: Data and Results of test for Scores of Gender Role Perception of Adolescent Girls

Sample	*Sample size*	*Mean*	*Standard Deviation*	*t value*
Hindu	227	34.87	4.39	9.57**
Muslim	245	30.37	6.03	
Christian	128	35.94	2.6	12.95**
Muslim	245	30.37	6.03	
Christian	128	35.94	2.6	2.97**
Hindu	227	34.87	4.39	

** indicates a significant mean difference at .01 level.

Similarly, significant difference exists in the gender role perception between Christian and Muslim girls, with the Christian girls having progressive and Muslim girls having traditional perceptions about women's role in the society. As compared to Christian girls, Hindu girls possess less progressive outlook on gender roles. Thus, the analysis shows adolescent girls belonging to Christian community have the most progressive and those belonging to Muslim community the least progressive, outlook on gender roles of women.

Conclusion

The position of women in India today is much better than what it used to be 50 years back. But there is still a long way to go. The world has changed, culture has changed, lifestyles have changed, the notions of development and happiness have changed, but the cultural image of woman remains unchanged. The fact that religion plays a critical role in sustaining this cultural image is indisputable. Religion being the most potent agent to bring about change in the mind-sets of people, it should take it up as its responsibility to promote egalitarian relations between men and women and fulfil the mission of ensuring peaceful coexistence of all genders. The fallacy behind biological determinism and the impurity assigned to women in all religions is to be exposed by intellectuals. Gender division of labour sustained by religious teachings does much harm to women's emancipation. Denial of religious leadership to women even in the twenty first century can in no way be justified. The codes of morality must be made equally applicable to men and women and respecting the individuality of women as equally capable human beings is to be emphasized. Timely modifications and corrections are required in the approaches and policies of all religions so as to facilitate unity and peace rather than discord and conflict whereby the concept of secular India could be made meaningful.

REFERENCES

Bakombo, Schwab, 2013, *How Religion and Society Contribute to Gender Inequality*, Enquire Publication, 29 January, (Available at http://inquireblog.blogspot.in/2013/01/)

Bartkowski, John, P. One Step Forward, 1999, One Step Back: 'Progressive Traditionalism' and the Negotiation of Domestic Labour within Evangelical Families, in *Gender Issues*, September, Vol. 17, Issue No. 4, pp. 40-64.

Bartkowski, J. P., and Read, J. G. 2003, Veiled Submission: Gender, Power, and Identity among Evangelical and Muslim women in the United States, in *Qualitative Sociology*, Vol. 26, No. 1, pp. 71-92, Spring.

Guterman, M., Mehta, P. and Gibbs, M. Menstrual Taboos among Major Religion, in the *Internet Journal of World Health and Societal Politics*, Vol. 5, No. 2. (Available at https://ispub.com/IJWH/5/2/8213)

Kelly, M. Clothes, (2010), Culture, and Context: Female Dress in Kuwait, in *Fashion Theory, Journal of Dress, Body and Culture*, Vol. 14, Issue 2, June 2010, p. 215.

Khan, Fawzia-Afzal. 1997, Introducing a new course: Muslim women in the Twentieth-Century Literature, in *NWSA Journal*, Vol. 9, No. 1, Spring pp. 78-77.

Kuruvilla, M. (2010), Challenges and Coping Strategies for Women in the Globalised Society in *Women's Link,* Vol., 16(4), 13 October, 2010, pp. 39-43.

Kuruvilla, M. (2011), Discrimination a*gainst Girl Child: The Trajectory of Missing Girls,* New Delhi: Gyan Books, pp. 46-47.

Kuruvilla, M., 2012, Religion and Son Preference, in the *International Journal of Multidisciplinary Educational Research*, Vol. 1, Issue 2, June, pp. 63-71.

Kuruvilla, M., 2013, Gender Studies Components in Teacher Training: An Essential Requirement for Teacher Empowerment and Gender Justice in the twenty first Century, in *International Journal of Education and Psychological Research,* Vol. 2, No. 2, pp. 46-50.

Kuruvilla, M. and Aswathi, N, 2014, Contraceptive usage among women in Peruvayal Panchayat, Unpublished PG Dissertation, Department of Women's Studies, University of Calicut.

Kuruvilla, M. and Nisha, P. (2015), Religion and Gender Role Perception: An Empirical Study among Adolescent Girls in Kerala, in *International Journal of Education and Psychological Research*, Vol. 4, Issue 2, pp. 78-83, June 2015.

Kuruvilla, M. and Seema, S.P. (2016). Role Conflict and Coping Strategies of Women Managers in Higher Education in Kerala, in *Zenith International Journal of Multidisciplinary Research,* Vol. 6 (1), January 2016, pp. 195-205.

Morin, K.M., and Guelke, J.K. (2007) *Women, Religion, and Space: Global Perspectives on Gender and Faith*, Syracuse, N.Y.: Syracuse University Press.

Saha, A.K., and Dey, S.K. (2014), Attitude Towards Marriage among the Students of Higher Learning in West Bengal: An Empirical Approach, in *Indian Journal of Social Work*, Vol. 75 (3), pp. 349-364, July 2014.

Sherkat, Darren E. (2000), That they be Keepers of the Home: The Effect of Conservative Religion on Early and Late Transitions into Housewifery, in *Review of Religious Research,* Vol. 41, Issue 3, March 2000, p. 344.

Sullins, D. Paul (2006), Gender and Religiousness: Deconstructing Universality, Constructing Complexity in *American Journal of Sociology*, Vol. 112, No. 3, November 2006, pp. 838-880.

15

Private Participation in Higher Education

Interpreting 'Quality' from the Perspectives of Stakeholders

M. MANISHA

Introduction

Higher Education in India today stands at a cross road. A burgeoning young population, prosperous middle class and the desire for social mobility together with policies of affirmative action have created demand for education at all levels. Being at the top of educational pyramid, Higher Education has faced increasing demand for availability, access and appropriateness. The Gross Enrolment Ratio (GER) has grown at a healthy pace, with 3.6 million students being added over the last four years. The GER stood at 13.8 per cent in 2010, up from 11 per cent in 2005. India has a long way to go when compared with China and Brazil and also when compared to the world average. USA, for instance, has a GER of 83 per cent while China's is 23 per cent and Brazil's 34 per cent. The Ministry of Human Resource Development has set a target of achieving 30 per cent GER by 2020. Nearly 85 per cent of the total enrolment in higher education is for undergraduate courses.

A cursory glance at the higher education scenario in India gives us an idea of the size and complexity of higher education in India and the challenges that it faces. Nearly 634 Universities are recognized by the University Grants Commission (UGC) with almost 20,000 affiliated colleges that teach programmes developed and examined by State Universities. In addition, there are around 250 specialized teaching and research institutions, established to provide training in medicine, engineering, agriculture, and computer science, and to conduct high-level research (Jayaram, 2004). The system as a whole employs more than 4,00,000 teachers and caters to almost 10 million students (Rizvi & Gorur, 2011). This makes India self-reliant in terms of educated human resources and establishes it as exporter of this resource to the world. India is the third largest system in the world after China and USA in terms of enrolment and largest in the world in terms of number of higher education institutions (UGC, 2011).

The process of globalization associated with the advent of technology has changed the nature of education. Apart from distance education, Massively Open Online Education (MOOC), class room without walls, e-learning and non-formal learning have changed the nature of teaching/learning process. This has opened up large vistas to the hitherto marginalised and created new markets for the new and existing entrants to the educational sector.

Private Sector Participation in Higher Education

Private investment in higher education is not new. In Asia, private institutions have always been a central part of higher education. Private higher education has been playing a major role in Japan, South Korea, Taiwan, Taipei, Indonesia and the Philippines, where up to 80 per cent of the students attended private institutions. Private higher education is reported to be rapidly growing in China, Vietnam, Cambodia, and other Central Asian Republics as well (Gupta, 2004).

Private investment in higher education in India comprises institutions specializing in fields of management, technology, or education, with the sole aim of offering high quality academic degrees having market acceptability. The NIITs in India fall in this category. There are also some institutions sponsored by private, non-profit religious groups or ethnic organizations. Most of the private colleges are affiliated to the open schools or public universities. There are also instances of new private universities being set-up under the Private Universities Act.

Private higher education is growing in response to a number of factors viz., increasing young population with a variety of goals, demand for advanced levels of knowledge and technological skills; providing more choices to meet the specific demands of students and industry. This enables the government to focus on its primary duty towards increasing literacy and providing basic education and save on public subsidies.

The share of unaided private institutions in higher education has increased from 43 per cent in 2000 to 63 per cent in 2006. As of 2006-07, private sector participation ranged from 50 per cent to 95 per cent of the total number of institutions offering various professional courses. According to the Department of Industrial Policy and Promotion of the Government of India, a total amount of US$ 1,171.10 million has flown into the education sector in India from April 2000 to June 2015. According to Urmi A. Goswami, approximately 90 per cent or more of the colleges in IT, engineering, and management sectors are private. (*Economic Times,* New Delhi, 5 May, 2003). Large scale private investment in higher education has met with mixed results. While it has increased the choices available to students in certain areas and has made higher education more accessible, it has also raised issues relating to unregulated fee, poor quality, and lack of accountability. The discourse on higher education centres around three dimensions namely; Excellence, Equity and Access.

In the above context, we propose to look into the concept of quality in higher education in India from the perspective of those who are directly and indirectly involved with higher education and understand the various parameters of quality in India's private educational institutions. The chapter is divided into four sections. The first section looks into definitions of Quality and Higher Education, the second section identifies the parameters of quality from the point of view of multiple stakeholders, the third section looks into existing parameters of assessing quality in higher education in India and the final section tries to identify the parameters of assessing quality in liberal economy.

Notion of Quality

The concept of quality has become a focal point in the debate on Higher Education. However, a brief look into the development of idea of quality may help us in raising some issues relating Quality in higher education in India.

The notion of "quality" became important with the advent of industrialization and mass production based on division of labour. The adoption of new scientific approach to management by F.W.

Taylor may be regarded as a starting point of discussion on quality. With mass-production, and breaking down of work into smaller and repetitive tasks handled by machines, the role of workers for ensuring of quality was reduced. In the days of craftsmanship, the responsibility of quality remained almost solely with the worker and to a marginal extent with the consumer who validated the workers' perception of quality. Industrialization and mass production in the later stage necessitated the need for inspection of the products, often by a third party to ensure they met specifications before they left the factory. Statistical input remained the primary determinant of quality in USA, Japan and elsewhere in the world. This came to be known as 'quality control'. Walter A. Shewhart (1931) of Bell Laboratories used statistical process control (SPC) to study variation in the performance of systems. Later, W. Edwards Deming, a student of Shewhart, using SPC helped engineers during the World War Second to produce bullets. In the Post-World War period, Deming focused on his theory of management based on quality principles. He became a pioneer both in Japan and America (Mishra, 2006). From 1960s onwards the concept of quality was associated with total quality management (TQM) principles which emphasised the culture of continuous improvement, organization-wide quality management.

Quality in industries was defined as adhering to the stated or implied performance requirements of the customer. Although, the quality management concepts in business and in education remain same, there are certain limitations in adopting the corporate methods of quality management because educational institutes cannot be considered as industry and the students are not the products, but they lie with the quality of education imparted to the students. Students, their parents, and their future employers are the customers of this product (education). In Quality management, the customer is defined as the next person in line. In an educational institute, students directly receive the teaching services and hence, are the customers of the teacher, whereas the faculty and the Institute's administrators are the suppliers of the services. Even the supplier-customer concept of Quality management cannot be applied in education because the customers do not understand what is to be acquired, or what is of good Quality. With increasing involvement of the private sector in Education sector, the notion of management or industries has gradually taken root. But with interpretations as varied as the individuals, it is rather difficult to define the quality in (higher) educational institutions.

Despite such issues, the concept of quality as associated with management has moulded the understanding of quality in higher education in India.

Definition of Quality of Higher Education

The concept of Quality in Higher Education has been interpreted in a number of ways and a crystallized definition of the term has not yet evolved (Aspin and Chapman 1994, Williams 2001, UNICEF 2000). It is descriptive and normative, measurable yet not quantifiable. It is known, yet not understood; it can be experienced but is difficult to explain.

Quality in educational context is a complex concept, for it deals with multiple stakeholders, their requirements in diverse geographical locations and socio-political context. It also involves issues of financial and social capital. It refers to the achievement of learning/ skills that may be considered desirable in a particular time and a socio-political context.

There are both relativist and objective interpretations of quality. Those who are relativists in their orientation believe that it may be considered desirable in a particular time and some others believe quality has specific quantifiable attributes. It is therefore not surprising that, it has been referred to as a quality concept (Peffer, N. & Coote, 1991).

It is both an absolute and relative term. When we consider quality as absolute, it is given and considered as the highest possible standard. Quality as relative term suggests that the quality of a product or service can be described in relative terms. According to Mukhopadhyay (2005), "adherence to product specification is actually the minimum conditions for quality, but not the sufficient condition. The sufficient condition is customer or user satisfaction and beyond." (p. 19)

In a chapter entitled "Quality in Professional Education: Role of Teachers", D. Venkateshwarlu, Priyanka Pathak and Ritu Arora defined Quality as under:

(1) *Quality means degree of excellence.* Quality in education is about what students have learnt as a result of their interaction with their teachers and University.

(2) *Quality is a value.* It is not a unitary concept but a multiple concept which embraces the quality of inputs such as students, infrastructure and the process of education, covering learning activities, extra-curricular activities, community development activities and the quality of the output in terms of students and graduates.

Quality is also about perception (Mukhopadhyay, 2005). It is the stakeholders and the socio-political context that create perceptions about quality. These perceptions are transient and not eternal or universal. It could vary from excellence to satisfying, from perfection to standard. It could be relating to efficiency or effectiveness (R.K. Srivastava and Anil Kumar).

Quality as a process, suggests that in order to achieve quality of a product or service it must undergo certain processes and conform to the procedural requirements. Thus, quality is the outcome of systems and procedures laid down for the purpose. However, quality could also be related to the people who provide education and not just the process.

Finally, quality, as culture, recognizes the importance of organizational view of quality as a process of transformation, where each entity is concerned and acknowledges the importance of quality. In this context it is apt to quote Barrnet (2010):

> ...a high evaluation accorded to an educative process, where it has been demonstrated that, though the process, the students' education development has been enhanced...not only have they achieved the particular objectives set for the course but, in doing so, they have also fulfilled the general education aims of autonomy of the ability to participate in reasoned discourse, of critical self-evaluation, and of coming to a proper awareness of the ultimate contingency of all thought and action." (p. 61)

Harvey and Green (1993) identify four parameters for quality:

1. Quality as excellence which aims at providing the best teaching;
2. Quality as value for money focusing on satisfying the demands of the customers;
3. Quality as fitness for purpose aiming at accomplishing goals; and

4. Quality as transforming which attempts to make students apply the knowledge.

Quality of higher education can be determined based on five interrelated dimensions, as put forth by Harvey and Knight:

1. Quality as *exceptional*, implying that quality of higher education should be determined by high standards;
2. Quality as *consistency*, meaning that quality of higher education lies in providing coherent and compatible knowledge transforming students into skilled and competent graduates who can effectively perform in the world. The authors more commonly call it as "zero defects";
3. Quality as *fitness for purpose*, implying that quality education is reached when the knowledge provided fulfils the purpose, i.e. the goals and expectations of both internal and external parties are met;
4. Quality as *value for money*, focussing on the stakeholders involved benefiting from return on investment, i.e. they should get the value for the money they have invested; and
5. Quality as *transformative*, whereby quality should be dynamic and adaptable ensuring that the students are able to apply the knowledge and be transformed into skilled individuals (Harvey & Knight, 1996).

From the forgoing, one would realize that the concept of quality is amorphous and contextual. It ranges from meaning 'standard' to 'excellence'. It is a set of elements which is a combination of input, process and output in terms of education which seeks in satisfying the stakeholders by theirs services.

Higher Education: Objectives

In interpreting and understanding the idea of quality in higher education, a preliminary definition of higher education and its objectives may be imperative. Ronald Barnett (1992) included the following in his understanding of the objectives of Higher Education:

1. *Higher education as the means for the production of qualified human resources:* In this view, higher education

is seen as a process in which the students are counted as "products" absorbed in the labour market. Thus, higher education becomes an input to the growth and development of business and industry.

2. *Higher education as training for a research career:* In this view, higher education prepares qualified scientists and researchers who would continuously develop the frontiers of knowledge. Quality within this viewpoint is more about research publications and transmission of the academic rigour to do quality research.
3. *Higher education as the efficient management of teaching provision:* Many strongly believe that teaching is the core of educational institutions. Thus, higher education institutions focus on efficient management of teaching-learning provisions by improving the quality of teaching, enabling a higher completion rate among the students.
4. *Higher education as a matter of extending life chances.* In this view, higher education is seen as an opportunity to participate in the development process of the individual through a flexible, continuing education mode (National Assessment and Accreditation Council).

It could be debated whether the notion of higher education as a service is largely the result of a market oriented view, whether it should be solely concerned with supplying labour power to the market or personnel to research. The existing regulatory mechanism too seems to have accepted this definition of quality in higher education, when it concerns itself only with increasing life chances of an individual, equipping him with requisite skills that the market demands. It also could be debated whether the process of managing the teaching-learning process is the primary goal. Such aims of higher education seem to harp on the notion of education as a product and emphasise less on education as a process; a journey. In this context higher education for itself, for knowledge creation, for innovation and for the euphemistic joy of learning are lost sight of.

Direct and Indirect Stakeholders and Varying Perceptions of Quality

It is possible to identify two categories of stakeholders in higher education: direct stakeholders, who include students, facilitators and administrators. The indirect stakeholders would include the alumni, industry, and policy-makers. To each category the objective of education is different in the larger context of the society, the polity and even posterity and hence their interpretation of what constitutes quality in higher education in a globalised world is varied. Tam (2001) found that all stakeholders hold their own view of what quality in education means to them. There is a lack of correlation between the main stakeholders' views of quality in higher education (Telford and Masson, 2005). Many of these interpretations were closely associated with the market notion of quality in a globalized world; others went beyond what is normally understood as quality.

Students

Students are the most important stakeholders of higher education along with faculty, administration, educational institutions, parents and government. However, there is hardly any systematic study on what the students regard as quality, nor has there been a significant assessment of whether there is a correlation between the needs of the students and what is supplied to them by the market.

Students, both in the private and public institutions, have a consumerist ethos towards higher education, wanting 'value-for-money'. It is the reputation of the institution that becomes fundamental in the students' choice of institutions in a marketized environment. The reputation of an institution is tangibly seen in terms quality of the faculty: The knowledge of the teachers (both their own and what they bring to the class), their experience and the accessibility of the faculty to the students and infrastructural resources, such as library and laboratory that are available and abstractly through institutions' investment in students, learning spaces and the educational community.

The primary purpose for students entering higher education is to improve their career prospects and as a means for career enhancement. However, interestingly a large number of students opt for higher education because of low investment and easy availability. Students expect institutions to offer sound knowledge of the discipline, advice and guidance to support them in developing their formal course. The curriculum therefore is of vital importance. They express the need for personalized higher education experience, with small teaching sessions, opportunities to meet other staff and students, acknowledgment of their individual circumstances, which are to be accommodated with flexibility and some degree of authorship over their degree experience. A student's interpretation of quality is associated with several of the requirements of the students:

- Does the education give adequate knowledge?
- Does it have a good faculty?
- Is the course updated and relevant?
- What is the process of learning?
- Is it cost effective? Is it value for money?

Accordingly, the notion of quality includes the following (not necessarily in that order):

- *Faculty*: Adequate in number and with specialization, updated knowledge and approachable;
- *Infrastructure*: Includes classrooms, computer labs, library, books, hostel, transport, canteen facilities, IT infrastructure, etc.; and
- *Ambience*: Created through enough opportunities for extracurricular and co-curricular actives, and placement opportunities.

Faculty

The faculty has multiple roles to play as teachers, researchers and leaders in higher educational institutions. However, in the current educational scenario in India the faculty is often viewed as a commodity, employed on the basis of perceived needs of the institute. The faculty provides students with opportunities for personal growth and presides over the transformation of inputs to outputs of greater value to the institute and to the ultimate customer. Though the faculty forms the institute's true competitive edge, teachers perceive themselves as having very little autonomy, are generally passive contributors, and do nothing beyond what they are told.

The interpretation of quality in higher educational institutions by the faculty is more subjective in terms of their personal and professional requirements in the educational process. It finds tangible form in the opportunities available to them for personal and professional advancement, autonomy and independence from political and administrative forces as well as from organized students, time and resources available to them for research. The faculty's conceptualization of quality therefore includes:

- Availability of opportunities,
- Quality of resource (including students),
- Autonomy and Independence; and
- Rewards.

Not surprisingly, the faculty's interpretation of quality is largely unidimensional. In higher educational institutions that emphasize largely on teaching, the situation is slightly different and herein the faculty's interpretation of quality coincides with that of parents.

Administrators

From the stand point of administrators, quality is a process oriented and involving smooth conduct of academic exercise. This would involve:

- Well laid out procedures,
- Clarity of rules,
- Non-interference,
- Autonomy, and
- Resources (Funds) for students and faculty.

Administrators confine themselves to increasing the strength and reputation of the institutions. Liaison between the highest level of management, faculty and students remain the top most priority of the administrators. Faculty is perceived as agents and association with industry is highly prioritized to the exclusion of faculty and students.

Industry

Industry is the most important determiner of the nature and quality of higher education. In a market economy where the objective of higher education is creation of opportunities, the industry provides the framework for the educational system. Thus, the course structure, curriculum and nature of skills to be imparted are all based on the needs of the industry. The industry recognizes that by the time a student arrives at the workplace it is too late to make any corrections. Unlearning and relearning both become difficult and require additional time, energy, materials, and human efforts. Errors can be prevented and wastage can be eliminated by improving the educational and training process. Further, the industry receives educated and trained manpower without any significant investment of its own in the process. In its conceptualization of quality, industry takes into account:

- Skills
- Attitude
- Knowledge
- Discipline

In the industry's estimation, quality is determined by the quality of:

- Faculty
- Nature of curriculum
- Interface with industry
- Quality of pass outs

This would require a standardized syllabus aligned to the needs of the current market and technology. It would also involve adequate exposure to extracurricular and non-curricular activities which involve application of knowledge, inculcation of scientific and market oriented values and attitudes (PRS India, 2011). Hence, industry's conceptualization varies from that of the faculty, administrators or students/parents. It is not surprising that the regulatory agencies, especially in the post-liberalization period have focused on skill development, training and liaison with industry as major parameters for assessing the quality of education.

Existing Parameters for Assessing Quality: What They Look for?

Aligning quality to the needs of each of the stakeholders is a difficult, though not impossible, task. However, it is possible to identify the elements that are central to quality. These would include:

- Curriculum
- Teaching–learning Process
- Attitudinal Issues
- Resource and Administrative Concerns

The faculty, the administration and to some extent even the industry believe that quality measures should be implemented in the educational institution. Hence, there is little challenge as far as the focus on the quality is concerned. However, the process suffers because of the considerably different perceptions about how to implement quality.

The approach of the UGC is clear: Quality and excellence in higher education are not activities, but are products of an environment which has to be built bit by bit and at all levels. The UGC recognizes that quality in higher education hinges on (a) physical infrastructure, (b) number and quality of teachers, and (c) academic governance in universities and colleges. Furthermore, the UGC has, under the Eleventh Plan, put in place a manifold strategy: Sensitize institutions on quality and excellence, support them to evolve institutional arrangements for the purpose, provide institutional arrangement at the apex level for their periodical assessment and accreditation, and make development grants contingent upon their being assessed and accredited. Towards improving quality and promotion of excellence in higher education, the UGC strategy under the Eleventh Plan has been: (a) General development grants with a substantial allocation for improving the infrastructure in universities and colleges; (b) New initiatives; and (c) Strengthening of State Universities and college sector.

In addition to the UGC and AICTE which are among the most important multiple agencies regulating higher educational institutions in India, the notion of accreditation has been first mooted since, the late 1980s. Accreditation in India owes its origin to the National Policy on Education (NPE) and the Programme of Action of 1986. As a follow-up of the recommendations, the National Assessment and Accreditation Council (NAAC) was established on September 16, 1994 as an autonomous body of the UGC. The NAAC assesses and accredits institutions of higher learning on the basis of the following key criteria:

1. Curricular aspects,

2. Teaching-Learning and Evaluation,
3. Research, Consultancy and Extension,
4. Infrastructure and learning resources,
5. Student support and progression,
6. Governance, Leadership and Management, and
7. Innovations and best practices.

The above criteria are further divided into "Key Aspects." Certain important Assessment Indicators are identified under the Key Aspects and the Seven Criteria which encompasses them, as probes or leads for the Peer Team members to capture the micro-level quality parameters. These indicators facilitate the computing of the Key Aspect-wise Grade Points (KA-GPS) and the Criterion-wise Grade Point Averages (CR-GPAs) in order to arrive at the quality status of the institutions.

In Lieu of a Conclusion

It would appear from the foregoing discussion that the objectives of higher education are determined by the market. The management-oriented definition of quality which regards education as a commodity, the educational institution as the service provider and the students as the consumer, has been accepted by all the stake holders in the process, notwithstanding their divergent stakes in the process and their varied requirements from it. Such alternations tuned into the system have raised many questions on the very idea of the role and scope of higher educational institutions in general and on 'quality' in particular. In the existing scenario the ability of higher education to meet the utilitarian requirements of supplying trained manpower to the industry assumes primary significance and the entire system and its stakeholders seem to be geared to it. It follows therefore that the notion of what constitutes quality in higher education is also market determined.

Apart from the fact that the entire discourse on quality in higher education is aligned to the global market, the access to higher education is also market driven. Private educational institutions, mostly imparting technical education, with often high fee structure, limit the access of education to a large section, while increasing choices and chances for some. That this 'some' constitutes a large number in the population in a populous country with large appetite for education makes it a lucrative investment opportunity.

The only regulation comes from the state and the state-led regulating agencies. The regulation agencies too, as discussed, have responded to the requirements of the globalized market and focussed on skill based education, technical education and interface with industry—important categories in assessment. This indicates a synergy of state, educational institutions and students at one level; it reduces the autonomy of education. Education from the time of independence till 1990s was based on social consensus providing access and opportunities, a political aspect in creating awareness and raising overall level of education, and an economic aspect in resource development. This consensus has now broken down due to a greater emphasis on the need for higher education to respond to the needs of the industry.

However, within this narrow framework there have been demands, especially from the students, to re-interpret the purpose and goals of higher education. This finds reflection in the desire of stakeholders to redefine what constitutes quality in the Teaching-Learning Process. Students favour institutions, private and public, which have invested in rigorous teaching-learning process. Within the framework of this, there appears to be an increasing move towards intensive guided learning and self-learning, knowledge creation, and autonomy.

Interestingly, autonomy has been interpreted as autonomy in the choice of courses, learning methods, and assessment methods as well as autonomy from market demands. There is an increasing desire to move away from the model of knowledge transfer to knowledge creation and from knowledge creation to knowledge autonomy. The challenge to the established educational system as well as its market oriented interpretation of quality in the globalised world is coming from the student community. While this is process is still in its infancy it may still be the beginning of a move towards establishing the autonomy of knowledge seeker.

REFERENCES

Altbach, Philip G. (2002), *"The Private Sector in Asian Higher Education"*, Centre for International Higher Education, Boston College, Fall Sense Publishers, Rotterdam and Taipei.

Altbach, Philip G., and Yoshikazu Ogawa (Eds.) 2002, Higher Education in Japan: Reform and Change in the 21st Century. Also published as a Special Theme Issue of Higher Education 43(1), January.

Asha Tewari, *Implementing Quality in Higher Education*, http://www.qcin.org/nbqp/qualityindia/Vol-2-No2/specialreport.htm

Barnett, R. (1992), *Improving Higher Education: Total Quality Care,* Society for Research into Higher Education Ltd., Buckingham: Open University Press.

Cheong, Y.C. and Tam, W.M. (1997), Multi-models of quality in education. *Quality Assurance in Education*, Vol. 5, No. 1, pp. 22–23 (on line Emeraldinsight.com)

Government of India, (1988), *BIS Quality system vocabulary. ISI 14000 quality system: Guidelines for selection and use of standards on quality system,* New Delhi: Bureau of Indian Standards.

Government of India, University Grants Commission. (Available at http://www.ugc.ac.in/)

Gupta, Asha (2005), International Trends in Higher Education and the Indian Scenario Centre for Studies in Higher Education, University of California at Berkeley, *Research and Occasional Chapter Series*, 11-05, 2005, pp. 1-35.

Harvey, L. and Green, D. (1993), Defining 'quality,' *Assessment and Evaluation in Higher Education,* Vol. 18, No. 1, pp. 9-34.

Higher Education in India: Strategies and Schemes during Eleventh, Plan Period (2007-2012) for Universities and Colleges, New Delhi, January 2011.

Jayaram, N. (2004), Higher Education in India: Massification and Change, in Altbach, P. and Toru Umaakoshi (Eds.) *Asian Universities: Historical Perspectives and Contemporary Changes*, p. 91, Baltimore and London: John Hopkins University Press.

Mishra, S. (2002), Guest Editorial: Does technology advancement mean better Education? *Media and Technology for Human Resource Development, 2002-2003,* Vol. 14, Nos. 1 and 2, pp. v-viii.

Mishra, Sanjaya (2006) *Models and Practices Widely Used in the Context of Quality Assurance in Higher Education.*

Mukhopadhyay, M. (2005), *Total Quality Management in Education,* (2nd Ed.) New Delhi: Sage Publications.

Nigvekar, A.S. 1996, Quality Assurance in Higher Education: An Indian Dilemma, in *Journal of Higher Education,* Vol. 19, No. 3, pp. 353-64.

On the Internet. Available at http://www.prsindia.org/billtrack/the-national-accreditation-regulatory-authority-for-higher-educational-institutions-bill-2010-1140/ accessed on July 30, 2013.

Peffer, N. and Coote, A. (1991), *Is Quality Good for you? A critical review of quality assurance in the welfare services,* London: Institute of Public Policy Research.

Pirsig, R.M. (1974), *Zen and the Art of Motorcycle Maintenance*, New York: Vintage.

Reeves, C.A. and Bedner, D.A., 2011, Defining quality: Alternatives and implications, *Academy of Management Review,* Vol. 19, No. 3, pp. 419-45.

Rizvi, Fazal and Radhika Gorur, 2011, *Challenges Facing Indian Higher Education in India,* Occasional chapters, Australia India Institute, Melbourne, Volume 2, Winter.

Tilak, J.B.G. (2013), *Higher Education in India: In Search of Equality, Quality and Quantity,* New Delhi: Orient Black Swan.

16

Impact of Globalization in the Life and Livelihood of the Poor

G. PALANITHURAI

Introduction

Globalization, decentralization and democratization (democracy promotion) are the three very big movements initiated in the world simultaneously. They are dynamic and produced series of consequences, both intended and unintended, in the lives of the people and more particularly in the life and livelihood of the poor. Any event in the world will produce both negative and positive impacts in the life of the people. To make any event to produce positive consequences and to arrest negative impact, human beings have to work through knowledge and governance. Globalization, democratization and decentralization have several promises to the poor and the marginalized human collectives. How to make all those movements to produce the intended consequences for the benefit of the poor is a daunting question in the minds of the knowledge community who has a concern for the poor.[1] The answer lies in governance; that too democratic participatory governance. In a multi ethnic, diverse society with extreme disparities and differences, establishing fair democratic participatory governance is a challenging task. On the issues of globalization the world is divided into pro-globalization defenders and anti-globalization protesters.[2] In the beginning, arguments were projected without a strong evidence base as to how people were arguing that globalization had produced negative effects. Market works only through the policies of the Government.

In a democracy policies and decisions are taken only through a process of consultation and debates in authoritative bodies. Globalization works through government by policies, programmes, reforms, laws and regulations of the state. Hence, it is not only a subject of market, but also subject of political democracy.[3] Globalization has got a tendency to impact both negatively and positively and it has the potential to do harm to the poor and environment.[4] But while governing globalization through a process of democracy and democratic decentralization, positive results could be delivered to the benefit of the poor. Handling all the three movements by the state requires perspective, understanding and strategies as it happens in a democratically governing country. People are being mobilised fast and politically on events and issues. Issues are being brought before the people both by print and electronic media. Despite many limitations, Indian democracy provides enough scope for mobilising people either to support or to oppose the state based on decisions, policies and resource allocation. If the political class is really interested in finding solution for the problems of the poor, it could be done through a democratic process.

Against this background, all these movements take place in the country. Protest against globalization is visible and louder but support for decentralization and democracy is also visible and louder and yet one is unable to see much progress in decentralization, but at the same time fast initiatives are on to promote globalization activities. It is a perplexing question in Indian politics and it is in this backdrop that how globalization and democratic decentralization would work for the poor is a major issue to be investigated. Globalization and democratic decentralization have been working in the Indian society for the past two decades very intensively. To make statements either in favour or against globalization or decentralization, we need evidence.

Hence, an attempt was made to study the impact of globalization in the life and livelihood of the poor. To conduct this study Tamil Nadu was chosen as a field for not only investigation, but also for intervention as we do action research. It is because Tamil Nadu has evinced keen interest in operationalising globalization and decentralization fast and simultaneously.[5] It is to be noted here that Tamil Nadu is regarded a well-placed state in terms of achieving development more specifically in social development sector and thereby it is in the 4th place in Human Development Index among 15 major states in India.[6]

Against the above background, an empirical investigation was planned as more and more of rhetoric on globalization—both positive and negative-appeared in the media. Many of them were drawn from case studies and micro-analysis.

Issues Investigated

This investigation has the following basic objectives:

(a) studying the implications of economic globalization on the livelihood security of the poor which have come up with the backing of the mediated policies and programmes of the State Government;
(b) identifying opportunities for the poor, if any, from globalization and to initiate an action plan for better utilization of such opportunities;
(c) identifying threats, if any, from globalization and to initiate action plan to avoid them or to mitigate them through local governance;
(d) establishing effective models of governance for Panchayati Raj Institutions to address the challenges brought about by globalization process to protect the livelihood security and to promote the interest of the rural sectors; and
(e) initiating a dialogue among different stakeholders especially with the leaders of local governments and policy-makers at the state government level to establish effective governance to tackle globalization.

To carry out this research the following sectors were selected: (a) water resources and services, (b) river sand mining, (c) agriculture, (d) food security, (c) plantation sectors, (f) rural artisans, (g) Dalits, (h) rural health, (i) public distribution system, (j) special economic zone, (k) Mahatma Gandhi National Employment Guarantee Act Scheme, and (l) handloom weavers.

It was decided to investigate all the above sectors as problems have been reported in the media. Credible media reports were kept in view while taking a decision to conduct the investigation in these sectors. The investigation was conducted in the rural areas of Tamil Nadu with an unbiased manner and based on the perspective of the Institute.

Methodology

It was decided to adopt a different approach in research methodology to investigate the problem and collect data from the field for analysis. A combination of methods and tools has been adopted for this study. Some of them are conventional and others based on improvisation of new methods to suit the requirement. The research exercise was started only based on newspaper reports. Active media brought to light the problems emerging from globalization. The stories reported were considered as issues and the areas from which such stories were reported were taken up for investigation. In research methodology this approach is known as emperico-inductive approach. It contrasts sharply with conventional social science research hypothesis testing approach. It sharply focuses on the livelihood of the poor. Variables that are malleable to rural livelihoods and globalization process were taken up for analysis. Hence, the research process has had a bearing on certain normative values of society such as equity, accountability and sustainability. The study has used a combination of methods, both quantitative and qualitative. The whole exercise was undertaken with a set of pre-designed questions based on theories of globalization and decentralization. Methodological nuances varied from issue to issue. Nature of the issue decides the mode of investigation and nuances and tools of data collection. Besides extensive field work, intensive interviews were conducted with opinion makers and policy-makers. In this study we have extensively used the secondary data drawn from various sources and more particularly the Government Departments.

Results of the Studies[7]

Following are the summary of findings and conclusions drawn from the research reports on the issues selected for investigation.

- It is found out that water has becomes a tradable commodity and thereby companies have entered into the market for water trade.
- Such trade in water takes place at the cost of the common man.
- It has done harm to the environment and the natural resources are depleted, thus affecting the resource base of the communities.

- The companies have maintained accountability to their shareholders. Ignoring the interest of the stakeholders.
- By using intensive technologies, water has been taken from different sources by the companies without considering the deep and long term implications.
- Companies are driven by profit and not by social ethics.
- Water is a public property but now it works for private profit.
- Natural resources are in peril because the market forces are exploiting natural resources.
- While it is a fact that laws and policies exist for protecting the common and natural resources in Tamil Nadu, natural resources are being exploited relentlessly for private profit.
- There is resistance and intimidation by the stakeholders, but the state's role on these issues is minimal.
- It has been noticed that the state has proactively supported the market initiatives by negating the voices of the poor.
- While establishing companies in the rural areas helps the economic development, the implications of the activities of the companies have been causing havoc in the community.

It is to be understood in this context that the state is fully aware of the implications, but yet has been allowing the entry of companies in the water trade. Resistance and protest from the people surfaces only after they realise and understand the real implications to their lives. But, the State continues to protect the companies however bad they are in their activities. Even violations of the contract provisions are not viewed as a serious issue by the state. Neither the companies exploiting the water resources have been providing employment to the rural poor nor protecting the livelihood of the poor. One could not see any market ethics in this commercialization process. On the other hand ordinary people have been oriented to change their attitude and behaviour towards the use of bottled water as we see in the west. Rural populace including the poor have joined the market as a water consumer. As marketization of water is on, we found in the villages the waste emanating from selling of bottled water. If a realistic analysis is done one could see the reason for all such activities. The local bodies are not in governance. They are considered as the implementing agencies of the government schemes and programmes. The local bodies are involved in service provision. They are not involved in micro-level planning. Further, the local bodies are not effectively trained on environmental management. Local body leaders are unaware of the link between environment and poverty. The weak conditions of the local bodies are being exploited by the water companies.

In Tamil Nadu, agriculture has also been commercialised and has undergone a significant change. Farming as a way of life is disappearing and "agri-business" is taking its place as a result of liberalised policies of the government in the agricultural sector. Thus, agriculture sector becomes vulnerable to external shocks and there is no policy mechanism to face the shock from external forces. Agriculture productivity has increased but profits have drastically reduced as the cost of inputs has increased enormously while the output price is subjected to the global market prices.

In the meanwhile, under the 11th plan, the Government of India decided to change the farm practices with a view to increasing productivity and profitability. This resulted in the throwing out of unskilled labourers from agriculture, as they were unsuited for the new methods of farming. The idea was to reduce the labour force by infusing technology into the farm practices. After the introduction of MGNREGA, farming has undergone a change and large machinery has been used in farming operations. Since, there is no labour budgeting the scheme has affected the farm operation. A new set of farmers originating from the IT sector have come to be involved in farming; both in agriculture and establishing marketing mechanism for the produce, with the sole aim of making profits. They are not traditional farmers. But it is to be noted here that area of cultivation has decreased.

Food security has been fairly achieved in Tamil Nadu. It may be recalled that rice shortages in the State in 1967 resulted in Congress Party losing power in favour of the DMK. Since then, the State Government has focussed its attention on food security. All structures, institutions and policies are in place to ensure food security to the people; more specifically to the poor. The State's poor are conscious and active in defending their entitlements. They are sensitive over certain services provided by the state government and agitate against the State when they are not getting all such services. Of the issues PDS is one.[8]

Besides agriculturists, rural artisans have lost their livelihood and they have lost their values. They have been excluded in the process of development. Their condition has worsened as sufficient protective measures have not been put in place. Rural artisans who were engaged in competitive commercial ventures were able to face any external shocks. Their continuous skill-upgradation enabled them to face the competition. But, traditional artisans are in deep crises. As there is no system in place to upgrade their skills in making their products, they are in distress. Besides the government, even the community has lost its affinity towards rural artefacts because of a change in their behaviour towards urban culture and consumerism. Even the rural communities have become aggressive consumers.

The handloom sector is yet another area affected by globalization. The handloom sector had offered lot of opportunities for profitable employment to the rural population so that they could improve their per capita income. Having become steeped in crisis, the handloom sector is no longer in a position to generate jobs. Similarly, the fishing community is yet another segment affected by globalization.

One could see opportunities in every aspect of globalization. But to make use of such opportunities arrays of steps are needed from policy-makers to the local bodies. In ushering in globalization, absolutely enabling conditions have not been created. At one level one could see the poor capacity of the policy-makers to tackle the issues through policies. Equally, the local bodies are clueless as how to help the rural poor in the context of globalization. An analysis of the field reality shows that the poor are not deriving any benefit from globalization. Globalization has systems, institutions, frameworks, regulations and approaches to allow unlimited economic activities and flow of goods and services across the world. In order to allow the new practices, existing governance regulations have been changed. While reforming governance and administration to suit the requirements of the market, it is imperative on the part of the state to find ways and means to reform governance practices and processes to enable the poor to get advantage out of globalization. The question is how to do it? It has been witnessed in the past twenty years that laws have been identified which are acting as hurdles for the promotion of big businesses which need to be amended and/or abrogated. Together more than five thousand such laws have been identified both at the Central and State Government levels. Steps are on to amend them or repeal them altogether.

There are laws which are against the process of decentralization of powers and empowerment of poor both at the Central and State

Government levels, but there is no initiative at the State Government level or Central Government level to remove them or to amend them. The Second Administrative Reforms Commission report contained a modicum of recommendations to both Central and State Governments to reform governance at the local level. But, till date no action has been taken on the recommendations either by the State Governments or by the Central Government. Hence, decentralization efforts have produced more unintended consequences. Despite all the drawbacks and obstacles, the local bodies have been delivering services. Women and Dalit segments have started asserting themselves and claiming their entitlements without fear. In this process one would notice the reduction of corruption; but the number of people involved in corruption has increased. In the same way, paradoxically, the per capita bribe has increased and per capita tax has reduced. In the absence of empowerment, the capacity of local bodies is poor in terms of governance. Local bodies have to perform four functions viz., governance, planning from below for economic development, administering social justice and democratising the communities. The local bodies are unable to perform these core functions. That is why we see lot of unintended consequences from the local bodies.

The special economic zone (SEZ) is intended to promote industrial corridors and technology parks. The SEZ are wiping out local livelihood resources and edging the poor land holders virtually to the margin. It has loosened their traditional strongholds. There is yet another interesting finding that emerges from research about the conditions of Dalits in Tamil Nadu. Globalization has helped the Dalits indirectly or inadvertently in some respects. Slowly the Dalits have been acquiring lands. Land gives recognition and identity in the rural areas. When many farmers found that farming was not a profitable proposition, they started selling their lands. These lands are being purchased by the Dalits. Yet they could not make any profit out of it. The social safety nets and domestic reform measures carried out in various sectors have helped the Dalits to remain protected by the possible damage that the market forces could exert on the poor in general and Dalits in particular. One could see the transfer of land to Dalits. The level of their assertion over their rights is increasing.[9] Newer technologies have transformed their life. Yet the discriminatory practices against them in the rural areas have not reduced.[10]

The above observations and findings have prompted us to work on this issue as the Rajiv Gandhi Chair for Panchayati Raj Studies is committed to action oriented research to find solutions for many of the problems. The chair is involved in a series of activities not only to strengthen the rural local government but also to enable the system to work for the poor and marginalized.[11] In fact, the chair has been created with the objective of strengthening rural local government and work for the empowerment of the poor.

Managing Globalization

Decentralization is an opportunity to empower the poor and to avoid threats from globalization. The success depends on the process of governance.[12] Decentralization is viewed from two perspectives. One, it is antithetical to globalization and secondly it is complementary to globalization. Whether it is contradictory and complementary depends on the use of both by the human collectives. Globalization has to be managed and mediated to deliver goods for the poor. Hence, as a part of the action project, a training module has been prepared to conduct training programme for Panchayati leaders to manage globalization.[13] It has been a highly professional task. Hence, a training programme was designed for the Gram Panchayat leaders. The training module and manual have been prepared and published. An orientation training programme has been given to civil society organizations to conduct training programme for the rural local body leaders in their areas.

Local body leaders have been drawn from many districts; particularly from the areas affected because of globalization. In the training programmes lasting for five days, awareness is created on the available legal and programmatic opportunities to enable the poor to make use of the opportunities and effectively prevent the threats and negative effects of globalization. Further, they are also told as to how they could get support of the civil society organizations. Periodical refresher courses have been organised for the village Panchayat leaders who have been facing a series of problems because of the market forces involved in trade activities in the rural areas and exploiting natural resources. The Rajiv Gandhi Chair has started acting as a resource agency to give hands-on support to the Gram Panchayats and communities to overcome the problems they face in Panchayat governance and administration. Series of operational guides have been prepared for the use of Gram Panchayat leaders to protect the natural resources and to track the resources flowing from Central Government to local bodies through State Government. They have also been told as to how they could safeguard their rights and make use of the Right to Information Act. All the operational guides have been published and distributed to different stakeholders through civil society organizations.

Functioning of all the village Panchayats has been monitored and necessary support extended to enable them to manage the fall-out of globalization. After a period of time, the whole process of tackling globalization has been captured and documented. Many of the Gram Panchayats emerged successful and become models for others.[14] Rajiv Gandhi Chair for Panchayati Raj Studies has adopted two pronged approach while conducting action research on "Globalization and Decentralization". One, doing policy advocacy, after carrying out field studies and preparing report a validation workshop was organised. The concerned Minister and the Secretary, along with other higher officials were invited to these workshops with a view to ascertaining their opinion on the findings of the study and their inputs and suggestions for acting on the issues.[15] Second, disseminating the findings to the people through media and preparing the civil society organizations to work with the Panchayats in managing globalization by publishing a periodical newsletter "Global and Local."[16] In the whole exercise, one could see the proactive nature of the state towards globalization. Not only the state but also the intellectuals who guide the policy-makers had only 'growth' in their vision and not environmental protection or safeguarding the interest of the poor.[17] There was reluctance on the part of the State to work for the poor despite the pressure exerted on the state by the civil society organizations.

Conclusion

The present study has brought to light the implications of globalization in the lives and livelihood of the poor in Tamil Nadu based on field studies and analysis of the field reality through this research project. Globalization is best understood by those who are in an advantageous position in the market, society and state. Hence, they work vigorously for pushing globalization to work fast as they derive huge benefits. All their activities are in silent mode despite noisy resistance from the anti-globalization forces. Decentralization and democratization provide enormous scope for the poor to empower themselves to avoid any threats and use them for the benefit of the poor. But the poor have not been able to understand the best opportunities of decentralization despite the best efforts of the civil society organizations and the media. The political parties and the intellectual classes supposed to work for the transformation of the poor have not adopted strategic approach to enable the poor to take advantage of decentralization. It is because of this reason that the poor cannot make use of democracy and decentralization and as a result they could not claim any benefits out of globalization. When local body leaders are trained in managing globalization and supported institutionally, Panchayats can overcome threats. This is demonstrated unequivocally through the action research project. To get benefits out of globalization and decentralization, series of steps are needed from the federal government to local government. As we find loopholes at every level, it is only by working with local bodies that threats of globalization could be avoided. It is in this context that the support of civil society organization is an imperative need.

REFERENCES

1. Joseph E. Stiglitz, (2006), *Making Globalization Work,* New Delhi: Penguin Books; James Manor (1999), *Political Economy of Decentralization,* Washington DC: The World Bank; Krishna Kant, (2003), Inaugural Address in the National Seminar on "Impact of Liberalization and Globalization on Rural Livelihoods" organised by National Institute of Rural Development, Hyderabad; and G. Palanithurai, (2001), *Towards Decentralization of Powers*, Gandhigram Rajiv Gandhi Chair for Panchayati Raj Studies,
2. Chanda, Nayan, 2002, Coming Together: Globalization means reconnecting the human community, in *Yale Global Online Magazine*, November.
3. Nayar, Deepak (Ed.) (2002), *Governing Globalization Issues and Institutions,* New Delhi: Oxford University Publications.
4. Bhagwati, Jagdish, (2004), *In Defence of Globalization,* New Delhi: Oxford University Press; Ha-Joon Chang, (2008), *Bad Samaritans: The Myth of Free Trade and the Secret History of Capitalism*, London: Bloomsbury Press.
5. *Business Line*, "Tamil Nadu plans to Move IT into Small Cities and Towns", 29th July, 2006.
6. Government of Tamil Nadu, *Human Development Index 2001,* Chennai.

7. Palanithurai, G. and R. Ramesh, (2008), *Globalization: Issues at the Grassroots,* New Delhi Concept Publishing Company (P) Ltd.; G. Palanithurai and R. Ramesh, 2011. *Globalization and Rural Development,* New Delhi: Concept Publishing Company (P) Ltd.
8. *Citizen's Audit of Basic Services in Tamil Nadu,* (2008), Chennai: The Catalyst Trust.
9. Manor, James. (2011), "Local Governance" in Niraja Gopal Jayal and Pratap Bhanu Mehta (Eds.) *The Oxford Companion to Politics in India,* pp. 61-79, New Delhi: Oxford University Press.
10. Palanithurai, G. (2013), *Dalits and Dalit Representatives in Rural Local Governance,* New Delhi: Concept Publishing Company (P) Ltd.
11. *A Decade of Experience in Decentralization* (2007), Gandhigram: Rajiv Gandhi Chair for Panchayati Raj Studies.
12. Werlin, Herbert H., 2003, Poor Nations, Rich Nations: A Theory of Governance" in *Public Administration Review,* Vol. 63, No. 3, May-June, pp. 329-42.
13. Palanithurai, G. and R. Ramesh, (2007), *Actionable Learning Handbook for Local Self Government: Globalization and Decentralization,* Gandhigram, Rajiv Gandhi Chair for Panchayati Raj Studies.
14. Palanithurai, G. (2009), *How Some Panchayats Become Model?* Gandhigram: Rajiv Gandhi Chair for Panchayati Raj Studies.
15. *Validation Report: Report of the Validation Workshop on Globalization and Decentralization* (2009), Gandhigram: Rajiv Gandhi Chair for Panchayati Raj Studies.
16. Rajiv Gandhi Chair, "Addressing Globalization", *Global and Local,* Gandhigram: Rajiv Gandhi Chair for Panchayati Raj Studies, No. 8, January-February, 2007.
17. Palanithurai, G. and R. Ramesh, (2009), *State Points on Globalization and Decentralization,* pp. 14-16, New Delhi: Concept Publishing Company, (P) Ltd.

Note: This chapter is prepared from the Reports submitted to the Ford Foundation on the Project Globalization and Decentralization supported by the Ford Foundation, New Delhi. The author profusely thanks the Ford Foundation, New Delhi for its generous grant to conduct studies in Tamil Nadu on Globalization and Decentralization.

17

Globalization, Inequality and Violence in India

TEJ PRATAP SINGH

Globalization is a multi-layered process impacting economy, society, polity, religion, culture, etc. Globalization refers to global integration of economy, society and polity due to drastic fall in the cost of transportation and communication, transforming the world into a global village. Globalization has been defined as unhindered movement of goods, services, capital and technology but not labour. Intergovernmental organizations such as IMF, World Bank, WTO and MNCs have played key role in the spread of globalization. Globalization is not a new phenomenon. Since time immemorial, the process of interconnectedness and getting closer of different communities cutting across the cultural, ethnic, social and geographical boundaries has been underway, but the term globalization is usually associated with the process of interconnectedness unleashed by the end of cold war bipolar world and disintegration of Soviet Union. Globalization in contemporary world politics refers to post-Soviet, post-Communist unipolar world of post-1990s.

Globalization is twin edged sword. It has benefitted many states, communities and adversely impacted many others. If East Asia has benefitted from it then Africa has suffered a lot. If it has pulled millions of people out of poverty, it is also alleged to have pushed millions into misery and poverty. Globalization has sharply divided intellectual community. If Jagdish Bhagwati writes in defence of globalization, Joseph Stieglitz finds discontents in it. Friedrich Hayekand Milton Freedman support unrestricted globalization, but neo-Keynesians such as John Rawls, Amartya Sen, and Paul Krugman argue regulation of globalization to mitigate the rigours of globalization. Thus, achievement of globalization has been mixed. However, globalization is unavoidable in the contemporary world.

In India, advent of globalization has coincided with many events, which reshaped Indian polity, society and economy. First, advent of globalization in India coincided with the advent of fractured mandate leading to coalition politics and resultant political instability. Extension of policies of affirmative action culminated in the implementation of Mandal Commission Report, which ushered in an era of identity politics, which further reinforced the caste identity and led to further churning of caste politics, manifesting itself into sharp polarisation of castes. This generated the fear of further fragmentation of already deeply divided Hindu religious community into various castes. Menace of Mandal politics to Hindu religious community was countered by *Kamandal* politics articulated through Ram Janmabhoomi movement led by Vishwa Hindu Parishad and Bharatiya Janata Party, which culminated into Rath Yatra and eventual demolition of Babri mosque. This triggered sharp reaction from the Muslim community resulting in communal violence throughout the country. Competitive caste and communal politics unleashed by the pursuit of *Mandal-Kamandal* politics led to deep social, cultural and religious divisions and social instability. Thirdly, volatile polity and sharply divided society coincided with unstable economy. Failure of Nehruvian model of development manifested in the licence-permit *raj* led to loss of global trust in India's development story and withdrawal of money by foreign investors leading to severe foreign exchange reserve crisis and the prospect of default by India. Chaos and turmoil in the Indian economy forced the government led by the then Prime Minister Narasimha Rao and his finance minister Dr. Manmohan Singh to usher in economic reforms under the aegis of IMF and World Bank, popularly known as Structural Adjustment Programme. This is the politico-socio-economic background of globalization in India.

Economic reforms led to stability in the economy and put Indian economy once again on the growth trajectory. Liberalization, privatization and stabilization in the economy under the ideology of globalization brought rich dividends to Indian economy. But growth registered under globalization was uneven, benefitting only a small section of already well-off Indian society and impoverishing the vast majority of Indian population, both rural as well as urban. Shining India competed with the suffering India, further dividing the people on the basis of privileged elites and underprivileged masses. Proponents of globalization claim that rising economy pulled vast masses of people out of poverty. However, this claim is refuted by the critics of globalization. Critics accepted benefits of globalization, but argued that very few benefited at the cost of many others.

Critics of globalization argue that globalization in India and the world at large has resulted in the rich getting richer and poor getting poorer, thereby further increasing the inequality of wealth and opportunity, widening the gap between the rich and the poor. This rising inequality manifested in rising poverty, deprivation, misery has created a situation of helplessness, despair, discontent leading to conflict, violence and insurgency.

We propose to explore the connection between globalization, inequality and violence. All three are connected and are mutually reinforcing each other. All three conflict zones in India viz., separatist religious insurgency in Kashmir, ethnic conflict in the Northeast and left wing extremism in the so-called Red Corridor in Central India, have been impacted by globalization. To be precise, we will focus on revolutionary violence in India, popularly known as Naxalism and Maoism.

There exists close parallel in the introduction of neo-liberal policies through economic reforms and the spurt in revolutionary violence in the vast swath of territory extending from Indo-Nepal border in the north to Telangana-Andhra in the Deep South or in the words of former Home Minister L.K. Advani, from Pashupati to Tirupati.

Causes of Naxalism/Maoism

Left wing extremism (LWE) in India, popularly known as Maoism and Naxalism, has its origins mainly in governance deficit, democratic deficit and development deficit or rather on account of the triple crises of governance, democracy and development. All three deficits and crises are interlinked and form a vicious triangle, which has led to the formation of violence triangle, where the triple deficits/crises trigger apathy among the vast section of society in the midst of hopelessness/helplessness and also violent/aggressive behaviour by the tiny few who take up arms and challenge the whole system created by the state with the tacit and active support of the masses.

Since "state is a human community that (successfully) claims the monopoly of the legitimate use of physical force within a given territory"[1], no state can allow the use of force by the non-state actors (Maoists) in the name of redistribution of wealth or for the abolition of inequality on the basis of any ideology or dogma. The result is the spiral of violence between the state and Maoists, which has spatial and human implications. Both are engaged in a fierce competition to bring more and more geographical terrain and people under their influence and control. Both are engaged in an area domination strategy to wrest the control of more and more geographical territory and win the hearts and minds of people to succeed in the ultimate objective of decimating each other completely. This is basically a political war with political objectives, but fought with military means.

Since, it is an insurgency, spatial factors become secondary to human factor. Rather than wresting the territory from the state, insurgents aim at winning the people to their side. Whoever succeeds in winning the people to their side will also succeed in gaining control of the territory too. It is not a conventional inter-state war, but intra-state unconventional war waged between state and non-state actors (insurgents). It is a low intensity guerrilla war, where combatants are state's own citizens. People are challenging/resisting their own state, which has created a civil war type of situation. Consequently, the state finds its hands tied as it is fighting its own people (citizens). State cannot resort to disproportionate use of force as it will alienate its own people and undermine its legitimacy. It will lead to enormous collateral damage and fuel insurgency further. Till this date, the Indian state has not used its armed forces in its fight against Maoists. Indian armed forces have been used extensively in Kashmir and the Northeast to suppress insurgency. The rationale behind the use of armed forces in these two regions is that they are separatists, whereas Maoists are not. However, the new National Democratic Alliance government led by Narendra Modi is revising the policy of the UPA Government and planning to use armed forces against Maoists.[2]

Neo-liberalism and Maoist Insurgency

There is a direct correlation between the adoption of neo-liberal policies by India in the wake of globalization, liberalization and privatization and the rise of Maoist insurgency in India. Indira Gandhi initiated liberalization process after her return to power in 1980 and the People's War Group formed in 1980 undertook the task of reviving Maoist movement from Telangana region of Andhra Pradesh. As liberalization process accelerated during Rajiv Gandhi's regime, Maoists also began consolidating in Andhra and Bihar. During 1990s with full-fledged embrace of the Washington Consensus and neo-liberal policies under the duo Narasimha Rao-Manmohan Singh, the Maoists also rapidly increased their area of influence.[3]

Globalization, liberalization and privatization led to rapid economic growth, where a tiny section of the population benefitted whereas large sections of the population were excluded from the growth process. The exclusion of the vast number of people from growth process created lot of resentment and discontent amongst the masses swelling the ranks of Maoists. India was divided into 'shining India'.[4] and 'suffering India'[5]. Inequality increased and the gulf between rich and poor widened. During this phase of neo-liberalism, Maoists recorded rapid expansion and spread to one third of the country by the time the architect of neo-liberalism in India Manmohan Singh transited from Finance Ministry to the office of Prime Minister in 2004. While addressing Chief Ministers of Naxal-affected States, on April 13, 2006, Manmohan Singh observed: "it would not be exaggeration to say that the problem of Naxalism is the single biggest internal security challenge ever faced by our country".[6]

With the advent of neo-liberalism, the public sector ceased to enjoy the "commanding heights of the economy"[7] and the role of private sector increased. Disinvestment led to the privatization of public sector enterprises or dilution of state control. Natural resources owned by the state were auctioned or allocated to corporate houses arbitrarily, resulting in an enormous loss to the state exchequer. All this led to ushering in an era of crony capitalism and massive corruption. Instead of protecting the interests of poor people, particularly Adivasis and poor peasants, the State was often perceived to be protecting the interests of corporate houses and thus eroding the faith of poor Adivasis and other marginalized people.

Corporate interest increased in mining and other spheres of the economy. Minerals lie buried in the areas inhabited by the Adivasis. Corporate houses needed large chunks of land for mining and to establish power plants, factories etc. State facilitated the acquisition of land by the corporate houses for mining and industrial purposes in the tribal areas which resulted in the displacement of Adivasis. This was described by a Committee set-up Ministry of Rural Development as "the biggest grab of tribal lands after Columbus."[8] This pitted corporate houses against the Adivasis. Extraction of minerals from tribal areas polluted their water sources, made their land infertile and destroyed their habitats and sources of livelihood resulting in alienation of Adivasis from the state. This provided a fertile ground for the Maoists to exploit the situation to their own advantage. They organised the Adivasis against the state and transformed the tribal areas of India as "the heartland of rebellion."[9]

Theoretical Perspectives

Various theoretical frameworks have been used for understanding and explaining LWE in India. However, most popular among them is the greed and grievance theory.[10] This theory has been developed in binary terms of either-or (either greed or grievance). Greed theory suits the state and grievance theory the insurgents (Maoists). Before going beyond these two theories, it would be pertinent to explain these two theories and their application for the understanding of the Maoist violence.

The Greed theory subscribed by the state postulates that insurgents (Maoists) are a bunch of criminals, who are using ideology as mask to conceal their true criminal face. They use violence to intimidate the people and create an atmosphere of fear. Their ultimate objective is to make money and lead a comfortable life. They develop vested interests in insurgency and want its continuance. Insurgents do not want the end of insurgency as it has become a source of livelihood for them. It is fashionable in insurgency ravaged areas for the youth to pick-up guns and become rebels. Ideology is a smokescreen, which provides legitimacy to their violence in the name of redistribution of wealth and social justice.

State treats the insurgents as hardened criminals and extortionists and LWE as a law and order problem and advocates the use of violence or counter-violence (counter-insurgency) to put an end to insurgency. Indian state is no exception and so from the very beginning of Naxalism in the late 1960s, the state has been resorting to disproportionate use of force to crush Naxalism. Indian state succeeded initially to crush Naxalism in 1970s. With the death of the top Naxal leader and the chief ideologue Charu Majumdar in 1972 in Police custody and killing or arrest of top leaders like Kanu Sanyal, Jangal Santhal, etc. it appeared that the Naxal movement has fizzled out. But since the root causes of Naxalism were not addressed, it bounced back with vengeance in 1980s and since then it has been spreading without any let up. According to the Ministry of Home Affairs data, one third of the country, i.e. more than 220 districts out of 624 districts in India are affected by the Maoism. Out of these, 68 districts are worst affected and for these regions the Government of India has launched Intensive Area Development (IAD) programme to address the issue of development deficits. Since, these regions suffer from security deficits caused by development deficit and so IAD has security component too. IAD has been especially designed to address the issue of LWE.

The rival theory of greed is grievance theory of violence. Insurgents have genuine socio-economic grievances against the society and polity. Since, their grievances have not been addressed satisfactorily by the state, these people have been left with no option but to pick-up arms and rebel against the state. Naxalism/Maoism has provided ideological justification to their armed struggle against the state. Maoists argue that protracted armed struggle is the only way to redress the grievances of impoverished, oppressed and exploited people. Maoism is spreading and deepening only in those regions of the country, which are most backward and poverty stricken. The so-called red-corridor is referred to as compact revolutionary zone (CRZ) by the Maoists, where the Maoists are running or striving to run a parallel government and intend to oust state completely; a state characterised by the triple deficits of governance, development and democracy.

In more than seven decades of Independence, there has been no significant change in the lives of people living in this vast stretch of land extending from Nepal in the north to Andhra in the Deep South. Of late, Maoist violence has been reported in Kerala too. All these areas are forested, hilly and inaccessible and mainly inhabited by the indigenous people, who live a wretched life. Maoists have taken up the grievances of the oppressed people who in the Indian context are mainly Adivasis (indigenous people) and Dalits (lower caste people). These two social groups constitute the main support base of Maoists. The day the state succeeds in winning these two social groups viz. Adivasis and Dalits to its side by addressing their grievances, the Maoist insurgency will come to an end.

Beyond Greed and Grievance

Theoretical framework of greed and grievance for explaining Maoist insurgency is oversimplification of complex issue of Naxalism/ Maoism in India. Both the theories have some elements of truth but both fail to offer satisfactory explanation of Maoist insurgency. Criminalisation has crept into the movement and many criminals have joined the movement, who have nothing to do with ideology justifying the greed theory. This is particularly true in the case of Jharkhand, where dozens of Maoist outfits with different names are primarily extortionists and indulge in all kinds of criminal activities. Most of the splinter groups are basically vigilant groups and indulge in serious human rights abuses. These splinter Maoist groups are engaged in fierce turf war with other splinter groups and the parent party. But to paint all the insurgents with the same brush will be unfair to the ideologically committed insurgents, who have sacrificed everything for the sake of their belief and ideology. They can be anything, but greedy or criminal. Similarly, all insurgents are not motivated by grievances. Many insurgents join the insurgency for selfish considerations. For these kinds of insurgents, insurgency is a source of livelihood. Thus, both the theories have some elements of truth and are flawed as well. These two theories have to be supplemented by other factors/theories.

Maoist insurgency is the cumulative result of various factors, of which, organization and leadership are most critical. In critically examining the role of the organization (agency/party) and leadership (actor) in the Maoist movement in India, it is observed that from the very beginning the radicals felt the need of a strong organization and party. They felt disenchanted by the moderates among the Communists, who had taken the parliamentary path and had deviated from the revolutionary path. Instead of challenging and changing the system, these mainstream Communist Parties viz. Communist Party of India (CPI) and Communist Party of India (Marxist) had become defenders of the system/state.

The history of Maoist parties can be traced back to the Andhra Committee of the CPI, which advocated a most radical path against the newly independent Indian state under the leadership of Prime Minister Nehru and the action taken by the state during the Telangana peasant rebellion against the Nizam of Hyderabad and later the merger of Hyderabad into Indian Union. The Andhra Committee was in favour of intensifying the agrarian struggle against the state and spreading it to other areas beyond Telangana to prepare the ground for Communist takeover of India for the emancipation of masses. Communists led by S.A. Dange and B.T. Ranadive argued in favour of giving more time to Nehru to bring agrarian reform by radical land reforms and Zamindari abolition. The Dange group later consolidated themselves into present CPI. However, the radical communists led by Ranadive split from the parent CPI to form CPI (Marxist). Most radical among the communists formed the CPI (ML-Marxist-Leninist), which led the Naxalite movement of the late 1960s and early 1970s.

Split in the Indian Communist Movement

The first split in the Indian Communists occurred in 1964 in the wake of Chinese aggression and growing differences between the Communist Parties of the Soviet Union and China. The most radical Andhra Committee joined the Ranadive group of Communists by breaking away from the parent party, the CPI. They named the newly created political party as CPI (Marxist). However, Communists toeing the line of revolutionary path of China could not continue for long with the moderates. Serious differences in the CPI (M) arose over the issue of government formation in West Bengal by the Bengal Congress led by Ajoy Mukherjee, who had broken away from the Congress Party. Radicals in the CPM led by Charu Majumdar opposed CPM participation in the government led by Ajoy Mukherjee. The Radical group led by Charu Majumdar, Kanu Sanyal, Jangal Santhal and others formed a Coordination Committee of Communist Revolutionaries (CCCR), who extended wholehearted support to agrarian struggle against landlords in Naxalbari in West Bengal and Srikakulam district in Andhra Pradesh. These radicals, who were later thrown out of CPM, announced their intention to form a new Communist Party on Lenin's birthday April 23, 1969. In a rally organised by these radicals in Calcutta on the International Labour Day (May 1, 1969), Kanu Sanyal formally declared the formation of a new Communist Party called the CPI (Marxist-Lenin-ML) in the presence of Charu Majumdar and other leaders. This party led the primarily agrarian and partly urban struggle called the Naxalite movement in the late 1960s and early 1970s till the death of its chief ideologue Charu Majumdar in 1972.

With the death of Charu Majumdar, the first phase of the LWE popularly known as Naxalbari or Naxalite movement (named after the place of its origin Naxalbari village in Darjeeling district of West Bengal), came to an end. The movement declined and it appeared during emergency and in its immediate aftermath in the late 1970s, that it was over for once and for all. After the death of Charu Majumdar, the CPI-ML disintegrated and its different leaders pulled in different directions and some even went to the extent of criticising its top leadership and its chief ideologue Charu Majumdar himself. S.N. Singh of Bihar, Nag Bhushan Patnaik of Orissa and Nagi Reddy of Andhra Pradesh not only criticised Charu Majumdar, but also diluted their extremist revolutionary line and tilted towards parliamentary path.

Fragmentation of CPI-ML

In the post-Charu Majumdar period, the CPI-ML (which led Naxalbari insurgency) was characterised by fragmentation and dissentions among its top leadership. There was intense turf war among top leaders, which led to the fragmentation of Naxal/Maoist parties. Apart from CPI-ML, Maoist Communist Centre (MCC) formed by Kanai Chatterji was another prominent Maoist party, which never was part of CPI-ML. Most other Maoist parties were splinter groups of CPI-ML; such as CPI-ML Liberation (Jauhar Group), CPI-ML Party Unity, etc. Indian Peoples Front (IPF) was formed by Vinod Mishra and others to contest parliamentary elections. Later it was renamed CPI-ML. This group is the major Naxal party, which is still participating in the electoral process. Most of the Maoist parties boycott elections as they were of the firm opinion that elections were tools in the hands of the bourgeoisie to befool the masses and as such no purpose would be served by contesting elections.

The Peoples War Group (PWG) formed by Kondapalli Sitaramaiyah and K.G. Satyamurthi in 1980 in Andhra Pradesh was one of the most important Maoist outfits in the annals of Maoist history. The credit for revival of the Maoist movement in South India goes to the PWG. The MCC sustained the movement in Bihar after the collapse and disintegration of CPI-ML. Of all the Maoist parties the PWG and the MCC are the most important. Revolutionary Socialist Party was active in west India; mainly in Punjab and the Janashakti Party in Andhra Pradesh. Thus, there were more than a dozen Maoist parties active in different parts of India. They frittered away their energy by fighting each other rather than fighting unitedly against the state.

From Proliferation to Polarization of Maoist Parties

Maoist parties moved from proliferation to polarisation in the late 1990s. The idea of bringing all Maoist parties under one umbrella was mooted long ago by Kanai Chatterji of MCC and Kondapalli Sitaramaiyah in 1980s, but it could not make much headway because of serious differences among the top leaders and turf war among various Maoist parties in different parts of India. However, the process of unification of Maoist parties was undertaken seriously in the late 1990s. The lead in these efforts was taken by two leading Maoist parties; the MCC active in Bihar and the PWG active in Andhra Pradesh. Smaller Maoist outfits began uniting either with MCC or PWG. The most important breakthrough, however, came in September 2004, when the two most important Maoist parties, MCC and PWG decided to merge into a new party called the CPI (Maoist).

The formation of CPI (Maoist) in 2004 is an important milestone in the Maoist movement. Now, Maoists were united and well organised. They had also formed an armed wing of the party called the Peoples Liberation of Guerrilla Army (PLGA). By Government estimates, the number of PLGA guerrillas was more than ten thousand. They were equipped with sophisticated weapons snatched from security forces, looted from police armoury and procured from illegal arm-bazaars. Apart from PLGA, CPI (Maoist) had also formed a scantily armed people's militia consisting of local sympathisers, who provided logistic support to PLGA in its protracted struggle against the state. Masses living in the Maoists areas provide the intelligence to PLGA to help it in its fight against the state. Guerrillas shared cordial relations with the masses. Mao Zedong, the Chinese leader, had likened Guerrillas to fish in the water. As fish cannot survive if water becomes hostile, in the same fashion guerrillas cannot survive if masses become hostile to the Guerrillas. Continued existence of Maoist guerrillas despite counter insurgency operation launched by the state against Maoists is ample proof of Maoists enjoying considerable support of the masses.

Role of Organisation/Party in Maoist Insurgency

Since unification of all significant Maoist parties under a single party, the left wing extremists are posing potent challenge to the state. The area under Maoist influence has increased rapidly and now one third of the country is under Maoist influence. This compelled former Prime Minister Manmohan Singh to describe Maoist insurgency as the single largest internal security threat, bigger than terrorism, communalism and separatism. Coming together of all Maoist parties has given a new vigour and vitality to the movement, which is reflected in the increasing assertiveness of the Maoists and the spiral of violence and counter-violence unleashed by the Maoists and the State.

Politicization and mobilization of masses by the Maoist parties is an important factor in the expansion and deepening of the Maoist insurgency. Poverty, inequality, deprivation create fertile grounds for the emergence of LWE, but in absence of the organization/agency/party, these conditions need not necessarily lead to insurgency/violence. Bundelkhand region in Uttar Pradesh/Madhya Pradesh is an extremely backward because of the absence of politicisation and mobilization by any party/organization. Though the poor people had developed apathy to their deprivation and resigned to their fate, these factors, viz., inequality, poverty, deprivation of the region did not lead to violence. Similar is the case with the famine-stricken districts of Kalahandi and Bolangir in Orissa, which are relatively free from Maoist violence despite being the most backward districts of the state. On the other hand, Koraput and Malkangiri are the worst Maoist violence affected districts of Orissa, despite being relatively prosperous in comparison to Kalahandi and Bolangir. Here too the weak presence of Maoist party is the main reason for absence of violence in these two districts despite extreme poverty.

Role of Leadership in Maoist Insurgency

Apart from organization, the role of leadership is also critical in expanding and sustaining the Maoist movement. Imaginative and creative leadership is crucial for ushering in successful revolution against the exploitative and oppressive regime. Role of Lenin in Russia, Mao in China, Ho Chi Minh in Vietnam, Chi Guerra and Fidel Castro in Cuba, was critical in bringing successful communist revolution in these countries. In the Indian context, the role of Charu Majumdar was critical in Naxal movement. After his death in 1972, the whole movement collapsed in the absence of effective leadership. Kondapalli Sitaramaiyah, Kanai Chatterji, Ganapati, Kishen Ji in their own way influenced and shaped the Maoist movement in the contemporary period. Death of top leaders is always a great setback for the movement. The recent Lalgarh movement in West Bengal's districts of Midnapore, Purulia was practically single handedly organized and led by top Maoist leader Kishen Ji. Once he was killed by the West Bengal Police in November 2011, the whole movement collapsed like a house of cards. Now, the Maoists have been weakened considerably in the absence of Kishan Ji's leadership.

However, leadership and organizational factors have only multiplier effects. If other factors such as poverty, inequality, deprivation, etc. are already present only then the leadership and organization (party) can play decisive role. Party led by decisive leader will exploit the situation to politicise and mobilise the masses against the system/state and create conditions of insurgency with the eventual objective of capturing political power. The party and leadership cannot create the objective conditions for insurgency. The objective conditions have got to exist prior to the organization and leadership. Party and leaders enter into the picture to create subjective conditions for insurgency and successful overthrow of the existing oppressive system.

Geographical Factors

Geographical terrain is another significant factor in insurgency. Difficult terrain characterized by rugged mountains, dense forests, deep ravines etc. provide ideal environment to insurgents for their hide-outs, training camps and enable them to launch operation against the state represented by the security forces. Maoists intend to create their base in inaccessible areas. The Maoist compact revolutionary zone (CRZ) from the Nepal border in the north to Telangana-Andhra in the south is inhabited by indigenous people (Adivasis). Maoists intend to expand their bases from inaccessible areas and gradually engulf the whole of the country. It is easier for Maoists to engage their enemy in forested mountain areas and consolidate their positions. Inaccessible forest areas are a strong bastion of the Maoists. In China, Vietnam and other countries too rebels have chosen difficult inaccessible areas to launch their insurgency against the state. Urban areas are called graveyards of Guerrillas. Thus, the forested and rural areas of the Dandakaranya region stretching from Jharkhand, Orissa, Andhra, Telangana, Chhattisgarh, Madhya Pradesh, and Maharashtra is the stronghold of Maoists in India because of its rugged terrain and dense forest.

Similarly, the Koraput and Malkangiri districts of Orissa also illustrate the significance of geographical factor for insurgency. Since these two districts are at the tri-junction of Andhra, Orissa, and Chhattisgarh and falls in the Dandakaranya region, these two districts are worst affected by Maoist insurgency, whereas Kalahandi and Bolangir are little affected by Maoist insurgency despite being extremely poor and backward. This is mainly because of the geographical proximity of Koraput and Malkangiri to the conflict zone in Andhra and Chhattisgarh.

However, geographical contiguity and poverty are not adequate to fuel insurgency. For example, eastern Uttar Pradesh bordering Nepal is free from insurgency whereas the territory just beyond the international border in Nepal is firmly under the grip of Nepali Maoists. Despite the porous Indo-Nepal border, Maoists of Nepal have not been able to influence the poor people on the other side of the border. This is mainly due to the absence of effective organization (party) and leadership to mobilise the poor and the exploited against the state for Maoists revolution.

Conclusion: The Way Forward

There cannot be one single factor that can offer an explanation for Maoist insurgency. Greed and grievance, no doubt are most important causes of Maoist insurgency. But to consider only to these two factors and ignore all others will be oversimplification of the complex issue of Maoist insurgency. LWE is the cumulative result of various factors. Every region and every community have their own specific reasons to extend support or oppose Maoism. To unravel the causes of Maoism in a particular state or region, all relevant factors have to be taken into account by going beyond greed and grievance. Apart from greed and grievance, the organization/party/agency, actor/leader, geographical terrain/contiguity and other objective and subjective factors such as ideas, norms, morale, etc. have to be examined to identify the exact causes of Maoist insurgency.

Once the exact causes of Maoism are identified, they could be addressed by the state for a lasting solution to Maoist insurgency. Broadly, the causes have been divided into greed (law and order) and grievances (socio-economic). Since, the proponents of the greed theory treat LWE as a law and order problem, they advocate law and order approach to a solution of Maoist insurgency. They advocate enactment of new laws to deal with insurgents, devise innovative strategies to fight Maoist guerrillas like guerrilla (Greyhounds in Andhra, COBRA-CRPF, SOG, etc.), strategic hamletting (cutting off insurgents from masses by relocating civilian population), equipping security forces with sophisticated weapons, counter-insurgency operations (COIN), area domination strategy, clear-hold-build strategy, winning over heart and mind strategy, etc. to decimate Maoist insurgency.

Proponents of the grievance theory suggest the adoption of socio-economic measures to address the Maoist insurgency, as they treat LWE as a socio-economic problem. They hold triple deficits of development, governance and democracy responsible for Maoist insurgency and as such advocate addressing these three deficits by undertaking all-round intensive development of Maoist affected regions, improving delivery system of pro-poor social welfare measures and protecting and respecting the rights of the people. These measures will instil the confidence of the people in the state and address the grievances of the people against the state. Government has initiated a special development programme, the Intensive Area Development (IAD) Programme, for Maoist affected districts. Other socio-economic programmes related to health and education includes the National Rural Health Mission (NRHM), Sarva Shiksha Abhiyan (SSA), supplementary nutrition through Integrated Child Development Scheme (ICDS), Mid-Day Meal etc. Through Right to Information Act (RTI) and social auditing, the problem of corruption in social-welfare programmes and development works is being addressed and accountability fixed. Forest Right Act (FRA), 2006 and Panchayat Extension Services Act have been enacted mainly to redress the longstanding grievances of Adivasis. Under FRA, Adivasis have been given the land rights over the land in which they resided and were under their cultivation. Under PESA, community rights have been given to Adivasis and their Gram Sabhas. Land Acquisition Act 2013 has been enacted to address the land issue so that land issue cannot be exploited by the insurgents to foment trouble among the affected people as happened in Nandi Gram and Singur in West Bengal, POSCO and Vedanta land acquisition in Orissa, TATA, ESSAR in Chhattisgarh, etc. A judicious mix of law and order and socio-economic measures can go a long way in addressing the root causes of LWE. However, these two can only weaken insurgency but not root out it lock, stock and barrel.

Maoism is a political problem and as such there cannot be a military solution to the LWE. Government must engage the left extremists in a serious and sincere dialogue to address the issues of LWE. Both the state and the Maoists have to abandon the maximalist position they have now adopted. The state should abandon its strategy of decimating the Maoists, as, after all, they are its own citizens. They have certain genuine grievances and these grievances must be addressed. Maoists should also abandon their protracted armed struggle against the state. Indian state is not the state of Chiang-Kai-shek of China or Tsarist Russia. India has the second largest armed forces after China and its military is the third most powerful in the world. To humble the third most powerful state of the world and capture political power through protracted armed struggle seems to be impossible goal. The world scenario has also changed drastically since the twentieth century, when all these revolutions took place in the different parts of the world. The only feasible option seems to be capturing political power through electoral process as the Latin American countries have achieved through Bolivarian revolution. Maoist hero Chavez in Venezuela had come to power through election and not revolution. Even in the neighbouring Nepal, the Communist Party of Nepal (Maoist) led by Prachanda and Baburam Bhattarai came to power through election only. If Maoists of Latin America and Nepal could come to power through elections, why cannot Indian Maoists?

Before Maoists and state enter into any meaningful dialogue, the state has to lift ban on CPI (Maoist) and make it a legal entity. How can an illegal organization enter into dialogue with the state? The State should also not insist that the Maoists disarm themselves before entering into talks. It is absurd to expect Maoists to commit *hara-kiri* by disarming themselves before the success of talks. Both the state and the Maoists should declare cessation of hostilities against each other and enter into dialogue without any preconditions from either side. Discussion will pave the way for some sort of amicable solution, where the core concerns of both the state and Maoists are taken care of. If Maoists are so confident of the support of the masses they should test their popularity in the electoral battles and bring about the desired change as per their belief and ideology. This is the only way out of this vexed problem of Maoist insurgency in India.

NOTES & REFERENCES

1. Weber, Max, 2015, *Politics as a Vocation*, (Available at http://www.sscnet.ucla.edu/polisci/ethos/Weber-vocation.pdf,accessed on 16 January.
2. Nishit Dholabhai, 2014, Army Option *Vs.* Maoist on Table in *The Telegraph,* 18 October, (Available at http://www.telegraphindia.com/1141018/jsp/nation/story_18939180.jsp#.VLqfYyuUfwg accessed on 16 January, 2015)
3. Jal, Murzban, 2014, Strangers in the Dark: Neo-liberalism and Maoism in India, *Critique*, Vol. 42, No. 4, pp. 607-629.
4. Shining India was a slogan coined by BJP leader Lal Kishan Advani in the wake of 2004 General Election, which BJP lost unexpectedly. Election defeat was interpreted by critics as rejection of neoliberal policies by the Indian electorates.
5. Suffering India term was coined by critics of BJP to decry its neoliberal pro-rich and anti-poor policies of Vajpayee led government at the centre.
6. PM Manmohan Singh, in *Hindustan Times*, April 13, 2006. (Available at http://www.hindustantimes.com/news-feed/nm9/naxalism-biggest-challenge-pm/article1-86531.aspx accessed on 24 January 2015)
7. The term commanding heights of the economy was coined by Lenin and was used in Soviet Union in their planning. P.C. Mahalnobis and Jawaharlal Nehru borrowed it from Soviets and was extensively used in India's planned development of public sector enterprises, which was assigned pride of place in the mixed economy.
8. Committee on State Agrarian Relations and Unfinished Task of Land Reforms, Ministry of Rural Development, Government of India, Vol. I, Draft Report, New Delhi 2009, (Available at http://www.rd.ap.gov.in/IKPLand/MRD_Committee_Report_V_01_Mar_09.pdf accessed on 20 January, 2015)
9. Navlakha, Gautam, 2012, *Days and Nights in the Heartland of Rebellion*, Penguin Books India.
10. Collier, Paul and Hoeffler, Anke, 2015, *Greed and Grievance in Civil War, Policy Research Working Chapter* 2355, The World Bank Development Research Group, May 2000 (Available at http://www-wds.worldbank. org/servlet/WDSContentServer/WDSP/IB/2000/06/17/000094946_00060205420011/Rendered/PDF/multi_page.pdf accessed on 31 January.

18

Impact of Globalization on Nomads of Maharashtra

CHANDRAKANT PURI

Introduction

Nomads is an umbrella term used to describe the "Nomadic Tribes (NT) and De-notified Tribes" (DNTs) in India which is one of the most marginalized and vulnerable communities. According to a rough estimate, they constitute 11 per cent of the total population of India, but the exact figure is not known, as there has been no census of them after 1931. Administratively, they are scattered across the OBC, SC and ST category. A few communities are not covered by any of these three categories. Those who are covered are unable to avail benefits due to various obstacles such as absence of citizenship documents and their nomadic way of life. As a result, DNTs are among the most underprivileged and destitute communities facing multiple forms of exclusion. Among the DNTs, nomadic mendicants and entertainer communities have been further neglected when they interface with the highly dynamic contemporary world. Several commissions were appointed by the Central and State Governments to study and recommend policies and programmes to improve their socio-economic status but all these efforts have hardly achieved the desired goal.

In this context, a study was conducted by the author to understand the socio-economic and livelihood related issues of these communities. The focus was also on access to education of the children of the nomadic mendicants and entertainer communities in

Maharashtra in the context of the Education for All. The study identified their struggles for survival, including accessing public services, changing livelihood options etc. A team of investigators visited around one hundred villages in Maharashtra for data collection using mixed methodology.

This study has been a small attempt at creating a major data base of the DNT communities whose exclusion results from their historicity and its interface with contemporary processes such as globalization, deepening their exclusion. The study further locates the disadvantages resulting from such processes including education, changing livelihood patterns and multiple struggles faced by the communities. The research tried to build a data base of select communities and new knowledge based on peoples' lived experiences and suggestions for reworking the exclusionary patterns of the Nomadic Mendicants and Entertainer Communities in Maharashtra for their equitable and sustainable development. It was an effort to put these communities on the 'development' map from where they have been largely invisible. One of the key objectives also was to start a collaborative dialogue amongst various stakeholders to co-create ways and means for transformative change. Since the government efforts have miserably failed to develop these communities in spite of 70 years of Independence, the author felt that efforts were needed from all the stakeholders viz., Government, non-Governmental organizations, Political Parties and the Civil Society in general.

This chapter highlights some of the major findings of the study and suggests policy guidelines and action strategies for the inclusive development of these communities. The chapter also looks at the larger impact of LPG (Liberalization, Globalization and Privatization) on these communities.

Globalization and the Marginalised Communities in India

With the LPG policies, (Liberalization, Privatization, and Globalization), all protective cushions have been done away with. The other policies of the Central Government, especially in areas like education, health, public distribution system, and industrial policy have had far reaching consequence in the economy and society of the state, deepening marginalities of the existing marginalized communities, including the Nomads. The impact of globalization is strongest on these populations perhaps more than any others because these communities have no voice and are therefore easily swept aside by the invisible hand of the market and its proponents.[1] In most cases, development projects ignore the essential needs of the poor, misunderstand their socio-economic conditions and hardly bother about the spiritual-cultural bonding that these people attach to the natural resources.

Anita Pisal's study (2014) on the impact of modernization on the religion, customs and traditional work of the *Vadar* Community has observed that the *Vadar* Community was facing problems in the shape of loss of identity on account of the establishment of industries that bring in development in the technology and its concurrent side-effects.[2] The DNT communities have been pushed to a corner by the economic interest of various dominant groups.

Globalization has led to exploitation of labour. Safety standards are ignored to produce cheap goods. And most of them from vulnerable communities such as DNTs. Increased job competition has led to reduction in wages and consequently lower standards of living. The increase in prices has reduced the government's ability to sustain social welfare schemes in developed countries. All these are further marginalizing the DNT Communities because of their historicity, stigma that many of them face and traditional livelihoods and knowledge which is not recognized in a so called 'globalized' world.

Nomads in India

Nomadic Tribes (NT) and De-Notified Tribes (DNT) are the most neglected and discriminated marginalized sections of the Indian Society. They are also one of the socially excluded groups. They were branded as criminal tribes by the British. DNT were traditionally pastoralists, hunter gatherers, traders, transporters, craft workers, entertainers, foragers etc. They are losing their traditional livelihood and are unable to equip themselves with new skills and techniques for survival.

One of the key problems in putting these communities on India's developmental map is their invisibility due to non-availability of authentic data as post-1931, no caste-wise Census was undertaken in India. Since most of these communities are nomads—they are unlikely to get enumerated in the census and other data collection processes. Hence, they continue to be excluded from the process of development.

They also experience atrocities, but since they do not have constitutional protection, they are not covered under the Prevention of Atrocities Act unlike the Scheduled Castes and Scheduled Tribes. There are also large scale Human Rights violations. A sizable number are denied basic entitlements due to non-availability of basic documents such as land titles, ration card and Below Poverty Line (BPL) card and Aadhar Cards (Puri, Chandrakant, 2015).[3]

Around 200 communities were notified by the British Government as "criminal tribes" through a notorious piece of legislation called the Criminal Tribes Act, 1871 (Jadhav, Narendra, 2014).[4] The rationale behind the Act was that as per the European view, all gypsies are criminals, and following that logic, all Indian nomadic communities who were gypsies were also believed to be potential criminals. For this reason, there is a large overlap between communities that were declared criminal tribes and those that were nomadic. The Criminal Tribes Act 1871[5], identified the following six categories as belonging to "criminal tribes":

(i) Petty traders who carried their merchandise like salt, forest produce etc. on the back of animals and supplied to villages;
(ii) Communities that entertained the public through performing arts. Among these were musicians, dancers, singers, storytellers, acrobats, gymnasts, puppeteers and tight rope walkers;
(iii) Communities that entertained the public with the help of performing animals such as bears, monkeys, snakes, owls, birds, etc.;
(iv) Pastoral groups and the hunting, gathering, shifting-cultivator communities within forests that traded not just in the forest produce, but in animals as well. They were also herders and traded in meat and milk products;
(v) Artisan communities that worked with bamboo, iron, and clay etc. and made and repaired a variety of useful articles, implements and artefacts. They traded or sold them to settled villagers; and
(vi) Nomadic individuals who subsisted on charity, or were paid in kind for spiritual services rendered to the traditional Indian society, such as *sadhus, fakirs*, religious mendicants, fortune tellers, genealogists and traditional faith-healers etc., who had a low, but legitimate place in the social hierarchy of settled people.

Some carried medicinal herbs and provided healing services as well. Describing the Criminal Tribes Act 1871 as a blot on the law book of free India, the then the Prime Minister Pandit Jawaharlal Nehru annulled it after Independence. As a consequence, these communities were "de-notified, and hence, are now referred as "de-notified tribes" (Jadhav, Narendra).

There has been no census of the "De-notified and Nomadic Tribes" (DNTs) of India after 1931, though their numbers run into millions. They are found in almost all the states, and belong mostly to the OBC category in major states. They are also spread across the SC and ST categories in others. Some communities are not covered by any of the three categories, i.e. SC, ST and OBC. Even those covered under the three categories are often not able to avail of the benefits because of not having caste certificates, or because the quotas are used up by the non-nomadic/non-de-notified communities in the reserved categories. Moreover, a number of states have not prepared lists of either the de-notified or the nomadic communities, and the status of such people is unknown. As a result, DNTs are among the most under privileged and destitute communities facing multiple forms of exclusion.

As mentioned above, there is no authentic information available on the DNT communities. Also the National Commission for De-notified, Nomadic and Semi-Nomadic Tribes (NCDNSNT) set-up in the year 2006 under the Ministry of Social Justice and Empowerment, Government of India to study various developmental aspects of de-notified, nomadic and semi-nomadic tribes in February 2006 and the Technical Advisory Group appointed by the Ministry of Social Justice and Empowerment, Government of India, on 8th September, 2006[6] failed to give authentic data on the DNT.

Nomads in Maharashtra

As referred earlier, the above two groups were especially found to be vulnerable, hence were focused for the study. As the name suggests, the livelihood of the mendicants is based on begging in the name of God whereas the entertainer communities entertain people and earn their livelihoods.

Nomadic Mendicants: The traditional occupation of this community was preaching, teaching, singing devotional songs and seeking alms. They roamed from place to place leading an ascetic life and due to their religious links enjoyed a higher place in the caste hierarchy. Hence, most of them are classified as belonging to OBC in most of the states. As they were landless, most of them have adopted non-agriculture vocations to support them and a large number of them still continue to seek alms. They are found in the slums of cities and towns and a large section of them still lead a nomadic life. These communities are smaller in size and dispersed. Each of them claim allegiance to specific deities and have specific place where they return every year on the occasion of fairs and festivals. Rest of the time they move in small groups of families. The major communities under this category are: *Budbudki, Fakir, Gosavi, Bairagi, Dasari, Garpagri, Jogi, Kashikapdi, Tirumali, Nandiwala* etc.

Nomadic entertainers: The nomadic entertainers earned their livelihood through providing entertainment to the village communities through their acrobatic, jugglery or other cultural performances. The demand for their traditional entertainment skills has dwindled under the pressure of modernization. They have been stripped off their artistic dignity and are looked at as begging communities with obsolete skills of entertainment. The names of the major communities under this category are: *Mang Garudi, Madari, Nat, Bahurupi, Bal Santoshi, Bharadi, Davri Gosavi, Chitrakathi, Garudi, Ghisadi, Gondali, Kolhati, Madari, Vasudev, Bajikar* etc.

The traditional entertainers were landless and hence today they are mostly absorbed in the unorganized sector as unskilled workers and include petty peddlers, rickshaw pullers and other such menial works. Some of them still lead nomadic life practicing their traditional livelihood skills. They are dispersed in small groups and live with other marginalized groups in cities and towns which provide them opportunities of employment. Nomadic entertainer communities are small in size and in some of the communities children play a significant role in earning livelihood.

Patterns of Exclusion among the Nomads

The DNT communities today face multiple forms of exclusion. It ranges from denial of basic amenities, lack of assets of survival to non-availability of work at the village level which leads to their migration with family. The migration further excludes their children from education thereby creating generations of illiterates. The working conditions are unhygienic and lack proper facilities violating all labour laws. It is especially worst for women as they face even sexual exploitations from the landlords or the owners at the work sites. They are cheated and exploited financially. On the political front, there is no proper representation due to spread of the community in small settlements. There is also a lack of leadership which could unite them. They are getting alienated from their own culture and the rich tradition of music, folklore, and mythology. Oral traditions are getting wiped out due to the nomadic way of life and also due to impact of electronic media. One finds that all human rights violations are taking place and there is no one to protect their rights. This aspect is discussed in the figure below:

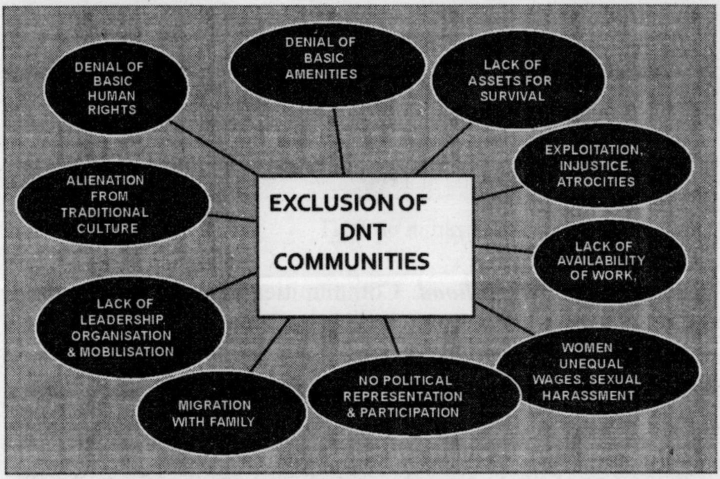

Fig 18.1: Exclusion of DNT Communities

The picture or Figure 18.2 was taken during the field work by the author at Jejuri, Pune district which is known for the annual market of Donkeys. While earlier the donkeys were used to travel from far off places on foot, the donkeys are now transported in tempos/trucks to the market; which says a lot about how globalization and modernization has affected the lives and livelihood patterns of the Nomads.

Based on the fieldwork with the Nomads in Maharashtra, the author has observed the following as the impact of globalization on the Nomads:

Fig 18.2: Impact of Globalization on DNT

1. Impact on Livelihood: Communities such as *Vaidu, Wadar* and *Lohar* were traditionally engaged in trade/profession in traditional medicine, construction and fabrications respectively. Since, the economy has become open it has adversely affected the traditional business of these communities. Uses of technology having reduced the cost of production, the traditional traders are unable to compete. Due to the size of production, the cost of production of the traditional traders remains high and as a result, the selling price is high. The market prefers the cheaper products which adversely affects the Nomads and their livelihood.

2. Impact of Forest Dweller Act and Wildlife Protection Act: Communities like *Nandiwale* who used to use decorated bulls and *Darveshi* who used to entertain with black bears cannot do so anymore because of the Wildlife Protection Act. The Communities which traditionally relied on the forest for residing/dwelling and for fuel and fodder can no longer do so because of these Acts. Also the *Vaidu* communities which used to find traditional medicinal plants in the forest are not able to freely access the forest which has directly impacted on their livelihood.

3. Impact on Entertainer Communities: Due to Environmental Protection Act, the Nomadic communities, particularly the Entertainers and Mendicants, have suffered a huge set back. Usually, the traditional entertainer communities start their performance after dinner. During the native fair (*Jatra*) procession of deities would start only after dinner and would continue throughout the night, where the traditional artists play a significant role. They are not able to do so now as they have to stop their performance by 10.00 p.m. This restriction is negatively impacting the livelihood of communities like the *Kolhati and Dombari.* Similarly, the *Gondhali* who were supposed to perform throughout the night have to stop their performance by 10 p.m. which cuts sharply their earnings.

4. Impact of Beggars' Act: The impact of Anti Beggary Act which prevents anyone from begging has badly impacted some of the Mendicants communities such as *Gondhali, Gosavi, Joshi, Mariaeewale* etc., who asked for alms in the name of God.

5. Skills at Crossroads: Old Skills vs. New skills: The skills which were used for survival by these communities have become redundant hence they have to adapt to new skills. Competing in the globalised world has become almost impossible for these traditional artisan communities.

6. Agriculture practices: Some of the communities were also traditional agriculturists who used to do traditional farming residing in and around forests. Due to the new methods of agriculture, which result in good yield, they have been forced by the market forces to adapt to the new agriculture practices using fertilizers and chemicals. This is the gift of globalization. This new practice has more production cost for which they have to borrow money which results in indebtedness, besides there being no guarantee of good production due to climatic changes. As a result, the Agriculture communities are at cross roads.

All these above factors are impacting the livelihood of Nomads making them further vulnerable.

Key findings of the study: The study has come out with the following major findings:

- Majority of the mendicant and entertainer communities were Hindus. Only the *Fakir* and *Darweshi* communities belong to the Muslim religion, which are equally poor and backward.

- Majority of the families are nuclear (56.6%) reflecting change in the family structure among the NT communities.
- Although more than 68 per cent of the respondents owned some sort of dwelling house or the other, 80 per cent did not own any agricultural land.
- Around 40 per cent respondents felt that their community concerns did not get reflected in the Gram Sabha. Majority (42%) of them resolve their disputes in the *Jaat* Panchayat, 20 per cent in Village Panchayat, while only 7.7 per cent approach the Police.
- Only 10 per cent said that they derived benefit from Government Schemes.
- Around 37 per cent respondents followed their traditional occupations, out of which a majority said that it did not generate adequate income. They knew that the traditional livelihood adversely affected their socio-economic and educational development besides getting excluded because of their traditional ways of living and the stigma associated with it. Around 77 per cent of the respondents desired to change their traditional livelihood patterns.
- More than 35 per cent still migrate in search of employment with their entire families which adversely affects even what little education their children get.
- Nearly 76 per cent respondents had no knowledge about the Right to Education Act, though all the parents expressed a desire to get their children educated. While the Mid-day meal scheme has made a positive impact on children's school enrolment, a sizable number of children of the DNT communities are still out of school, including 30.8 per cent children in the age group of 5 to 14 years. One third of the children drop out between classes 5 to 10, on account of poverty, lack of interest in education and the need to start earning. However, a significant improvement is seen in girls' education. Around 63.2 per cent girls belonging to NT communities are enrolled in schools.
- Contrary to popular view, 90 per cent of all respondents had Aadhar card; 88.5 per cent had voter card; 74 per cent had domicile certificate; 78 per cent had ration cards; 60 per cent had caste certificates and 54.5 per cent held bank

accounts, which means that they are now in a better position to avail benefits arising out of Government schemes.

Recommendations for the Development of Nomads

- There is an urgent need to undertake a census of the DNT communities to systematically plan policies and programmes for them. This also includes updating the ethnographic profile of these communities.
- Among the Nomads, a majority of the nomadic mendicants and entertainer families have so far been excluded from the development process and hardly avail any benefits from these programmes. A time bound plan of action and strategies should be worked out by the Governments for their development.
- Lack of livelihood opportunities is one of the major problems of the DNTs. As such, there is a need to develop livelihood generation programme for DNTs on priority basis.
- NGOs should consider inclusion of DNT in their work and promote small CBOs/activists working with them to take up their cause.
- Since a sizable number of children of the DNT communities are out of school and face exclusion at various levels, besides creating awareness of the provisions of RTE Act it is necessary to work out special strategies for their inclusion in the education process. Special attention needs to be paid for the education of the girls of Nomadic communities.
- School teachers should be sensitized towards the problems of the DNTs and instructed to pay special attention for their inclusion in the education system (Puri, Chandrakant, 2015).[7]

Conclusion

The processes of globalization as mentioned earlier are making them further invisible and marginalized. There is therefore an urgent need to focus our understanding on these communities. Today, the Nomadic communities are struggling for their basic survivals hence all stake holders must come together to make a change in their lives.

REFERENCES

1. On the Internet. Available at http://www.rgics.org/test/wp-content/uploads/2012/09/Technical-Advisory-Group.pdf
2. Volume 19, Issue 7, Ver. III (July, 2004), pp. 37-43 e-ISSN: 2279-0837, p-ISSN: 2279-0845.
3. Puri, Chandrakant, (2015), Evolving Humanity, Emerging Worlds, 17th World Congress of the International Union of Anthropological and Ethnological Sciences, 5-10 August, 2015, University Manchester, Manchester UK, Panel SE-24, "Exclusion of de-notified (ex-criminal tribes) and nomadic tribes in India: Issues and Challenges or inclusion" (Available at http://www.nomadit.co.uk/iuaes/iuaes2013/panels.php5?PanelID=1563).
4. On the Internet. Available at http://narendrajadhav.blogspot.in/(May 31, 2014)
5. *Ibid.*
6. On the Internet. Available at http://www.rgics.org/test/wp-content/uploads/2012/09/Technical-Advisory-Group...pdf
7. Puri, Chandrakant, (2015), Strengthening Right to Education Act Implementation for Children of Nomadic Mendicants and Entertainer Communities, Workshop on RTE of Children of Nomadic Tribes in Maharashtra, 18 February, 2015, Rajiv Gandhi Centre for Contemporary Studies, Mumbai (Sponsored by New Education Group-Foundation for Innovation and Research).

19

Violations of Human Rights in a Globalized World

HOMI DHALLA

Introduction

Though Globalization has brought in immense benefits to various people, it has ignored human rights. In fact, Globalization has resulted in violation of human rights in various forms. This chapter attempts to focus on the various forms of violations of human rights that are taking place today in a globalize world. Besides the Indian scenario, a few examples from other countries will also be relevant. Similarly, the constructive work being done by individuals and organizations for safeguarding the rights of women, children, minorities and prisoners need also be mentioned. According to the Human Rights Watch, many governments today view human rights as a "luxury" that they cannot afford. But these abuses lead to crises in different parts of the world and run parallel to globalization benefits.

Nelson Mandela had said: "To deny people their human rights is to challenge their very humanity." In recent times, Ban Ki-Moon, the UN Secretary-General has said: "All are born free and equal. We oppose discrimination against lesbian, gay, bisexual. We oppose arrests, imprisonments they suffer." Decades after the liberation of the Nazi death camps and the Cambodian killing fields, the promise of 'never again' is ringing hollow in view of the tragedies in Darfur and disasters in Bosnia and Rwanda. Emphasizing that human rights are basic and inviolable, Kofi Annan, former UN Secretary-General had asked: "Can justice be sometimes scarified for peace? No. There should never be amnesty for genocide, crimes against humanity and violation of human rights."

Addressing the World leaders who had gathered in Dubai to attend the World Government Summit on February 8, 2016, through video conference, US President Obama assured that governments across the Middle East which make a "commitment to justice and human rights will continue to have a friend in America." Visiting Cuba in March 2016, he stated: "Voters should be able to choose their governments in free and fair elections." Describing this as consistent with what the US wants for countries around the world, he reiterated: "Not everybody agrees with me on this, not everybody agrees with the American people on this, but I believe those human rights are universal. I believe they are the rights of the American people, the Cuban people and people around the world."

In a Fox News interview (April 10, 2016) President Obama was remarkably self-critical, when he admitted that the failure to plan for the aftermath of the toppling of Dictator Muammar Gaddafi of Libya, in October 2011, was the "worst mistake of his seven years in office." It is Libya's tragedy that post-Gaddafi it is a failed state. This has also destabilized its neighbours and the presence of ISIS on Libyan soil is daunting. Similarly, speaking at Peshawar University on May 31, 2016, Alexei Dedov, Russia's envoy in Pakistan described the 1979 Soviet intervention in Afghanistan a "tragic mistake." Though both the US and Russia have frankly admitted their mistakes, the fact remains that so much harm, destruction, loss of lives and property have been inflicted on Libya and Afghanistan, besides the gross violation of human rights.

From the end of the Nuremburg trials in 1949 till the 1970s, hardly any head of a state or a government official has been held responsible for violations of human rights. But in the last few decades, the possibility of punishment has increased and those in power may be more cautious before assassinating or torturing their political opponents.

- The plight of Hosni Mubarak, the former Egyptian President held in a cage in a Cairo court should discourage government officials in other regions of the world; to think twice before adopting repressive measures against their own people.
- In 2010, Cambodia issued its first war crimes conviction, after 30 years over the horrors of the killing fields. Similarly, Uruguay courts took 20 years to award 30 years in jail to Juan Maria Bordaberry, former authoritarian leader for violations of human rights.

- In 2014, two former Khmer Rouge leaders stood their second trial at a UN-backed court in Cambodia on charges of genocide. They were charged with killing of an estimated 1,00,000 to 5,00,000 ethnic Cham Muslims and 20,000 Vietnamese. On August 7, 2014, they were awarded life sentence for crimes against humanity.
- On March 24, 2016, the International Criminal Tribunal at The Hague awarded a 40-year sentence to the former Bosnian Serb leader Radovan Karadzic for orchestrating Serb atrocities throughout Bosnia's 1992-95 war that left 1,00,000 people dead.
- On May 11, 2016, Bangladesh hanged Islamist party leader Motiur Rahman Nizami for genocide, rape and crimes committed during the 1971 war of Independence during which about three million people were killed and thousands of women raped.

In September 2012, Nobel laureate Desmond Tutu said that Tony Blair and George Bush should be prosecuted for their role in the 2003 US-led invasion of Iraq. "They should be made to 'answer for their actions.' The Iraq war has destabilized and polarized the world to a great extent than any other conflict in history."

In March 2016, the US and 11 other countries demanded at the UN Human Rights Council in Geneva that China should release all the activists and lawyers that it had detained in violation of human rights. China rejected the charge and countered by stating that "the US is notorious for prison abuse at Guantanamo prison, its gun violence is rampant and racism is its deep-rooted malaise." By and large, human rights prosecutions would lead to more just societies in the long run.

I. Women

Globalization has affected women in several ways. Women in ancient India were more liberated. If girls wanted to join *gurukuls* there was nothing stopping them from doing so. The *Upanishads* (written about the 7th century B.C.) contain accounts of very learned women. The composers of the *Rig Vedic* hymns included a number of women. More than 20 women number among the authors credited with the composition of these hymns. However, in modern India, women have a long way to go before they can enjoy all their rights. Vidya Dehejia, Professor of Indian and South Asian Art at Columbia University, rues that that while we worship *devis* in temples, outside the temples women are treated like second-class citizens. She asserts:

> "We worship the *Devi* in so many forms and with such reverence but do not accord women at home or on the streets any respect or dignity. You celebrate menstruation in a goddess because it is about the power of procreation, but when it comes to women, it becomes a dirty thing...there is a great disconnect between feminine divinity and the place women are given in society".[1]

However, it is encouraging that there are some brave women in India who are not content with expecting change, but demanding it.

Women in Parliament

Globalization has not brought political rewards to women all over the world. This equally applies to India. While 62 women were elected to the Lok Sabha in May 2014, and four more were added through by-elections, globally, India's rank stood at 144 among 191 countries in early 2016 in the matter of women's representation. While making a strong pitch for reviving the Constitution Amendment Bill to give 33 per cent reservation to women in Parliament on March 6, 2016, President of India, Pranab Mukherjee lamented: "It is a sad commentary on us that India has not been able to achieve more than 12 per cent representation for women of the total membership of Parliament since Independence." Earlier in October 2015, he had said that India needs more women in top positions in government, academia and business.

Melinda Gates had an occasion to observe that "a lot of African nations actually have quotas for their Parliaments, so they are better than most countries. Rwanda has over 60 per cent quota for women in their Parliament." She lamented that even in US Congress women constitute less than 20 per cent of the members.[2]

India Slides in Gender Equality Ranking

According to a survey of 142 nations released on October 28, 2014, Indian women still face some of the world's worst inequality in terms of healthcare, education and work in spite of the great strides in economic growth. The annual Gender Gap Index conducted by World Economic Forum showed that India had slid to 114th place, after being ranked 101 out of the 136 countries surveyed in 2013. India ranked a high 15th for female political participation, as some of its most important positions in government recently were occupied by women. But it was among the bottom 20 in terms of income, literacy, work force participation and infant survival.[3]

Atrocities against Women: Domestic Violence

According to the National Crime Records Bureau (Crimes in India 2014), the highest number of cases recorded was under the rubric "Crimes against Women." These crimes were perpetrated by husbands or his relatives. In all, 1, 22,877 cases of domestic violence were recorded in 2014 as against 1,18,866 in 2013.[4]

Rape and Compensation to Survivors

An August 2014 report by the Commonwealth Human Rights Initiative states that between 2001-2013 there have been 2,64,130 rapes in 28 states; an average of almost 56 incidents of rape per day. Delhi recorded the highest number of rape cases among the 28 states, compared to the figures reported in 2001.[5] On February 11, 2016, the Supreme Court of India took a significant decision to provide succour to the victims of rape. It asked the states and Union Territories to frame rules to grant compensation up to Rs. 10 lakh to women subjected to sexual exploitation. Justice Iqbal, who wrote the judgement for the bench said: "indisputably, no amount of money can restore the dignity that the accused took away from the survivor. No amount of money can erase the trauma and grief the survivor suffers. This aid can be crucial in the aftermath of crime."[6]

Dowry deaths

On April 29, 2016, Union Minister Maneka Gandhi told the Lok Sabha that over 24,700 dowry deaths were registered during three years between 2012 and 2014. She also stated that most states in India have appointed dowry prohibition officers. The government regularly conducts awareness programmes and public campaigns on various laws related to women including Dowry Prohibition Act 1961 through workshops, seminars and cultural programmes.[7]

Condition of Mentally Retarded

A study conducted by the National Commission for Women and NIMHANS found that the condition of women in mental health institutions was deplorable. There was a shortage of psychiatrists, trained attendants and sanitary conditions were poor. Many women had been abandoned by their families over false pretexts.[8]

Justice H.L. Dattu, Chairperson, National Human Rights Commission stated that when he was a Judge of the Supreme Court, he had found that at a government-aided home for the disabled, 49 children were using a single toothbrush and were provided one tube of toothpaste. He further stated that such was the condition in most government-aided homes for disabled children, who are the most neglected lot.[9]

Hindu, Muslim and Jewish women fight for their Rights to enter Places of Worship

Addressing a fundamental issue of gender equality, the Mumbai High Court issued a clear and unambiguous order in March 2016 stating that women must be allowed to enter Maharashtra's *Shani Shinganpur* temple. Thanks to Activists the centuries old custom of not allowing women enter the temple was brought down. Such obscurantism existed in ancient times, but it has no place in modern days. On April 8, 2016, for the first time in 400 years, the temple opened its *chauthara* (platform) to women also. Similarly, on April 21, 2016, for the first time in 500 years, three women activists entered the sanctum sanctorum of the *Tryambakeshwar* temple near Nashik.

Muslim women too have been agitating about their not being allowed into the sanctum sanctorum of the Haji Ali Dargah in Mumbai. Nasreen Contractor's (founder of *Haji Ali for Everybody*) petition filed before the Mumbai High Court in November 2012 asking for access for women to the Dargah's *mazaar* is still pending.

In April 2016, a group of Jewish women in Jerusalem challenged the tradition at Jerusalem's "Western Wall" where the blessing is usually conducted by men. The Jewish women (of the "Women of the Wall" group) pushed for equal prayer rights at the site. The ultra-orthodox Jews, who oversee the Western Wall, strongly have been opposing the attempt stating that it would be a desecration under the strict interpretation of the Jewish law.

Muslim Women Protest against Triple *talaq*, *halala*, Child marriages and Gendered Polygamy

Increasing number of Muslim women are demanding a ban on triple talaq, where a man can legally divorce his wife by saying talaq thrice in one go. They are also protesting against *halala*, a custom under which a woman divorced thrice by her husband, cannot remarry him unless she marries someone else and has intercourse with him. Muslim women have also been raising their voice against child marriages and gendered polygamy where men are allowed to marry four times.[10] On June 1, 2016, a petition signed by 50,000 Muslim women and men sought the intervention of the National Commission for Women to end these "un-Koranic practices." The agitation was spearheaded by the Bharatiya Muslim Mahila Andolan. Supreme Court gives green signal to dance bars. The Mumbai High Court had struck down an order issued by the Maharashtra Government banning dance shows in bars. On an appeal by the State Government, the Supreme Court ruled that women dancing in bars had a right to pursue their profession. On March 2, 2016, the Supreme Court asked the State Government to start issuing licenses to dance bars which it had forced to close down. It is stated that it is better for women to perform in dance bars than beg on the streets or indulge in some objectionable activities to make ends meet.

The witches of Assam

In some of the remote corners of Assam, women and sometimes men, are routinely considered witches and killed, beheaded, raped and force-fed excreta by desperate mobs. Enacting a law by the State abolishing witch-hunting has had little effect. According to Mamoni Saikia, an activist with the Assam Mahila Samata, there are instances of sons beating up their own mothers. Villagers who had close contact with the victim for decades turn a blind eye when they are tortured.

The issue of witch-hunting is not confined to Assam alone. According to the Ministry of Home Affairs, 2257 people across India have lost their lives since the year 2000. National Crime Records

Bureau data shows that there were 1045 such deaths in India with Jharkhand alone accounting for 222 deaths between 2008-13. The other states where this horrendous practice still persists are Haryana, Andhra Pradesh, Madhya Pradesh, Odisha, Rajasthan and Chhattisgarh.[11]

Trafficking

July 30 is observed as UN World Day against Trafficking in Persons, meant to raise awareness of the plight of victims of human trafficking and promote and protect their rights. UN Secretary-General, Mr. Ban Ki-Moon warned that conflict, terrorism, economic turmoil and natural calamities have led to unprecedented crisis giving a business opportunity to human traffickers. Millions of women and children are being exploited and coerced into working in fields, factories, brothels and begging, pushed into armed conflict or forced marriages; trafficked for their organs. The Global Report on Trafficking in Persons by the UN office on Drugs and Crime found that the trafficking victims identified in 124 states were citizens of 152 different countries.[12]

'Nirbhaya' (The Fearless)

The ghastly gang rape of a young woman on December 16, 2012 in a New Delhi bus shook the conscience of India. An inspirational play entitled '*Nirbhaya*' was premiered at the Edinburgh Fringe Arts Festival in August 2013. I witnessed this play on March 19, 2014 in Mumbai—a heart wrenching performance which left the audience deeply moved and disturbed by the graphic enactment of this incident. Director Yael Farber said: "We will never truly know what that young woman endured. But it is our work to depict the enormity of the savageness of what happened on that bus and the epidemic of sexual violence." The play also wove into it the searing personal testimonies of five of the cast members based on their real life experiences. The play won accolades abroad and it is hoped that '*Nirbhaya*' would ignite a global dialogue and awareness of sexual crime triggered by the Delhi rape.

'Thumbprint'

In January 2014, the world premiere of an opera entitled 'Thumbprint' took place at a basement theatre in Manhattan, New York. It was inspired by the terrible gang rape of illiterate Pakistani woman in 2002. She survived the tragic incident and her metamorphosis is an inspiring story. She was raped to avenge her 12 year old brother's alleged impropriety with a woman from a rival sect. [13]

'Burqavagnaza'

Pakistani theatre has been holding a flag of protest with plays depicting repressive social and political practices. Madeeha Gauhar, theatre activist and director of one of the most celebrated theatre groups, 'Ajoka' said: "Military dictators have tried to suppress it with censorship laws, victimization of theatre activists under the Dramatic Performances Control Act. At present, the major threat comes from religious extremists whose agenda is to stifle freedoms." The group received threats for its play '*Burqavagnaza*', a spoof on the fundamentalist's insistence on the *Purdah.* The play was later banned in Pakistan. The group also enacted other plays focusing on taboo topics in Pakistan viz., "*Dekh Tamasha Chalta Ban*" on blasphemy law and persecution of minorities, "Hotel Mohenjo-Daro" on *Talibanisation*, *Maiku Kari Karneday Nee Mai* on honour killings.[14]

II. Children

Tragic Plight of Children

According to WHO report of 2012, over 6,50,000 children develop tuberculosis every year in 22 countries. Research published in the Lancet Global Health suggests that about 15 million children are exposed to TB every year and roughly 53 million are living with latent TB infection. TIME magazine reports that Vitamin A deficiency blinds some 3,00,000 children annually and is linked to the deaths of about 7,00,000 others. This problem is very serious in East Africa where bananas are a staple food but lack essential nutrients.[15]

According to the National Family Health Survey-3, about 40 per cent of Indian children are underweight and 45 per cent are stunted due to malnourishment. According to the 2011 census, there were at least 4,68,680 reported cases of female foeticide. Over one million children under 5 die in India every year. According to the Home

Ministry Report released in July 2014, 3.25 lakh children went missing between 2011 and 2014, i.e. nearly 1 lakh children going missing every year. There are about 49,00,000 child labourers across the country. Thousands of child labourers toil in Jharkhand and Bihar's illegal mines, who are at risk of head injuries, silicosis and TB. According to a July 2014 UNESCO report, there are 57.8 million children who were out of primary school globally and India, with 1.4 million children, ranks among the top five nations with kids aged 6-11 out of school.

Child abuse

In February 2014, a UN Human Rights Committee Report denounced the Vatican for systematically adopting policies that allowed priests to abuse tens of thousands of children over decades. The report added that Church officials had imposed a "code of silence" on clerics to prevent them for reporting to the police and moved abusers from parish to parish in an attempt to cover-up such crimes. Pope John Paul II had apologized for child abuse and Pope Benedict XVI defrocked nearly 400 priests for molesting children. An article in Newsweek ("The Chosen"), describes how the Jewish ultra-orthodox school system muzzles survivors of child abuse and protects the criminals who prey on them.[16]

Child soldiers

Some of the countries around the world use youth as child soldiers. In March 2016, the US State Department spokesperson stated that the ISIS group is relying more heavily on child soldiers as growing numbers of adult fighters desert the organization. In Syria and Afghanistan, children are also being used as child soldiers.

Denial of Girls' Right to Education

A February 2015 report by the UN Human Rights office in Geneva depicted a grim picture of the suffering inflicted on girls in some parts of the world who wish to get educated. Most such attacks on girls were carried out in the name of culture or religion, although some were gang related, notably in El Salvador and other parts of Central America. Veronica Birga, Chief of the Women's Human Rights and Gender Section at the UN human rights office who made this report said that this form of violence was on the increase. She cited instances of acid attacks and poisoning by the Taliban in Pakistan and Afghanistan. Many of the attacks between 2009 and 2014 involved rape and abduction. Birga stated that some of the attacks were due to opposition to girls' education as a means for social change and in other cases schools were seen as imposing western values including gender equality.[17]

Malala Yousafzai, a Pakistani teenage girl was shot in the head by the Taliban on October 9, 2012, for promoting education for girls. On December 16, 2014, the Taliban butchered 132 kids and 7 others by storming into a Pakistan Army-run school at Peshawar. On April 14, 2014, 276 schoolgirls were abducted in Northern Nigeria by the Islamic extremist group the *Boko Haram*. The term *Boko Haram* may be roughly translated as "Western education is unclean". The group's leader Abu-Bakr Shekau stated in 2 videos that "We will give their hands in marriage because they are our slaves. We will sell them in the market". On January 20, 2016, the Taliban militants attacked the Bacha Khan University in Charsadda in North Western Pakistan killing 25 students and teachers in classrooms and hostels.

Child Marriages

On November 21, 2014, the UN General Assembly resolved that all members should pass and enforce law banning child marriages, thereby putting an end to the practise that was affecting about 15 million girls every year. There are more than 700 million women who have been married before the age of 18. Child marriages are very common in South Asia and Sub Saharan Africa. Bangladesh has the largest number of girls married under 15 and India has 1/3rd of all child brides worldwide.[18]

However, there is another positive side to this story. A study released by Plan Asia Regional office in April 2013, entitled "Asia Child Marriage Initiative: Summary of Research in Bangladesh, India and Nepal", states: "There are a few cases where child brides are able to continue with their education after getting married and sometimes even after having a child...many girls are even annulling their child marriages. They are approaching schools and police for help."[19] According to the 2011 Census data released on May 27, 2016, there has been a dramatic decline in child marriages in India, across various religious communities and even among less educated sections. The share of girls getting married before reaching the legal marriage of 18 years fell steeply from 44 per cent in 2001 to 30 per cent in 2011.

Archbishop Tutu and the 'Girls, Not Brides' Campaign

Archbishop Desmond Tutu, Human Rights activist and anti-Apartheid campaigner, who won the 2013 Templeton Prize, played a pivotal role in the abolition of apartheid and subsequently worked to heal the wounds in South Africa's traumatized society. In an interview to *The Times of India,* he spoke about the crucial 'Girls, Not Brides' campaign and said:

> "Child marriage was a problem not only in India but also in Africa. We are unlikely to achieve six out of the eight Millennium Development Goals if we do not deal with this huge problem. If we do nothing, at the present rate, ten million girl children will become forced brides in just one year—that's one hundred million in the next decade. We are flouting the human rights of these young children, the world's most vulnerable, most invisible people. Girls under 15 years of age forced into sex, bearing children, are five times more likely to die than 20 year olds and above…it's a crisis. We decided to found a global movement to end child marriage—girls are not brides. Religious leaders must state their religion does not approve of exploiting children thus. Political leaders must stand up. Brothers must stand up for their sisters' rights."[20]

Female Foeticide

While launching a report on the status of girls in India in November 2014, Union Minister Dr. (Mrs.) Najma Heptullah painted a grim picture of their condition as they are still faced with deep discrimination. The findings indicate that for the girl child the struggle for survival begins in the womb itself. We bear the tragic burden of being a nation of disappearing daughters. The census of 2011 shows that overall there are 38 million missing women. A report entitled "Disappearing Daughters" by Action Aid (June 2008), stated that

Indian parents have killed more than 1 crore female fetuses in the last two decades.[21]

The *Beti Bachao, Beti Padhao* (Save the daughter, Educate the Daughter) Programme for which Rs.100 crore has been allocated should become a mass movement. There are a number of other projects which have been launched to save the girl child.

An article in *The Times of India,* Mumbai entitled "*Nakusa—Burden of Unwanted Girls*" states that in Marathi language it means 'Unwanted'. Many girls in Satara district are given this name. In a Survey conducted, nearly 70 per cent of girls said that they faced humiliation because of their name.[22]

'*Khatna*'—Female Genital Mutilation (FGM) is Violation of Human Rights

The ancient practice of Female Genital Mutilation (FGM) of girl children as young age 4-5 is called '*Khafd*' or '*Khatna*' by the Bohra community. This is being strongly opposed in circulars by local representatives in India and elsewhere in the world. The latest edict comes from Detroit US, stating explicitly: "You are strictly directed not to engage in *'Khafd'*. The Jamaat in Australia also issued an edict outlawing FGM."

Masooma Ranalvi, who spearheaded the anti-FGM campaign, said that the UN has categorically declared FGM a violation of the rights of the girl child, apart from being an outright breach of human rights. The UN declared February 6 as the International Day of Zero Tolerance for FGM and it was on this day that the advocacy group "Speak Out to FGM" launched the "Each One Reach One" campaign. According to UNICEF, there are 200 million girls and women alive today who have suffered FGM in 30 countries. According to the report of World Health Organization (WHO) of May 16, 2016, new guidelines for managing complications from FGM have been released. It dismisses any health benefit from FGM and lists the grave physical and emotional harm arising from it, besides declaring it as a violation of human rights of the girl child.[23]

After the US declared FGM illegal in 1996, in 2006, Khalid Adem, an Ethiopian immigrant in Atlanta, became the first person to be convicted for performing FGM on his 2 year old daughter. UK has criminalized FGM in 2003 and made it mandatory for health professionals and teachers to report 'known' cases to the police.

Global Child Sex Tourism and Pornography

Sexual abuse of children by tourists and travellers is a growing scourge around the globe. More than 70 child protection agencies, charities and academics contributed to the UN-backed "Global Study on Sexual Exploitation of Children in Travel and Tourism" report released in 2016. Dorothy Rozga, Executive Director of ECPAT International stated that "despite 20 years of hard work... exploitation in travel and tourism has expanded across the globe, outpacing attempts to stop it."

According to TIME (April 18, 2016), pornography is a $ 97 billion industry around the globe. Over 40 per cent children in the age group of 10 to 17 years are exposed to porn online; many accidentally. The Government of India plans to setup a Rs. 400 crore cybercrime control hub to check all cybercrimes including child pornography and online abuse in the country. On February 26, 2016, the Supreme Court of India directed the Centre to block all child pornography websites.

Organizations and Individuals Working for the Rights of Women and Children

It is heartening that there are a large number of organizations all over the world which have been working for the rights of women and children. Some of these may be mentioned here:

- Eve Ensler, American playwright and activist has travelled to 182 countries bearing witness to horrific testimonies from women. On February 14, 2013, millions all over the world took part in "One Billion Rising" which is an international movement launched by Ensler for women's rights. Statistics show that in India there are 250 million women who face violence and these are only the reported cases.
- Great changes are sometimes initiated by one single person. The "Somaly Mam Foundation" of Cambodia was launched with the purpose of ending sex slavery and empowering the survivors. A multifaceted approach has resulted in supporting those who have been rescued and establishing recovery centres, grassroots activism and the constructive role played by the media. All this has been due to the vision and work of Cambodian survivor and anti-trafficking activist Somaly Mam.

- A very moving documentary entitled "Everyday in Cambodia" sponsored by the CNN Freedom Project, in which Mira Sorvino, an actress and activist plays the leading role, depicts how girls between 8 and 12 are trafficked for sex. Large number of children are often sold by their own parents who are in deep debt. Don Brewster of the Agape International Mission has been playing a leading part in rescuing these children and educating them for jobs. He has also been rehabilitating traffickers.
- "Global Summit to end Sexual Violence in Conflict" was held in London in June 2014. It was the result of a two year campaign by Angelina Jolie and The Hague who had visited the Democratic Republic of Congo and Bosnia to meet victims of rape during conflict.
- Michelle Obama, who launched the "Let Girls Learn" initiative in Japan in March 2015, told the audience that there was a global crisis which left 62 million girls without the chance of an education. Both Japan and the US are big donors for this initiative.
- The largest women's conference of the decade "Women Deliver" was held in Copenhagen from May 16-19, 2016. It launched a new 12-point global campaign "Deliver for Good" to boost investment in girls' health, education and empowerment.
- Britain is planning to make emotional cruelty towards children a crime, punishable by up to 10 years in jail as part of a new "Cinderella Law". This is to protect children's emotional, social and behavioural well-being.
- "Girl Rising India" is part of a global campaign about changing the mind-set and bringing behavioural changes among people to promote girls' education.
- "Global Fund for Women" supports women who break stereotypes every day. It is one of the world's leading foundations for gender equality, building a world where every women and girl is strong, safe and powerful.
- *"Majlis"* is an organization which has taken on the challenge of engaging with legal processes. Launched in 1991 as a legal and cultural resource centre by Flavia Agnes, this NGO has fought for the rights of almost 50,000 women.

- "Giving Back Foundation" was launched by Meera Gandhi, a philanthropist and socialite, who has dedicated her life to work towards empowering women and girls.
- Project *"Nanhi Kali,"* jointly managed by K.C. Mahindra Education Trust and Naandi Foundation addresses the educational needs of underprivileged girls in nine Indian states. Its goal is to educate every rural Indian girl child for at least ten years which would reverse centuries of deprecation—it would also lead to a fair and equitable India. This project has already educated over 1,00,000 out of its targeted 17,98,87,312 illiterate girls in India. It inspires the donors to sponsor the girl child for at least a year. It has collaborated with government schools to provide educational support beyond what is done in rural schools. An extra class focuses on mathematics, science and language.
- Formed in 1984, the Naga Mothers Association deals with drug and alcohol addiction ravaging Nagaland. In the 1990s, it played a pivotal role in tackling HIV and AIDS. It has also been dealing with the rights of women and focusing on the atrocities by the Indian Army against civilians.
- In Manipur, the *"Meira Paibi"* ('women with flaming torches') is the largest grassroots civilian movement fighting state atrocities and human rights violations. Launched in 1970, initially as a drive against alcoholism and drug addiction, it has also been dealing with crime against women and the Armed Forces Special Powers Act (AFSPA). Another prominent figure from Imphal, Manipur is Irom Sharmila, the Ion Lady of India. She has now been protesting non-violently to oppose the AFSPA for the last 16 years.
- Another scourge that has been facing some villages in India is honour killings ordered by the *Khap Panchayats*. The latter's ordering and endorsing such heinous crimes drew severe criticism at a session during the Literary Carnival held in Mumbai in December 2013. Chander Suta Dogra spoke about the brutal death of the young couple Manoj and Babli central characters in her book (*Manoj and Babli: A hate story).* The killers of Manoj and Babli were put behind bars. The Indian judiciary has also been taking a very stern view of this and those responsible for the death of these innocent persons are imprisoned for life.

- Singers and poets in Ahmedabad are making a silent statement to new parents. Lullabies which have been sung glorifying the birth of a son are now including the mention of a daughter too. Noted Gujarati singer Manhar Udhas stated that the change was prompted by the skewed child sex-ratio in Gujarat which is 886 girls per 1000 boys. Poet Madhav Ramanuj who has also changed the lyrics of three traditional lullabies said "When a mother sings to her child, people around too absorb the love and affection. This love cannot be limited to boys, especially in times when people are killing the girl in the womb".
- The draft National Policy for Women 2016 released on May 17, 2016 by Union Minister Maneka Gandhi aims to tackle new technological challenges like cyber crime, protection for women using artificial insemination and surrogacy techniques on health, education and social security.
- On May 31, 2016, it has been reported that Women and Child Ministry has come up with an anti-trafficking bill which assures legal rights for the victim and goes beyond the existing legislation that only deals with trafficking for prostitution.

III. Minorities

"A civilization can be judged by the way it treats its minorities."

—***Mahatma Gandhi***

Minorities in different parts of the world are being targeted. Expressing serious concern over violence against religious minorities in India, 34 leading American lawmakers requested (letter dated February 25, 2016) Prime Minister Modi to protect their fundamental rights and bring the perpetrators to justice. In the Catholic Secular Forum's Report, it is stated that a minimum seven pastors have been killed and 8,000 victims have suffered other atrocities. Over 500 clergy and community leaders have been targeted. 85 major incidents across 20 states have taken place in 2015 which is an increase of 20 per cent since 2014.[24]

At the World Sufi Forum organized in New Delhi On March 20, 2016, prominent Sufi leaders condemned extremism and urged Muslim youth not to be misguided by incorrect interpretation of Islamic scriptures. They also stated "there is a sense of fear among

Muslims due to riots. Government should alleviate this fear and Union Home Ministry should spell out what steps have been taken with regard to all small and big communal incidents that have taken place in different parts of the country".

Minorities in other parts of the world also feel unsafe and are persecuted. Some of these incidents are cited here briefly:

- In March 2013, the main opposition leader of Bangladesh, Khaleda Zia condemned attacks on the Hindus in different parts of the country and demanded punishment to the perpetrators. In February 2016, a Hindu head priest was hacked to death in Dhaka. Similarly, an elderly Buddhist monk was killed in May 2016.
- Protesting against harassment, Hindus living in Pakistan have moved the Supreme Court of Pakistan against attacks by extremists on Hindus and their temples in Sindh province. In May 2014, lawmaker Ramesh Kumar Wankwani told the Pakistani National Assembly that about 5,000 Hindus migrated from Pakistan to India and other countries every year due to religious persecution. Over the years, there have also been systematic attacks on Christians. On March 28, 2016, Christians who were celebrating Easter in Lahore were attacked by Pakistani Taliban. In the suicide bombing that took place at a popular park, resulted in 72 deaths including 29 children. Condemning Pope Francis demanded the authorities protect the religious minorities.
- In April 2016, Reema Abbasi, author of *"Historic Temples in Pakistan"* stated that "Largely, places of worship under attack are Shia; Ahmadis are attacked for calling themselves Ahmadi Muslims; Zikris are attacked because they resist being called Zikri Muslims; Ismaili Muslims too are not spared though Jinnah was one."[25]
- A October 2014 report of the Minority Rights Group International stated that several minority communities including Christians, Yazidis and Turkmen had been subjected to assassinations, kidnappings and sexual violence and were in danger of extinction in Iraq. Till October 2014, more than 12,000 civilians had been killed in Iraq mainly by ISIS. In August 2014, an ISIS video entitled "convert or die "showed a number of Yazidis being converted to Islam.

In March 2016, Chaldean Catholic Bishop Antoine Audo stated that of the 1.5 million Christians in Syria before the conflict started in March 2011, two-thirds had already left due to the insecurity.

- The Roma community in Europe suffers discrimination. In Hungary, they live in poverty, are unemployed and suffer from poor health. Lacking education and skills, they remain marginalized and unemployed, which breeds a cycle of poverty leading to crime. Their children are frequently classified as mentally handicapped, even if they are not. In August 2013, the Hungarian Government has produced a Europe wide strategy to integrate the Roma.
- On May 7, 2016, London made history by electing its first Muslim Mayor, Sadiq Khan, the son of a Pakistani bus driver. He celebrated his landslide election victory in a multi-denominational ceremony at an Anglican Cathedral where members of other communities were also invited. He hailed his victory as a triumph of "hope over fear and unity over division" and said: "I am not a Muslim leader or a Muslim spokesperson. I speak for the city of London."

IV. Racism

Fifty three years after Martin Luther King's speech, racism still continues to exist in the US. On August 28, 1963, he had stated "I have a dream that my four little children will one day live in a nation where they will not be judged by the colour of their skin, but by the content of their character".

In May 2015, Law Professor Paula Johnson of Syracuse University was speaking before the UN Human Rights Council in connection with the US Universal Periodic Review, which reviews the human rights records of all 193 member states. She criticized the US over its 'racist' policies and said that "most of the problems raised by member states in the UPR of the US reflected a common theme of an embedded racist structure with no real mechanisms for accountability."[26]

In recent months, racism has created an acute crisis in the US. It is well known that the US has a historical problem of racial inequalities, but the palpable inequity in dealing with, especially, blacks by the US police has led to shocking incidents. These events have exposed the underlying racial prejudices. The death of Eric Garner in New York, Michael Brown in Missouri and Freddie Grey in Baltimore and many others has shaken the conscience of all Americans. On July 13, 2015, Sandra Bland, 28, who had been active in "Black Lives Matter" movement died in police custody after she was pulled over for a trivial traffic violation. This movement is a cry from the heart of the frustrated black population and has spread like wildfire across the entire country. The deaths of black Americans which continue to this day have clearly shown discrimination and racial prejudice. These incidents have forced President Obama to say that he too was mistaken for a waiter as well as a valet and more needs to be done to improve racial relations.[27]

Democratic presidential frontrunner Hillary Clinton confessed in March 2016: "We have got to be honest with ourselves. We have systematic racism that is really at work inside of the criminal justice system. We have got to be willing to stand up and question these inequities and then go ahead with the business of ridding them." On the contrary, on December 7, 2015, Republican Presidential candidate Donald Trump had declared that Muslim should not be allowed entry into the US. On another occasion, he said that a wall be constructed to restrict Mexicans from entering the US. He was snubbed on April 15, 2016, by Zeid Raad Al-Hussein, UN High Commissioner for Human Rights, by stating that "Bigotry is not proof of strong leadership. Hate speech, incitement and marginalization of the 'other' are not a tittering form of entertainment or a respectable vehicle for political profit...discrimination is a powerful and profoundly destructive force...this is also the rod to violence, not perhaps visible–not yet." Similarly, on May 18, 2016, UN Secretary-General, Mr. Ban Ki-Moon indirectly criticized Trum saying that "would-be leaders and politicians should not divide people and racist remarks by them are 'outrageous." If Donald Trump's call to keep Muslims from entering the US has created a flutter amongst Muslims living in America, as anti-Muslim sentiments against American Muslims are leaving a mark even on young students in American schools. Muslim parents say that their children hear disparaging remarks in their schools, see hateful bumper stickers and T-shirts and have had their friends abandon them because of their religion.

In the backdrop of increasing hate crimes against their community, the Sikh community in California has raised $ 4,00,000 for launching a national media campaign to generate awareness among Americans about their religion.

In January 2016, in the face of a major controversy over the second straight year when all the 20 Oscar nominees were white, the Academy of Motion Picture, Arts and Sciences assured sweeping reforms designed to help diversity. George Clooney and Chris Rock expressed their displeasure over the nominations. Macklemore in his new song "White Privilege II" raps about a white person's position in society with black people fighting injustice.

A recent article "What schools should learn from student protests" in *TIME* magazine (May 23, 2016) indicates how the issue of race has been taken up by black students in hundreds of US colleges. Bilphena Yahwon, a Towns on University senior protested racism on campus by stating "Being black on this campus...you know that there's a me and there's a 'them'. And you are always hyper conscious of everything you do. You are constantly editing yourself. I do not want to be too black." University presidents have pledged to address this problem through faculty diversity and by establishing an interdisciplinary centre devoted to the study of race and transnational migration.

On May 23, 2016, a coalition of more than 130 Asian-American groups have sought an investigation into admission practices of the prestigious Yale University, Brown University and Dartmouth College, alleging that they discriminate against students on racial grounds. This complaint was filed with US Department of Education and Justice. In May 2015, a similar complaint was filed against Harvard University by a coalition of 64 Asian-American groups alleging that applications from well-qualified Asian-American students for admission were 'unfairly' rejected because of their race.[28]

Records of UK's first national anti-Muslim hate crime helpline have revealed that there were 816 *Islamophobia* offences recorded in London up to July 2015; a 70 per cent rise in a year compared to the previous 12 months.[29]

Almost 102 years ago, the then Government of Canada turned away about 376 migrants, mostly Sikhs, from India due to discriminatory laws of the time. The *Komagata Maru* was a Japanese ship that was hired to bring the migrants to Canada to challenge the racist laws of the time in 1914. The ship was forcibly sent back by the Canadian Government. On May 18, 2016, the Canadian Prime Minister Justin Trudeau formally apologized for the "great injustice" done to them. Welcoming Trudeau's apology, the advocacy group, the World Sikh Organization has now demanded that the *Komagata* chapter be included in the school curricula in Canada.

Canada's first Sikh Defence Minister Harjit Sajjan was heckled in the Parliament by opposition member shouting that MPs needed an English-to-English translation as Mr. Sajjan spoke. Other members in the Parliament dubbed this as 'racist'.

But Indians too are racist. Racial prejudice is exhibited against people of North East because of their unique facial features. African students were targeted in January and May 2016 in Bengaluru, New Delhi and Hyderabad over trivial matters. African envoys have taken up these incidents with the Government of India, expressing their deep anguish and stating that "the brotherhood concept between us will ring hollow unless these issues are addressed." The acting High Commissioner of Nigeria stated that "Racism against black Africans in India is a major concern. Ugly incidents, like what we consider barbaric attacks on Africans, murder in cold blood, have met with outrage."

V. Modern Day Slavery

Today, support for human rights having become global, prominent personalities and religious leaders have also been supporting human rights. The importance of human rights was highlighted by President Obama when he visited Goree Island in Senegal on June 27, 2013. He toured a slave house and gazed out at the Atlantic Ocean through what is known as the "Door of No Return." It is the point on this island from which Africans were shipped to the Americas and into slavery. Obama, the son of a Kenyan said that the tour helped him to "fully appreciate the magnitude of the slave trade." He said that "this is a testament to when we are not vigilant in defence of human rights what can happen. Obviously, for an African-American President, to be able to visit this site, I think, gives me even greater motivation in terms of human rights around the world".

- On July 29, 2008, the US House of Representatives issued an unprecedented apology to black Americans for the ill treatment meted out to them and their ancestors under slavery and the Jim Crow segregation laws. The resolution drafted by Tennessee Democrat Steve Cohen stated that the Africans who were pushed into slavery "were brutalized, humiliated, dehumanized and subjected to the indignity of being stripped of their names and heritage" and the present black Americans still suffer from the consequences of slavery.

- On June 18, 2009, the US Senate formally apologized for the "fundamental injustice, cruelty, brutality and inhumanity of slavery" of African-Americans." The unanimous voice vote came ahead of June 19, celebration of the emancipation of African-Americans at the end of the US Civil War in 1865.[30]
- Three prominent religious leaders, Pope Francis, Archbishop of Canterbury, Justin Welby and Grand Imam of Al-Azhar, Dr. Mahmoud Azab will collaborate to eradicate modern day slavery and human trafficking in India by 2020. Perhaps, this is the first time in the history that the Christian and Islamic leadership which covers over three billion people have teamed up for a common cause.[31]
- According to the recent Global Slavery Index released in 2013, India was ranked 4th worst country exhibiting the full spectrum of different forms of modern slavery viz., severe forms of inter-generational bonded labour across various industries, child labour, commercial sexual exploitation as well as forced and servile marriages. It is estimated that about 20 to 60 million Indian citizens are in forced labour due to debt bondage.
- The Global Slavery Index released on November 17, 2014 reports that 35.8 million people were enslaved across the world, with 23.5 million people in Asia alone. India and Pakistan accounted for over 45 per cent of the total global enslaved population and India is home to 14.29 million enslaved people. They are either pressed into forced labour or victims of trafficking.[32]
- According to the *Tanglin Times* of Singapore, "modern day slavery is a global business worth $ US 150 billion a year where most of the victims are sexually exploited."[33]
- On December 15, 2015, the Canadian Prime Minister Justin Trudeau apologized to the natives for more than a century of abuses at boarding schools set-up to assimilate Canada's indigenous people, saying the burden of those experiences weighs heavily. Beginning in 1874, 1,50,000 Indian, Inuit and Metes children were forcibly enrolled in 139 boarding

schools run by Christian churches on behalf of the Canadian Government in an effort to integrate them into society. The previous administration had officially apologized in June 2008 for the "cultural genocide."[34]

- The UN Assistance Mission for Iraq and the UN Human Rights office estimate that 3,500 people were "currently being held in slavery by the ISIS. They predominantly women and children and come primarily from the Yezidi community, but a number of them are also from other ethnic and religious minority communities."[35]
- According to the Global Survey of Slavery published in November 2014 by the Walk Free Foundation, Pakistan has two million bonded labourers trapped in "modern day slavery" condemned to a lifetime of hardship and toil. Although there are laws in place to outlaw bonded labour, still the cycle continues with thousands of children sucked in every year by their parents' supposed debts. According to this Survey, Pakistan has the third most 'slaves' in the world after India and China.[36]

There are a number of organizations working towards the emancipation of "modern day slavery"–two of which may be mentioned here. The Freedom Fund launched in 2013 by Andrew Forrest and the Global Fund to End Slavery is doing commendable work in this field.

An article in *Newsweek* by Max Kutner ("Sex slaves on the Farm") states that every year, thousands of women are trafficked from Mexico and forced to have sex with America's millions of undocumented farm labourers. For several months, they are housed in barracks or trailers invisible to the outside world.[37]

VI. Discrimination against Dalits

> For us today there can be no sacrifice higher than to forget distinctions of high and low and to realize the equality of all men.
>
> —*Mahatma Gandhi*

The National Crime Records Bureau data reveals that crimes against Scheduled Castes rose steadily to 47,064 in 2014 from 39,408 in 2013 and 33,655 in 2012. In 2014, 744 Dalits were murdered, up from 676 in 2013 and 651 in 2012. Rape of Dalit women stood at 2,233 in 2014 up from 2,073 in 2013. The Dalits have been bearing the brunt of recurring atrocities over a long period of time. At the root of these crimes against them is the new found independence of Dalits. Observers state that the retribution inflicted by the upper caste is to send a strong message to the Dalits as to who dominates in society. Sexual attack on Dalit woman is a form of weapon to show domination.[38]

A bench headed by Justice Mukhopadhyaya of the Supreme Court of India which was hearing a public interest litigation for the rehabilitation of Dalit families of the 2010 Mirchpur (Haryana) riots in which Dalit settlements were burnt by the upper castes on April 21, 2010, observed: "Ideally all castes should be living together. Now, that has become a *pravachan* (sermon). All people should be living without fear. Now, there should be at least four policemen with them at all times to protect them."[39]

The dark shadow of caste has penetrated even the educational institutions. The suicide of a Dalit scholar, Rohit Vemula on January 17, 2016, at Hyderabad University has led to nation-wide protests. His suicide brings into the open the deep-rooted caste biases and discrimination against Dalit students even in the institutions of higher learning in the country. Over the last decade, 9 Dalits have ended their lives because of discrimination and caste politics at the University of Hyderabad campus. In Tamil Nadu, the prejudice against Dalits continues in various forms right from the schools. In November 2015, the National Human Rights Commission issued a notice to the Tirunelveli District Collector asking for a response to reports that school students should wear coloured wrist-bands to indicate their caste. This shows how caste-based assertion has gradually been institutionalized in schools to mark out the Dalit community. This shows how caste fault lines have muddied higher education and the government's erratic decision-making are adding to the grievances.[40]

But there is some light at the end of the tunnel. In a complete departure from tradition, some temples in Kerala are gradually casting out prejudice and supporting human rights. After centuries, they are chanting a new *mantra* of inclusiveness. This move has led to a silent revolution which has broken the last bastion of casteism—many non-Brahmins are now allowed to preside over *pujas* hitherto performed only by Brahmin priests. In 2012, this was implemented by the Travancore Devaswom Board which has about 2000 temples under its control. In September 2015, in a sharp departure from tradition, the Tirumala Tirupati Devasthanams, the world's richest temple, has decided to train non-Brahmins in temple rituals and practices. About 200 persons from Dalit and backward communities were trained for three months as part of a pilot project. For almost 400 years, Dalits and women had been barred from entering the famous Parasuram temple in Garhwal's Jaunsar Bawar region in Uttarakhand. They have now been granted entry into this famous temple but there are other 339 temples in the area which still enforce the ban.[41]

The battle against the caste system has now gone global. Caste-based discrimination and the battle against untouchability have drawn supporters from around the world. Kevin Brown, a faculty at Indiana University's Maurer School of Law has collaborated with India's Dalit intellectuals. He states that "we want to share our experience of overcoming racism in America with Dalits in India. We want to help build a culture of resistance to the caste system." Discrimination against Dalits is a serious violation of human rights.

VII. Abuse of Senior Citizens

The Tata Institute of Fundamental Research published in January 2015 the report of a survey of senior citizens. Presently, there are about 90 million senior citizens in India and by 2050, the number is expected to rise to 315 million. The survey points out that one out of ten elderly people are subjected to physical, verbal or emotional abuse. In Maharashtra state, 35 per cent of senior citizens complained of abuse, which was the highest among the all states surveyed. Such abuse was more in rural areas than urban. Half of those who were interviewed reported that the violence in rural areas was perpetrated by neighbours, followed by sons (41%) and relatives (34%) and daughters-in-law (32%). The abuse of senior citizens was lowest in Tamil Nadu (2%) and Kerala (3%). One out of ten elderly women lived alone. The majority of them are from poor and illiterate classes, making them more vulnerable.[42]

VIII. Atrocities of Khap Panchayats

For generations, village life in Haryana in India has been controlled by Khap Panchayats or what have been branded as "Kangaroo Courts." Matters relating to property, marriages, wearing of jeans and use of mobile phones by girls have been controlled through the *diktats* of a few powerful, unelected men. They have been blamed for provoking honour killings, public beatings and even arranging the purchase of brides. A report published in November 2014, states that about 1,000 young people are killed every year in the name of honour according to AIDWA. Punjab, Haryana and Uttar Pradesh together with 18 other states, have empowered the Central Government to introduce a law against honour killings. This would be an effective way to curb the powers of caste bodies which consider themselves to be the final arbiters of social mores and wrongfully arrogate judiciary power to themselves. Honour killings also occur in Pakistan. In recent times, the Indian judiciary has taken a very serious view of honour killings and those guilty have been punished. *Dehraadun Diary* was a film inspired by the honour killings of three real-life incidents.[43]

IX. Journalists in Peril

The watchdog group "*Reporters without Borders*" in its annual evaluation report released on February 12, 2015 stated that media freedom suffered a "drastic decline" worldwide in 2014. All parties in conflicts raging in West Asia and Ukraine were waging a "fearsome information war" where media personnel were directly targeted to be killed, captured or pressured to relay propaganda. The ISIS group active in Syria and Iraq, *Boko Haram* in Northern Nigeria and Cameroon used "fear and reprisals to silence journalists and bloggers who dare to investigate or refuse to act as their mouthpieces."[44]

In January 2013, 100 journalists went on a rare strike to protest against the Chinese Government censorship. The strike involved a major Chinese newschapter that sells 1.6 million copies in Guangdong province. The cause of the strike being that a New Year message listing challenges facing China was replaced by an article phrasing its new leader Xi Jinping. Because of this media gag, even people joined the journalists demanding freedom of expression.[45]

In July 2014, Myanmar journalists staged a silent protest in support of five journalists who were jailed for ten years. In December 2014, the International Federation of Journalists termed Pakistan, the most dangerous country for media because 14 journalists were killed in 2014.

During 2015, four bloggers in Bangladesh have become victims to the wrath of extremists who choose violence to articulate their differences. These killings have brought into sharp focus the conflict between liberal thought and extremist reaction.

On June 7, 2015, the Supreme Court of Saudi Arabia decided to uphold a cruel sentence imposed on the blogger Raif Badawi by the criminal court in Jeddah, which tantamount to sentencing Badawi to a torturous death for the "crime" of free expression. This has invited worldwide condemnation as he has been sentenced to ten years in prison and 1000 lashes. The social media in Saudi Arabia has been exploded among the youth, offering a rare outlet for free expression in a society that severely restricts it. The US has called this punishment 'inhumane.' The European Union has decided to make "every effort to engage the Saudi authorities in a dialogue on the need to recognize and respect freedom of speech for all."[46]

On August 29, 2015, three Al Jazeera TV journalists were sentenced to three years in jail by an Egyptian court. They have been charged on charges of broadcasting material harmful to Egypt and operating without a press license. This case has stirred an international outcry. Human Rights advocates state that their arrest formed a part of a crack-down on the freedom of speech initiated since the army overthrew President Mohamed Morsi. Human Rights lawyer Amal Clooney said that they would appeal this verdict and hoped that it would be reversed. Philip Luther, Director of Amnesty International for West Asia and North Africa stated that "the fact that two of these journalists are now facing time in jail makes a mockery of justice in Egypt."[47]

An article published in *Newsweek* reveals how Mexican journalists caught between drug cartels and corrupt officials were being blackmailed, threatened and murdered. During the reign of President Felipe Calderon from 2006-2012, one incident took place against journalists every two days. But under the present President Enrique Pena Nieto, the incidences have gone up to one in every 22 hours. Since 2000, 16 journalists have been reported missing and 88 have been killed; in 2015 alone, seven journalists have been murdered. Annabel Hernandez, author the best-selling book *Narcoland*, is one of Mexico's most prominent investigative journalists. Her house was broken into and she has received death threats for exposing the links between Mexico's drug cartels and corrupt government officials. She says that "these attacks against journalists are, above all, attacks against the fundamental human right of freedom of expression. The ultimate victim is a society that no longer has access to the truth."[48]

In February 2016, a report from Tehran stated that 40 state-run media outlets have joined forces to put a new bounty on the head of controversial award-winning British Indian writer Salman Rushdie who has been facing flak since the 1980s. The bounty is worth $ 600,000. The Swedish Academy has condemned this Iranian death warrant.

X. Curbing Religious Freedom

Speaking at Peking University's Stanford Centre on March 22, 2014, US first lady Michelle Obama emphasized the importance of universal rights and respect for freedom of expression and religion.

In January 2015, Brunei banned public celebrations of Christmas for fear of Muslims being led astray. China has banned the Biblical epic film 'Noah' without offering any reason although this is seen as an expression of solidarity with Muslim countries, many of which have banned this movie. *Boko Haram* has been attacking churches in Nigeria and killing Christians over the last few years.

Lobsang Sangay, Head of the Tibetan Government-in-exile stated in Delhi that there was no religious freedom in Tibet. In March 2016, the International Campaign for Tibet stated that at least 144 Tibetans have self-immolated in China since early 2009 in protest of Beijing's rule.

In its annual report released on May 23, 2016, the Congress-mandated US Commission International Religious Freedom stated that religious freedom in India was on a "negative trajectory" in 2015 as religious tolerance 'deteriorated' and religious freedom violations 'increased'. In a sharply worded rebuttal, India has refused to take cognizance of this report. The report also states that Pakistan is one of the worst places in the world as far as religious freedom is concerned. It records that "in the past year, the government grappled with a challenging security environment and initiated efforts to fight the Pakistani Taliban. However, despite these efforts Pakistan continued to experience chronic sectarian violence that targets Shias, Christians, Ahmedis and Hindus".

XI. The Indian Judiciary Safeguards Human Rights

> "True peace is not merely the absence of tension, but it is the presence of justice and brotherhood". —*Martin Luther King*

Through its landmark judgements, decisions and interim orders, the Supreme Court of India has come to the rescue of the aggrieved people from all walks of life, proving that an independent and efficient judicial system can create confidence in the society. The following are some examples where the Supreme Court and High Courts of India have safeguarded human rights of the citizens:

- Late Chief Justice of India, S.H. Kapadia ruled (September 1, 2012) that poverty is a violation of basic human rights and concerted efforts were needed to tackle the issue. This is a very serious matter as 1/3rd of the world's extreme poor are in India. A panel headed by the former Reserve Bank of India Governor, C. Rangarajan has stated that in 2011-12 the number of poor in India were 363 million.
- On October 15, 2012, a Supreme Court bench ruled that "Corruption is not only a punishable offence, but also undermines human rights, indirectly violating them and systematic corruption, is a human rights violation in itself, as it leads to systematic economic crimes".
- In a landmark judgement on April 15, 2014, the Supreme Court granted India's transgender community the right to be recognized as a third gender. Over the years, this community has faced extreme forms of violence, abuse, discrimination and disinheritance.
- On July 7, 2014, the Supreme Court ruled that *fatwas* issued by Shariat Courts or muftis had no legal sanctity and that their defiance will have no civil or criminal consequences. The Court also held that it would be illegal to impose religion-based opinions on personal issues on citizens in violation of their fundamental rights. It further held that "whatever may have been the status of *fatwa* during the Mughal or British rule, it has no place in independent India under our Constitutional scheme." It also observed that *fatwas* could cause "immense devastation".

- In January 2016, the Delhi High Court rightly upheld the role of women in managing a Hindu Undivided Family (HUF) property. Due to the raging debates on gender equality in India, the Delhi High Court has ruled that the eldest woman member can be a *'karta'*–a manager of a HUF. This landmark judgement will enable women to break another glass ceiling as according to tradition only men used to be a '*karta*' of the HUF.
- On January 11, 2016, the Supreme Court called child rape cases "atrocious, inconceivable and cruel crimes" and favoured tougher punishment for offenders. But it asked the Parliament to consider harsher measures, including chemical castration. Senior advocate, Mahalakshmi Pavani said that countries like South Korea, Russia and Poland had enforced chemical castration for such crimes.
- On February 5, 2016, the Supreme Court expressed serious concern over the plight of under trial prisoners languishing in jails across the country and asked the states to release on bail prisoners, who had served half the maximum term that they would get if they were convicted. As a result of this order, the Maharashtra Government released 4,923 under trial prisoners in May 2016.
- While hearing a batch of petitions challenging the ban on entry of women between the ages of 10-50 in the *Sabarimala* temple on April 13, 2016, the Supreme Court stated that customs are not above the Constitution and the denial of entry of women based on custom, faith or tradition cannot defeat the Constitutional principles of equality.
- On May 12, 2016, the Supreme Court awarded Rs. 10 lakh as damages to Ms. Jeeja Ghosh of Kolkata, a passenger suffering from cerebral palsy who was offloaded by Spice Jet. The bench stated that a little care, a little sensitivity and a little positive attitude on the part of Spice Jet would not have resulted in the trauma, pain and suffering of Ms. Ghosh. This led to the violation of her human right and dignity.

XII. The Denial of Justice

In India, the wheels of justice move very slowly leading to great frustration and violence. At times, litigation takes decades to settle.

On February 8, 2014 the President of India, Pranab Mukherjee commented: "Our system is weak in speedily dispensing justice. The 31 million cases backlog is disturbing."[49] In an interview to *The Week* on February 7, 2016, the Chief Justice stated that while in the US the ratio of judges for every million people was 151, in India the ratio stood at 12 judges per million. On May 8, 2016, the Chief Justice of India stated that the country required more than 70,000 judges to clear the mounting backlog of cases. He further added that "access to justice is a fundamental right and the government cannot afford to deny the people their fundamental right."[50]

XIII. Torture is a Human Rights Violation

June 26 is observed as International Day in Support of Victims of Torture. The words of the Universal Declaration of Human Rights remain as relevant as ever: "No one shall be subjected to torture or to cruel, inhuman or degrading treatment or punishment." In spite of this, torture continues to be inflicted in different parts of the world. Torture dehumanizes both the victim and the perpetrator. The terrible pain and terror deliberately inflicted on another human being leave permanent scars.

In January 2014, a Syrian military police photographer provided "clear evidence" of systematic torture and killing about 11,000 detainees. About 55,000 images provided by the photographer who fled Syria showed mutilated corpses, signs of strangulation and corpses without eyes.[51]

On August 1, 2014, President Barrack Obama acknowledged that US intelligence operatives had used torture and said: "We tortured some folks. We did some things that were contrary to our values. When we are engaged in some of these enhanced interrogation techniques, techniques that I believe and any fair-minded person would believe were torture, we crossed a line." These harsh methods were exercised owing to great pressure to prevent another 9/11.In April 2016, the CIA Director John Brennan promised that the US spy agency would not use "enhanced interrogation" techniques including water boarding against terror suspects; not even under a new President's orders to do so.

Prisons in different parts of the world continue to be a source of horrendous human rights violation. A recent UN report dated February 25, 2015 stated that Afghan authorities tortured or mistreated more than a third of nearly 800 suspected Taliban-linked detainees for human rights investigators interview. A top UN envoy to Afghanistan Nicholas Haysom stated that torture is prohibited by Afghan law but, widely used as a tool for extracting information.

Over the last year, there have been reported incidents of brutal torture, beheading, burning people alive, raping and forced recruitment of children perpetrated by the *jihadists* of ISIS and *Boko Haram*. Besides the UN, several Muslim religious leaders as well as Pope Francis have severely criticized these acts.

XIV. Horrendous Condition of Prisons

> "The degree of civilization in a society can be judged by entering its prisons".
> —*Fyodor Dostoevsky*

By and large, the condition of prisons in India is most deplorable. A report in *Frontline* magazine entitled "Horror Behind Bars" covering 58 prisons in Bihar reflects the denial of basic human rights and the urgent need for prison reforms throughout India. These prisons practiced forced labour. Over the years, a number of committees had made several recommendations but these have not been implemented.[52] In July 2012, the available capacity in Indian jails was 3,43,169, but the occupancy rate went beyond 112.2 per cent. In July 2014, the government had spent Rs. 3,500 crores on jails housing some 3,80,000 inmates, about 60,000 more than their capacity. The US State Department in its annual 2015 Country Report on Human Rights and Practices in India stated that the "most significant human rights problem involved police and security force abuses, including extra-judicial killings, torture and rape; corruption remain widespread and contributed to ineffective responses to crimes including those against women, children and members of scheduled castes or tribes."

The overwhelming incidence of custodial deaths in Maharashtra' state is the result of a culture of immunity that the police enjoy, signifying chronic failure in the system. In three years from 2012-2014, Maharashtra registered 94 deaths in police and judicial custody. In October 2015, the High Court directed the State Government to ensure zero custody deaths in six months. The Supreme Court has held that police brutality is gross human rights violation.

Prisoners in the Philippines are among the few allowed to surf the web, although closely supervised. As the Tanzanian Government was anxious about the high rate of sexual abuse in jails, it stated that it may introduce conjugal visits. In 2011, Brazil and Costa Rica formally extended that right to all gay prisoners and Israel did the same in July. China is quite active in teaching prisoners useful new skills. Scandinavian countries favour rehabilitation. Prisons in Norway offer bungalows, TV and mini markets to its 3,600 prisoners to prepare them for release. America, on the other hand, emphasizes retribution.[53]

This long chapter is intended to remind ourselves that the benefits and luxuries arising out of globalization should not blind us to the miseries of the vulnerable sections and the injustices perpetrated in a fast moving world where success is equated with money and money alone.

NOTES & REFERENCES

1. There's a disconnect between feminine divinity and a woman's place in society in *The Times of India*, Mumbai, January 17, 2016.
2. Mukherji, Anahita, 2016, Women in Parliament: India's rank slips to 144 among 191 countries in *The Times of India*, Mumbai, March 8.
3. Gender equality in India among worst in world: UN in *The Times of India*, Mumbai, October 29, 2014.
4. Anupama, Katakam, 2016, Law and Limitations in *Frontline*, April 1, p. 102.
5. Dhawan, Himanshi, 2014, India's shame: Two rapes an hour over past 13 years in *The Times of India*, Mumbai, July 28.
6. Choudhary, Amit, 2016, SC to states: Grant compensation of up to Rs. 10 Lakhs to rape survivor in *The Times of India*, Mumbai, February 12.
7. Over 24,700 cases of dowry deaths in 3 years in, *The Times of India*, Mumbai, April 30, 2016.
8. Dhawan, Himanshi, 2016, "Women in mental asylums live in inhuman conditions: Report in *The Times of India,* Mumbai, March 26.
9. Mahapatra, Dhananjay, 2016, 1 toothbrush, 49 disabled kids: State of Government homes in *The Times of India*, Mumbai, May 16.
10. Helar, Jyoti, 2016, Muslim women want to take the law to court in *Mumbai Mirror*, May 4.
11. Madhukalya, Amrita, 2016, The Witches of Assam in *DNA,* Mumbai May 15.
12. Fedotov, Yury, 2015, Trafficking growing amid turmoil, calamities in *Asian Age,* July 29.

13. Pakistan gang rape inspire New York opera in *Mumbai Mirror*, January 16, 2014.
14. On stage, in protest in *The Times of India,* Mumbai, September 21, 2011.
15. *TIME,* June 30, 2014.
16. Wolfson, Eligah, 2016, The Chosen in *Newsweek,* March 11, pp.24ff.
17. UN: Girls face rising violence in fight for education in*The Times of India*, Mumbai, February 10, 2015.
18. UN members to tackle scourge of child marriage in *Asian Age*, November 11, 2014.
19. Kurup, Saira, 2013, Early marriage a bane of young girls in *The Times of India*, Mumbai, April 17.
20. *The Times of India*, Mumbai, September 21, 2011.
21. India a nation of disappearing daughters: Study in *The Times of India*, Mumbai, November 20, 2014.
22. *Nakusa—Burden of Unwanted Girls* in The Times of India, Mumbai, January 4, 2016.
23. Das, Mohua, 2016, Female genital mutilation can cause grave harm: WHO in *The Times of India*, Mumbai, May 18.
24. Gohain, Manash, (2016), Attacks on Christians rose by 20 per cent last year: NGO report in *The Times of India*, Mumbai, January 18, 2016.
25. Pakistan is not Saudi in *The Times of India*, Speaking Tree, Mumbai, April 17, 2016.
26. UNHRC criticizes US over its racist policies in *The Asian Age*, Mumbai, May 13, 2015.
27. Obama says he was mistaken for a waiter, valet in *The Asian Age,* Mumbai, December 18, 2014.
28. Singh, Yoshita, 2016, Asian-American allege discrimination by Ivy varsities in *The Asian Age*, Mumbai, May 25.
29. Sinha, Kounteya, 2015, Hate crimes up 70 per cent in a year in London in *The Times of India*, Mumbai, September 8.
30. US senate apologizes for slavery, segregation in *The Times of India,* Mumbai, June 20, 2009.
31. Sinha, Kounteya, 2014, Top religious leaders vow to end modern slavery in India in *The Times of India*, Mumbai, March 18, p.18.
32. Sinha, Kounteya, 2014, India home to highest no. enslaved people in world in *The Times of India*, Mumbai, November 18.
33. *Tanglin Times*, Singapore, April 2015, p.26.
34. Canada PM sorry for 122 years of abuse of natives in *The Asian Age*, Mumbai, December 17, 2015.
35. IS holds 3,500 slaves in Iraq in *Hindustan Times*, Mumbai, January 20, 2016.

36. Lavallee, Guillaume, 2014, Trapped for $ 500 debt: The misery of Pakistan's 'slaves in *The Asian Age,* Mumbai, December 4.
37. *Newsweek*, February 13, 2015, pp. 34-37.
38. Jain, Bharati, 2015, Haryana upper castes envy rise of Dalits in *The Times of India*, Mumbai, October 22, p.13.
39. Caste equality has become just a sermon in *The Hindu*, Mumbai, August 28, 2014, p.12.
40. Grim shadow of caste over educational institutions in T.N. in *The Hindu*, Mumbai, January 22, 2016, p.12.
41. Singh, Kautilya, 2016, After 400 years, temple opens doors to Dalits in *The Times of India*, Mumbai, January 16.
42. 35 pc elderly in Maharashtra report abuse in *The Asian Age*, Mumbai, January 30, 2015.
43. Dhawan, Himanshi, 2014, 21 states, UTs back Centre's bill to curb honour killings in *The Times of India,* Mumbai, November 16.
44. Burleigh, March, 2015, Drastic decline in media freedom worldwide in *The Asian Age*, Mumbai, February 13.
45. Dasgupta, Saibai, 2013, Chinese rise against media gag in *The Times of India*, Mumbai, January 8.
46. "Clemency for Raif Badawi" in *International New York Times,* June 11, 2015.
47. "Jazeera journos get 3-year jail in Egypt" in *The Asian Age*, Mumbai, August 29, 2015.
48. Dying to tell the truth in *Newsweek*, January 1, 2016, pp.16f.
49. Backlog of 31 million legal cases is disturbing: Prez, in *The Times of India*, Mumbai, February 9, 2014.
50. Need 70K judges to clear pending cases in *The Asian Age*, Mumbai, May 9, 2016.
51. 11,000 tortured, killed in Nazi-style Syrian jails in *Mumbai Mirror,* January 22, 2014.
52. Horror Behind Bars in *Frontline*, January 8, 2016, pp. 4-37.
53. Gilding cage in *The Economist*, August 17, 2013, p. 51.

20

Globalization and Human Rights

ALLWYN D'SILVA

My chapter will focus on the economic aspect of globalization. In general, globalization refers to the intensification and acceleration of an ever more open flow of communication and movement of people, technology, money, goods, images and ideas across national borders. The cross-border interaction links individuals, organizations, countries, and cultures into a global economy.

The economic globalization process began in the late 1980s and early 1990s. Similar to preceding waves of globalization, there have been reductions in barriers to international trade that led to an increase of trade in goods. The reduction in barriers to the flow of trade and capital was accomplished mainly through international trade agreements. This process has effects on the environment, culture, political systems, economic development and prosperity, and on human physical well-being in societies around the world.

The chapter approaches globalization from a human rights perspective as set out in the IFSW/IASSW International Ethical Statement. The chapter recognizes the benefits and disadvantages of globalization for the most vulnerable people in the world. Our professional perspective focuses especially on how the economic and environmental consequences affect social relationships and individual opportunity.

The following global definition of the social work profession was approved by the IFSW General Meeting and the IASSW General Assembly in July 2014:

> "Social work is a practice-based profession and an academic discipline that promotes social change and development, social

cohesion, and the empowerment and liberation of people. Principles of social justice, human rights, collective responsibility and respect for diversity are central to social work."

Principles of Social Work and its Relation to Globalization

The overarching principles of social work are respect for the inherent worth and dignity of human beings, doing no harm, respect for diversity and upholding human rights and social justice.

Advocating and upholding human rights and social justice is the motivation and justification for social work. The social work profession recognizes that human rights need to coexist alongside collective responsibility. The idea of collective responsibility highlights the reality that individual human rights can only be realized on a day-to-day basis if people take responsibility for each other and the environment, and the importance of creating reciprocal relationships within communities. Therefore, a major focus of social work is to advocate for the rights of people at all levels, and to facilitate outcomes where people take responsibility for each other's wellbeing, realize and respect the inter-dependence among people and between people and the environment.

Social work embraces first, second and third generation rights. First generation rights refer to civil and political rights such as free speech and conscience and freedom from torture and arbitrary detention; second generation socio-economic and cultural rights include the right to reasonable levels of education, healthcare, and housing and minority language rights; and the third generation rights focus on the natural world and the right to species biodiversity and inter-generational equity. These rights are mutually reinforcing and interdependent, and accommodate both individual and collective rights.

In some instances "doing no harm" and "respect for diversity" may represent conflicting and competing values, for example where in the name of culture, the rights, including the right to life, of groups such as women and homosexuals, are violated. The Global Standards for Social Work Education and Training deals with this complex issue by advocating that social workers are schooled in a basic human rights approach, with an explanatory note that reads as:

"Such an approach might facilitate constructive confrontation

> and change where certain cultural beliefs, values and traditions violate peoples' basic human rights. As culture is socially constructed and dynamic, it is subject to deconstruction and change. Such constructive confrontation, deconstruction and change may be facilitated through a tuning into, and an understanding of particular cultural values, beliefs and traditions and via critical and reflective dialogue with members of the cultural group *vis-à-vis* broader human rights issues."

Globalization can be seen as a remote process, related only to the economic and commercial world. So how would greater attention to human rights change any of these realities? First, the human rights framework adds to the development policy the notion that education, food, adequate housing and health care are rights, not merely needs. This implies that the poor should not simply benefit from more resources, but must have legal and political space to claim their rights and take part in decision-making. It implies that government policies should ensure access to justice, protect against discrimination, and fulfill economic and social rights. In designing social safety nets, and poverty reduction strategies, their policies must respect the right to an adequate standard of living, including food, housing, health protection, education and social security.[1]

While recognizing the benefits of globalization, the Copenhagen Declaration and Programme of Action, cautions:

> "At the same time, the rapid processes of change and adjustment have been accompanied by intensified poverty, unemployment and social disintegration. Threats to human well-being, such as environmental risks, have also been globalized. Furthermore, the global transformations of the world economy are profoundly changing the parameters of social development in all countries. The challenge is how to manage these processes and threats so as to enhance their benefits and mitigate their negative effects upon people" (Report of the World Summit for Social Development, 1995).

These very same sentiments are expressed in the Statement of the Committee on Economic, Social and Cultural Rights on globalization issued in May 1998 (International Human Rights

Reports, 1999). The widely respected Human Development Index is advocated by UNDP as a means of realistically assessing levels of development. It is also affirmed by the Copenhagen Declaration and Programme of Action (1995) on social development (Report of the World Summit for Social Development, 1995).

The UNDP Human Development Report 1999 argues that reaping the benefits of a globalized economy cannot be done by merely forcing countries to open up their economies. To make the most of those benefits there has to be a policy package. Governments have to ensure that sound policies for social development and protection, poverty eradication, income distribution and environmental protection are put in place, just as well-thought-out macroeconomic policies and institutions have to be established to ensure sound economic management.

In the absence of that combination, sustained and sustainable development will remain illusory. It is also the case—as successive waves of financial crises have taught—that sound social policies have to be in place in order to absorb the shock of the vagaries of market forces (United Nations Development Programme, Human Development Report, 1999). The report also calls for a reorientation of global governance that ensures equity in international negotiations and that has as its central focus human development and human rights.

Globalization, Human Rights and the Indian State

There is no single way that the globalization is entering into the private sphere of the citizen (Giddens, 2000). It is true that due to globalization large numbers of populations became displaced and have lost their livelihood. The emphasis on competitiveness and economic development has had especially negative effects on such vulnerable groups as migrant workers, indigenous peoples and migrant women. Globalization has been cited as a contributing factor in violations of the right to life, the right to protection of health, the right to safe and healthy working conditions and freedom of association in many countries. The competitive pressures of the new international economy have had negative effects on the rights of workers. Low labour costs and low labour standards are important elements in the choice of location of branches or subsidiaries of transnational corporations or choice of suppliers for industrial development. The state has little or no incentive to improve working conditions. The violation of the rights of the indigenous people has been taking place for centuries. The recent emphasis on economic development and international competitiveness has resulted in new onslaughts on their rights. The link between the rights of indigenous people and globalization is contradictory. Natural resources are found through out the world on indigenous lands, and prospectors and entrepreneurs have been permitted to encroach on them in the name of economic development. Indigenous rights in all over world are under threat.

Globalization is the violating cultural rights of local people and actually imposing culture upon them. The process of globalization has affected the environment too. Due to high level of industrialization, the environmental quality has deteriorated more and more. High pace of deforestation violates the human rights of indigenous people. Another thing that has taken place is consumer culture, which is also a product of globalization. The agricultural sector has come under increasing threat with the patent regimes that globalization has introduced. Patent regimes have taken away the right to produce, sell and exchange seeds (Assadi, 2011: 377-86).

Globalization and Challenges to Human Rights in India

Globalization has posed so many challenges in the way of human rights all over the world. India is also facing the challenges of globalization in terms of human rights violation. Due to liberalization, privatization and globalization the human rights of workers, women, children and tribal are under question. Large scale displacement of tribal people, exploitation of works, low rate of wages, worst work conditions, trafficking in women and children, environment degradation and polluted rivers are some issues which can be recognized as human rights violations in our country. Human rights issues that arise include displacement, the poverty of rehabilitation, and often, the impossibility of rehabilitation, the impoverishment that results from displacement, the non-reckoning of cultural and community identity and of rights, what constitutes development has come into severe question in the country.

Due to these issues, several violent and non-violent protests have taken place. The Land Acquisition Act 1894 has been at the centre of protests. Maoist insurgents, a violent protest group, operate in 10 states and claim to fight for the rights of the marginalized tribal, Dalit, and landless communities. Governance has often been weak in regions where the Maoists have found popular support, with economic development-related corruption and illegal mining severely limiting the revenue available for public services and infrastructure in many of the areas. With government oversight and regulation of the mining sector often wholly ineffective, irresponsible mine operators also pollute vital water supplies, destroy farmland, wreck roads and other public infrastructure, and create other serious health and environmental hazards.

Globalization has posed major challenges to tribal rights in India. Despite of protective legislation, the tribal people's rights over land in the country are under question. After 1991, globalization demanded for an open market economy in India which changed the nature of the state; now it has become a protective state with limited welfare nature. The process of alienation of tribal land accelerated in this period, due to which, their livelihood is under threat. One major problem raised due to industrialization is the conversion of agricultural land for non-agricultural purposes. "The people most affected due to conversion are the tribals and other marginalized groups whose livelihoods are dependent on agriculture. Apart from large-scale conversion of their agriculture land, there are far more families that work as agricultural labourers whose livelihoods are threatened. Tribals and other groups already displaced still have not been provided any or adequate compensation. An estimated 40 million people (of which nearly 40% are tribals and 25% Dalits) have lost their land since 1950 on account of displacement due to large development projects. They still await compensation and rehabilitation. This situation is aggravating due to addition of more number of people in this 'inhumane' category every year. These people are immensely dissatisfied with government's apathy towards them" (Government of India, 2009).

Human rights of the Indian farmers are under threat. It is estimated that more than a quarter of a million Indian farmers have committed suicide in the last 16 years—the largest wave of recorded suicides in human history. A great number of those affected are cash crop farmers and cotton farmers in particular. In 2009 alone, the most recent year for which official figures are available, 17,638 farmers committed suicide—that is one farmer every 30 minutes. While striking on their own, these figures considerably underestimate the actual number of farmer suicides taking place. Women, for example, are often excluded from farmer suicide statistics because most do not have title to land—a common prerequisite for being recognized as a farmer in official statistics and programmes (CHRGJ, 2011). The farmers' suicide is due to the new forms of capitalist development that globalization has initiated in the sphere of agriculture. New patent law and hybrid seeds further aggravated this crisis and it is estimated that in India more than two lakh farmers have committed suicide between 1900s and 2000s.[2]

Impact of Globalization on Human Rights

There are groups of "human rights" in the form of economic rights, labour rights, cultural rights, civil and political rights etc. Globalization is considered to have an impact on the following rights: (Alan O Sykes, International Trade and Human Rights: An Economic Perspective, 2003. Available at http://chicagounbound.uchicago.edu/cgi/viewcontent.cgi?article=1278&context=law_and_economics)

- The admission to the WTO of nations that violate human rights extinguishes opportunities for valuable sanctions to discourage such violations.
- Open trade causes production to relocate to areas where environmental standards are lax and results in environmental degradation.

Likewise, the competitive pressures that result from open trade cause regulators to lose control over local regulatory matters and precipitate a race to the bottom over matters such as social welfare standards, environmental standards, and worker protection legislation. Open trade exacerbates inequality in the distribution of income. Similarly, the negative impact of globalization, especially on vulnerable sections of the community, results in the violation of various rights guaranteed by various Covenants, in particular:

- on the enjoyment of fundamental aspects of the right to life,—freedom from cruel, inhuman or degrading treatment, freedom from servitude, the right to equality and non-discrimination;

- the right to an adequate standard of living (including the right to adequate food, clothing and housing), the right to maintain a high standard of physical and mental health,— the right to work accompanied by the right to just and fair conditions of labour; and
- freedom of association and assembly and the right to collective bargaining, have been severely impaired. Developing States are, more often than not, compelled by the dynamics of globalization to take measures that negatively impact on the enjoyment of those rights (Oloka-Onyango & Deepika Udagama, 1999).

Globalization has not caused "developing" countries to catch up with the developed world. Inequality has risen during this present globalization period. The developed world—their intellectuals and policy-makers—views globalization as "providing good opportunities for their countries and their people." Globalization can be perceived from two angles. One angie is that globalization is a means of increasing the wealth of nations and promoting international trade. However, globalization is a direct cause for the widening economic gap between "developing" countries and "developed" countries (Waldron, 2010). There is a relationship between globalization and equality and non-discrimination in a more concrete fashion. The two concepts are central to the corpus and ethos of human rights instruments and practice. The Universal Declaration and other human rights instruments are unequivocal in their declaration that all persons are equal, and that the right to non-discrimination is a basic and fundamental human right. Inequality and discrimination unfortunately existed long before globalization was recognized as a distinct phenomenon on the international scene (Oloka-Onyango & Deepika Udagama, 1999).

Among the distinct groups of society upon whom globalization's impact has been most telling, women clearly stand out. Few observers will deny that the general issue of gender relations globally, and the question of women's human rights specifically, has undergone significant transformation. Spurred by the various international conferences, declarations and, most significantly, by the Convention on the Elimination of All Forms of Discrimination against Women, the respect for and recognition of women's human rights have made significant advances worldwide. The phenomenon of globalization adds greater complexities to this quest, particularly in the economic arena, and also within the context of culture and politics. Women in the agricultural sector have also been adversely affected by the promotion of export-oriented economic policies, trade liberalization and TNCs' activities in agriculture-related industries. Emphasis on export crops has displaced women workers in certain countries from permanent agricultural employment into seasonal employment. Subsistence farming has been severely affected in the new economic environment, leaving women farmers to seek seasonal employment (United Nations, 1999). Aside from the tenuous and low economic returns of seasonal agricultural employment, the Food and Agriculture Organization of the United Nations (FAO) has noted that the destruction of subsistence farming, increased industrial pollution and the loss of land to large commercial ventures, often financed by TNCs, have given rise to grave problems relating to food security and the health of the rural poor (Food and Agriculture Organization of the United Nations, 1998).

It is increasingly becoming clear that it is no longer tenable to draw a neat distinction between the nature of State obligations with regard to civil and political rights on the one hand, and economic, social and cultural rights on the other. Human rights mechanisms have debunked the traditional view that civil and political rights entail only negative obligations, while economic, social and cultural rights give rise to the more complex issue of positive State obligations which require resources to be expended. The United Nations Human Rights Committee has interpreted certain rights guaranteed by the ICCPR as entailing positive obligations. This is clearly the case with regard to the right to life. In General Comment on Article 6, the Committee interpreted (Report of the Human Rights Committee, 1982) the right to life in a broad manner that requires State-parties to take positive action, e.g. to reduce infant mortality, to increase life expectancy and to take measures to eliminate malnutrition and epidemics (McGoldrick, 1991). The negative effects of corporations on human rights in development can be divided into two categories. First, the corporation may directly violate human rights by itself or in conjunction with another actor. This typically involves civil and political rights, such as the right to personal security. For example, a corporation may hire state security forces to protect its facilities that engage in torture as occurred in Myanmar in association with Unocal Corp. Also, a corporation may directly violate rights by prohibiting collective bargaining or discriminating against minorities. The second category concerns indirect effects. This involves the corporation's influence on host governments. Corporations can undermine the state's ability to fulfill human rights law. They use their influence to encourage governments to adopt policies of liberalization, deregulation and privatization that ignore human rights consequences. This second effect concerns mostly economic, social and cultural rights, which are vital in developing states. Corporations are the engines of economic growth upon which states depend for the provision of the right to development. Increasingly, corporations are more economically powerful and influential than the developing host-states from which they extract their profits.

When negotiating and implementing international rules on trade liberalization, Members of the World Trade Organization should bear in mind their concurrent obligations to promote and protect human rights, mindful of the commitment made in the Vienna Declaration 1993, that human rights are the first responsibility of governments.

While the WTO agreements provide a legal framework for the economic aspects of the liberalization of trade, the norms and standards of human rights balance this by offering a legal framework for trade liberalization's social and ethical dimensions. The human rights violations resulting from globalization are failures of governance. Human rights law is capable of monitoring and regulating foreign investment. Respect for human rights requires governments to protect, promote and fulfill obligations. The right to development process can provide a framework focused on the implementation of a rights-based approach to development. The right to development is versatile and promotes global responsibility for globalization. The Declaration on the Right to Development requires states to guarantee rights in a manner applicable to globalization.

In order to be universal and remain relevant, human rights law must protect those marginalized by the exigencies of globalization by empowering local peoples (De Feyter, 2005). Development strategy consists of liberal trading regimes with a reduced role for the state. Despite the new challenges arising from the globalization process the state remains the only full subject of international law responsible under human rights law. It is the state, acting individually or collectively, that ultimately controls international relations. The protection of rights generally requires a legal system that is effective and credible, and such systems do not come free. Moreover, many rights require some additional sacrifice of other human wants—minimum wages, rights to unionize, environmental standards, and social security systems, for example, all come at the price of an increase in the cost of goods and services, or an increase in taxation. Not all effects of globalization will infringe "human rights," but some of them may (Sykes, 2003).

The authors of Global Issues had estimated that "the lives of 1.7 million children will be needlessly lost during 2002 because world governments had failed to reduce poverty levels and "Progress in life expectancy was also reduced for 4 out of 5 groups of countries, with the exception of the highest group (life expectancy 69-76 years), also progress in reducing infant mortality was also considerably slower during the last two decades than over the previous decades."[3]

T. Raja Moorthy states that "globalization resulted in the violation of the fundamental right to work. In their drive for profits, companies, in particular TNCs have been restructuring their operations on a global scale. The result has been massive unemployment. In 1995, the ILO announced that one third of the world's willing-to-work population was either unemployed or underemployed ....the goal of full employment, which was one of the pillars of the social consensus that prevailed after the Second World War, has been jettisoned by nearly all governments .... Globalization has also engendered or accentuated the process of the casualization and informalization of labour". He mentions that only 8 per cent of the labour force in India is in the formal economy while 90 per cent work in the informal economy with no legal protection or security and are subject to ruthless exploitation. Many companies, including TNCs got rid of their unionized labour force and moved their operations to low wage and depressed areas to avail themselves of the large supply of unorganized and unprotected, mainly female labour.[4]

Mathews George Chunakara describes the state of workers in developing countries after globalization as a race to the bottom, and the bottom means slave-like conditions. He explains this by the search of transnational companies for cheap labour in order to maximize their profits, so the governments of developing countries compete for the investors by providing cheaper labour.[5]

The right to education has been also adversely affected by the privatization policies and the turning of education into a profit generating enterprises in the developing countries. Due to the reduced governmental expenditure on education the quality of public free education has suffered a lot. Investors established educational institutes covering the entire range from kindergartens to universities offering better but much more expensive quality of education for the elites, motivated mainly by profit. However most developing countries still suffer a high rate of illiteracy and graduates of the governmental low quality educational institutions are not well prepared for the labour market so they suffer unemployment.

Danilo Turk showed that the globalization agreements and policies had its adverse effects on the right to work, the right to food, the right to health, the right to education and the right to development.[6] There is almost a consensus over the fact that the human rights are much more adversely affected by globalization in the south or the so called developing countries. One of those adversely affected fundamental rights is the right to development. "When countries lose their right to regulate the entry, behaviour and operations of foreign investment in the interests of their own people, it is not difficult to appreciate why it is bound to result in an impairment of the right to development."[7]

Consequences of Violations of Human Rights

No doubt that the widespread violation of human rights is related to the widening gap between the rich and the poor, both on the global and on the local levels. International Statistics prove this fact.[8] It shows that half the world–nearly three billion people–lives on less than two dollars a day. The wealthiest nation on earth has the widest gap between rich and poor of any industrialized nation. The top fifth of the world's people in the richest countries enjoy 82 per cent of the expanding export trade and 68 per cent of foreign direct investment, while the bottom fifth, barely more than 1 per cent. In 1960, the 20 per cent of the world's people in the richest countries had 30 times the income of the poorest 20 per cent; in 1997, 74 times as much. A few hundred millionaires now own as much wealth as the world's poorest 2.5 billon people. The combined wealth of the world's 200 richest people hit $ 1 trillion in 1999; the combined income of the 582 million people living in the 43 least developed countries is $ 146 billion. This leads to increasing feelings of deprivation and injustice among the populations of the different countries of the world which is enhanced by the rapid and unprecedented advance in communication and information technologies, which really turned the world in this respect into a global village. The deprived are exposed daily, if not every minute, to images and evidences of the huge gap in standards of living between the rich and the poor.

Some consequences of these deprivations of human rights are social and political unrest and even violence and counter violence. It also leads to an increasing resort to suppression and to chaos. Paradoxically the expenditure on suppressing protest and violence may be equal to or even exceed the ought-to-be expenditure on implementing economic, social and cultural human rights for all the peoples of the world. What matters more are the loss of human lives and the loss of constructive contributions which all the deprived could have offered to the economic, social, scientific and cultural advancement of humanity if they were granted their basic human rights. Racism, prejudices, and discrimination are negatively associated with justice and implementation of human rights.

There is enough evidence that the world wealth is in general, rapidly increasing due to the advance in science and technology and that it is more than enough to satisfy the needs of all the dwellers of the globe. What is needed is the globalization of human rights and prosperity, but how?

Globalization and the Human Rights Approach

Mary Robinson stressed the fact that "a key characteristic of economic globalization is that the actors involved are not only states, but private powers in the form of multinational or transnational corporations. It is now the case that more than half of the top economies in the world are corporations and not states, and international investment is increasingly private." She states that there is a trend towards holding companies accountable through legal rules for the human rights and environmental impact of their policies. She says that corporations should ensure that they uphold and respect human rights as reflected in the Universal Declarations of Human Rights and are not themselves complicit in human rights abuses.[9]

But if we acknowledge that transnational corporations are much more powerful than the states, particularly those of the dependent developing countries then who would issue those badly needed legal rules and who would implement them? Transnational corporations which are steering the economic globalization are not at all directed by ethical or humanitarian principles. Maximization of profit is the major if not the only driving force for all their activities.

To be logical, I tend to think like this: if economic corporations became transnational and that much powerful, what is needed is a powerful transnational government based on real democracy for all the countries and citizens of the world. A government which is capable of issuing and implementing global rules aimed at realization of the maximum use of all humankind achievements for the sake of all the dwellers of our globe; a government which is capable of making economy in the service of man, instead of making man a victim and a slave for the market economy.[10]

Conclusion

In an age of globalization, the struggle for human rights has become more complex and challenging. Realizing human rights, especially economic and social rights, is becoming increasingly difficult. One of the most profound challenges that we face as a community of nations is to understand better the emerging socio-economic forces and forms of globalization, to shape them to serve our needs and to respond effectively to their deleterious consequences. Human rights can balance forces of globalization within a just international legal framework. Maintaining balance between globalization and protection of human rights should be a priority. Human rights are what make us human. They are the principles by which we create the sacred home for human dignity. Human rights are what reason requires and conscience commands.

Suggestions

A global watch should be established to monitor and report the unethical transactions that take place between the governments of developing nations and global corporations. The governments of developing nations should not continue to get rich by selling their factors of production (land, labour) to global corporations. Requirements to become a free trading nation should be revised. Present requirements eliminate many developing countries. Developed countries need to do more to assist by making it easier for developing countries to benefit from trade and investments. Treaty-based mechanism focusing on the responsibilities of multilaterals as well as private actors in protecting human rights is an extremely significant step in the current economic environment. Efforts by states to create investment rules must be subjected to scrutiny and analyzed through human rights discourse.[11]

NOTES & REFERENCES

1. IFSW General Meeting and the IASSW General Assembly in July 2014.
2. Tripathi, Ambikesh Kumar, *Globalization, Human Rights and the Indian State,* Department of Political Science, Banaras Hindu University, Varanasi.
3. See:
   — Thomas L. Friedman: *The Lexus and the Olive Tree: Understanding Globalization*, Cairo: international Publishers, 1999;
   — Anthony Giddens: "Globalization", BBC Reith Lectures, (http://www.Ise.ac.uk/Giddens_99/week!.htm),
   — Leslie Sklair. *Globalization—Capitalism and its Alternatives*, Oxford University Press, 2002.
   — Gray C. Hufbaur, *Globalization Facts and Consequences*, Institute for International Economics, 2001. (Available at http://www.iie.com/chapters/hufbaur1000.htm)
   — Paul L. S.J., *Education for Globalization*, America Press, 2002 (Available at http://www.americapress.org/articles/locatelli.htm)
   — Vandana Shiva, *Violence of Globalization*, in *the Hindu* (New Delhi, India) March 25,2001. (Available at http://www.zmag.org/crisesCurEvts/shivaglob.htm
   — Theodore Levitt, *The Globalization of Markets, Harvard Business Review* 61 (3) (May-June): 92-102.
   — Diana Smith, *What Does Globalization Mean for Health*? Third world network,1999, http://www.globalpolicy.org/globaliz/special/health.htm
   Global Issues, Causes of Poverty. (Available at http://www.globalizationissues.org/Traderelated/Facts.asp
4. T. Raja Moorthy, *Development and Human Rights*. (Available at http://www.daga.org/press/ia/glob/glob04.htm
5. Mathews George *Chunakara Globalization and its Impact on Human Rights*. (Available at http://www.daga.org/press/ia/glob/glob06.htm)
6. Danilo Turk, How World Bank-IMF policies adversely affect human rights", Third World Resurgence, May 1993.

7. Global Issues, Poverty Facts and Stats, (Available at http://www.globalissues.org/Traderelated/Facts.asp)
8. Cited in: Poverty facts and Stats, Global Issues.
9. Mary Robinson, 2002, Globalization has to take rights into Account, the *Irish Times*, January 22.
10. This chapter was presented at the XV Congress of the International Sociological Association, Brisbane, 8-11th July, 2002. Dr. Samir Naim Ahmed is Professor of Sociology at Ain shams University, Cairo.
11. *American Journal of Humanities and Social Sciences*, Vol. 1, No, 1, 2013, 18-24 DOI: 10.11634/232907811301270 ISSN 2329-0781 Print/ ISSN 2329-079X Online/ World Scholars http://www.worldscholars.org Globalization and Human Rights: An Overview of its Impact Shabina Arafat Faculty of Law, University of Kashmir, Srinagar, Kashmir, J&K, India.

Index